Bursting the Bonds?

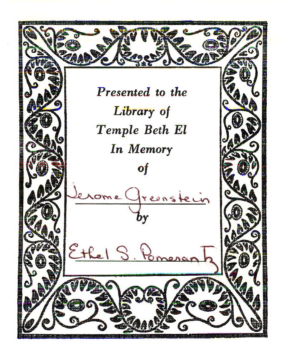

FAITH MEETS FAITH

An Orbis Series in Interreligious Dialogue

Paul F. Knitter, General Editor

In our contemporary world, the many religions and spiritualities stand in need of greater intercommunication and cooperation. More than ever before, they must speak to, learn from, and work with each other, in order to maintain their own identity and vitality and so to contribute to fashioning a better world.

FAITH MEETS FAITH seeks to promote interreligious dialogue by providing an open forum for the exchanges between and among followers of different religious paths. While the series wants to encourage creative and bold responses to the new questions of pluralism confronting religious persons today, it also recognizes the present plurality of perspectives concerning the methods and content of interreligious dialogue.

This series, therefore, does not want to endorse any one school of thought. By making available to both the scholarly community and the general public works that represent a variety of religious and methodological viewpoints, FAITH MEETS FAITH hopes to foster and focus the emerging encounter among the religions of the world.

Already published:

Toward a Universal Theology of Religion, Leonard Swidler, Editor
The Myth of Christian Uniqueness, John Hick and Paul F. Knitter, Editors
An Asian Theology of Liberation, Aloysius Pieris, S.J.
The Dialogical Imperative, David Lochhead
Love Meets Wisdom, Aloysius Pieris, S.J.
Many Paths, Eugene Hillman
The Silence of God, Raimundo Panikkar
The Challenge of the Scriptures, Groupe de Recherches
    Islamo-Chrétien
The Meaning of Christ, John P. Keenan
Hindu-Christian Dialogue, Harold Coward, Editor
Christianity through Non-Christian Eyes, Paul J. Griffiths
The Emptying God, John B. Cobb, Jr., and Christopher Ives, Editors
Women Speaking, Women Listening, Maura O'Neill
Christian Uniqueness Reconsidered, Gavin D'Costa

FAITH MEETS FAITH SERIES

Bursting the Bonds?

A Jewish-Christian Dialogue on Jesus and Paul

Leonard Swidler
Lewis John Eron
Gerard Sloyan
Lester Dean

ORBIS BOOKS

Maryknoll, New York 10545

232
5

The Catholic Foreign Mission Society of America (Maryknoll) recruits and trains people for overseas missionary service. Through Orbis Books, Maryknoll aims to foster the international dialogue that is essential to mission. The books published, however, reflect the opinions of their authors and are not meant to represent the official position of the society.

Library of Congress Cataloging-in-Publication Data

Bursting the bonds?: a Jewish-Christian dialogue on Jesus and Paul /
  by Leonard Swidler . . . [et al.].
    p. cm. — (Faith meets faith series)
    Includes bibliographical references and index.
    ISBN 0-88344-713-4 — ISBN 0-88344-712-6 (pbk.)
    1. Jesus Christ — Jewish interpretations.   2. Paul, the Apostle,
Saint — Views on Judaism.   3. Judaism — Relations — Christianity.
4. Christianity and other religions — Judaism.   I. Dean, Lester.
II. Series: Faith meets faith.
BM620.B87   1990
232 — dc20   90-39046
                                                           CIP

copy

Contents

v

Foreword

This book grew out of a number of formal and numerous informal dialogues among four scholars, two Jewish and two Christian. The occasion for precipitating these dialogues in this particular form was several extended dialogues — organized by Temple University's Religion Department — that occurred mostly, though not exclusively, in Germany, both West and East, between 1980 and 1986. It was in the latter of these dialogues — in West Berlin and the German Democratic Republic — that essentially the present structure of a dual set of dialogues, one on Jesus and one on Paul, took shape.

Although each set focused its major attention on either Jesus or Paul, the four of us not only read each other's written statements but also listened to each other's verbal dialogues — sometimes in English and sometimes in German — and also shared in them.

The response to our dialogues, by Jews and by Christians, was so generally positive that we were encouraged to put them in a form for publication as a book, which is what we have done here.

We perceive this whole enterprise as an exercise in dialogue. It is an encounter in which each partner comes *primarily* to learn from rather than teach the other, though obviously if learning is to occur teaching must also — *secondarily*.

The structure of our verbal interchanges takes the form of statements on a topic concerning either Jesus or Paul, on which there has been contention in the past. Each opinion section is followed by another author's response. The two parts of the book follow essentially the same format, with summary statements at the end of each of the two sets of dialogue. We have also added extensive footnotes and annotated bibliographies for those who wish to pursue the scholarly path further. Most of all, we hope that our readers will be stimulated to follow the path of dialogue.

Prologue

Why a book on this subject? Jewish scholarship is suspicious of treatments of Christian origins that stress Jewish roots. It tends to think that such works are covertly proselytizing in intent. Christian scholarship is suspicious of Jewish interest in the question, either supposing that those who address it will hold the gospel to contain little new or that only a confused approach is to be expected of Jews and Christians of such evident good will. As the learned in these matters know, the birth of Christianity from Israel was both painful and bloody. The relationship of the two religions to this day is that of a parent who asked for no such child and a rebellious, adolescent offspring. Can the story be retold in such a way as to foster any measure of reconciliation without studious avoidance of the facts?

The best reason for a dialectical exchange is that the hard-headed scholarship so much praised by both sides has often proceeded from a set of premises which led inevitably to polemics. There should be room for an approach based on mutual respect, since mutual suspicion has held the field for so long. Ignorance of the facts has also abounded, providing a perfect formula for misunderstanding. Add to this a lively suspicion of the other's motives, especially when either side puts forward positions other than the long-familiar ones, and the possibilities for continuing antipathy are limitless.

Participants in any conversation between Jews and Christians at a scholarly level must face the possibility that a fuller knowledge of history of the period, including the antagonisms expressed by each side, will lead to even more bitter feelings. A legend has long been cherished by each of the adversaries about the other. If historical research should disclose the offenses of the past to have been far worse than imagined, what then? "To know me is to love me" may be as foolish a claim in the exchange of religious histories as it is on bumper stickers.

Are inquirers into controversies of long standing to be trusted when they claim to lay bare all that they find? What if they are so bent on reducing tensions that their willingness to bring to light any data that could increase these tensions is questionable? Are the contributors to this volume, in particular, so predisposed to religious harmony that they are unable to make the case for Jewish-Christian dissonance? The period of the origins of the two traditions (since Judaism, as we know it, was an offspring of the religion of biblical Israel) was by any reckoning marked by certain oppo-

1

sitions. It remains to be seen whether the writers of this book are able to acknowledge them.

The writers are not only academic colleagues but friends. That is a suspicious detail in itself. To have an abhorrence of religious hatred and a love of religious peace may, as we have indicated, disqualify anyone for objective study. The persons engaged in this project are convinced that, whatever historical truth may signify, ignorance of that truth is its meanest counterfeit.

The data for a study of the Jewish parentage of Christianity are fragmentary. Except for the writings of the historian Josephus, there is on the Jewish side no contemporary mention of the Christian phenomenon. Josephus refers to John the Baptist, James of Jerusalem who was murdered in 62 C.E., and Jesus—the latter evidently edited theologically by Christian hands in such a way as to have Josephus acknowledge Jesus' messiahship. The original text is, however, recoverable in a tenth-century Arabic translation by a Bishop Agapius, much shorter than the suspect Slavonic version, the so-called *"Testimonium Flavianum."* Josephus' sycophantic currying of Roman favor (he adopted the name of the imperial *domus Flaviana* by whom he was employed) disqualifies him in Jewish eyes as an accurate reporter on Jewish history, especially regarding the war of 67–73 C.E. In that engagement he acted first the coward, then the braggart. He may have written in Aramaic but his work is preserved in Greek, and it was Christians who preserved it. This has provided grounds for its not being taken seriously by Jews until very recent times.

The far greater reason for the lack of Jewish data was that the Jewish community opted for the Mishnah and Gemara as the continuation of the report on their life as a people. It might be noted in passing that there is no Jewish account from the period on exactly who were the Pharisees, Sadducees, or the community of Qumran except its own report (Josephus' characterization of these "three philosophies" is too brief to be informative). We are left with the impression from Jewish sources that the Samaritans and those Greek-influenced, non-observant Jews designated "Epicures" were the only departers from Jewish centrality worthy of notice. There is a fair amount about Sadducees, Boethians, and Perushim in Jewish sources, but this information is of questionable worth and does not deal with most of the historical facts that interest us. It does, however, show a lack of Jewish unity during the period of Christian origins. Unfortunately, those who came to be called Christians did not figure in Jewish reckoning.

The Christian community's record of its own earliest activities is not very extensive. Religious and scholarly attention to this relatively small corpus has been so intense that it gives a different impression. The events of the years 30 to 50—the latter the date of Paul's first extant letter(s)—are sufficiently obscure as to be described by Christian historians as "the tunnel period." Nothing Christian whatever remains in Aramaic, the *lingua franca* of most Jews of Palestine who believed in Jesus. The early chapters of what is known today as Luke's Acts of the Apostles—what *he* called it we do not know, probably "my second book"—are largely a theological reconstruction from the late first century. Luke may well have had a Jerusalem source and Pauline journey-narrative sources, but, if he did, they were already worked up rhetorically in the manner of the historiography of that age.

The four gospels in their present form probably come from the last thirty years of the first century. All four derive from Palestinian traditions about Jesus' life and teaching, but in the form in which they reach us they are much influenced by Hellenist Judaism. The Septuagint version was the Bible of all who contributed to the New Testament, as it was of diaspora Jews generally. There is some witness to the Masoretic Text in those twenty-seven books and also to targums on the Holy Scriptures. The latter may have been better known popularly than the text itself. Paul's seven letters surely written by him are, paradoxically, the only testimony to Jewish life that we can positively date to the fifth decade of the century. These are, in what may be the sequence of their authorship, 1 Thessalonians, 1 and 2 Corinthians, Philippians, Philemon, Galatians, and Romans. Paul is the best candidate for having written the second Thessalonian letter; he provided the ideas if not the wording of Colossians. Ephesians is certainly a second-generation anthology of Pauline thought, as is 1 Peter; 1 and 2 Timothy and Titus were produced well after Paul's lifetime, in part in a spirit opposed to his, although claiming perfect fidelity to him. The remaining Christian writings that make up the canon can be safely dated to the period 70–135 (James; 1, 2 and 3 John; Hebrews; Revelation; Jude; 2 Peter). The same is true of the noncanonical material equally important to the reconstruction of Christian beginnings (1 Clement, the Didachē, the Shepherd of Hermas, and the epistles from shipboard of Ignatius of Antioch).

The Dead Sea scrolls are instructive as a reminder of the kinds of Judaism that may have been abroad in the first century. The Gnostic Christian library of Nag Hammadi on the upper Nile, discovered in 1945, can tell us something of gospel composition and the kinds of writing some Christians drew upon for their view of Christianity. None of the canonical books is extant in that collection. Highly germane to an exploration of Christian origins are the biblical books of the so-called "second canon," namely those of the LXX that the rabbis of Yavneh dismissed as "not soiling the hands" (viz., not numinous enough to affect the handler). The extensive collection of Jewish writings dating from 165 B.C.E. to 135 C.E. known as the Pseudepigrapha ("false writings" in the sense of not being acceptable guides to authentic Jewishness) shed light on the kind of Judaism in which the Christian movement originated. Listing the above sources requires immediately that a word be said about their status in their respective communities.

Jewish distaste for the writings of Josephus has already been mentioned. The same is even truer of the pseudepigraphic writings. They were either composed in Greek or else survived in Greek translation, the language of the despised oppressors (the ordinary Roman populace as well as the Greeks). Many feature apocalyptic dreams of a deliverance in the impending future that the Rabbis gradually repudiated. It took the Rabbis a full two centuries after 70 C.E. to accomplish this, but they eventually succeeded. This provides the paradox of Christianity as the preserver of the apocalyptic tradition of post-biblical Judaism while later Judaism officially let it languish. That has not kept it from flourishing as an underground stream in the kabbalistic tradition, but the Rabbis always professed to know little of it and have a poor view of what they did know. There remains, to be sure, a lively Jewish hope in the "days of Messiah," but this is interpreted variously. Meantime, because of the evolution in Jewish thought, the eschatological or apocalyptic character of Christianity provides sufficient reason why Judaism, which is identical with rabbinism, is convinced it need not take Christianity seriously. No claimant to the title "the religion of Israel" which understood Judaism any way but halakhically has been allowed the distinction since the turn of the second century C.E. That includes any tradition based on end-expectation or mystical experience more than on *halakhah*, "walking in the way."

The libraries from Qumran and Nag Hammadi were lost until our time. Historians knew of the movements only through the polemical remarks of their opponents, the "legitimate" streams within the Jewish and Christian traditions. With few exceptions, Jews and Christians alike have welcomed the discoveries from the Dead Sea and have accepted the scrolls as valuable witnesses to a sectarian group within Judaism. The same almost universal welcome cannot be found when we turn to the Gnostic writings. The literature is in Coptic, rather than in the more well-known languages of Hebrew, Aramaic, or Greek. But the problem extends beyond the difficulty of the language. These are writings that were judged to be heretical. Since they were rejected once before, should they not also be rejected now?

The Christian movement was increasingly influenced by Hellenism at the time the rabbis were throwing off this foreign cultural yoke. This means that by the year 200 the two had quite different vocabularies and practices. It might be thought that the ethnic basis of the religious community Israel, a basis that Christianity increasingly lacked after 70, would suffice to distinguish the two. In fact, however, Israel was significantly Hellenized in the days of Jesus, his disciples, and Paul, even in Palestine. Moreover, Judaism encompassed many Gentile proselytes and sympathizers, making it not easily distinguishable from the adherents to Jesus within it until after the fall of Jerusalem. The years 70–135 were critical ones for both communities, marking the time of solidification in self-awareness. The Christians defined themselves in terms of membership in Israel, although increasingly in contradistinction to Judaism. If Jews anywhere in the homeland or the diaspora defined themselves with reference to the new movement, there is no record of it. That is not to say, however, that when Paul was sending the epistles we have or when the roots of Mark's gospel were being put down, there was no Jewish writing in a similar spirit without the mention of Jesus. Several Jewish apocryphal writings in Greek come to us from just that time. The rabbinic repudiation of the *genre* was a subsequent development.

In brief, the absolutely clear-cut distinction between the kinds of writing found in the earliest parts of the Christian collection and contemporary Jewish writing is something that comes later. It could well have been preceded by the destruction of certain Jewish religious writings because they conformed so little to the new, halakhic pattern, or the suppression of certain Christian writings because they conformed so much to Judaism. In any case, the "non-Jewish" character of the New Testament and cognate first-century documents that Jewish and some Christian scholarship tends to speak of can be claimed only if the fairly large body of writing outlined above is repudiated as not being Jewish. For some, only the discovery of first-century writings in Aramaic or Hebrew from Palestinian groups that believed Jesus to be the messiah can definitely reverse the judgment that the movement was not Jewish. In light of the Qumran and Nag Hammadi finds of this century, the suggestion of such future discoveries is not foolish.

It is possible to deny that the bulk of the Christian testament has come from sectarian Judaism only because it does not meet criteria proposed by the Judaism of a later time. To be sure, a tradition should be able to define what falls within and without its own self-imposed limits. That is not a problem. The question is: was there ever a time that portions of the New Testament might have qualified as fully Jewish? The bitterness that developed between the two traditions after the Bar Kokhba revolt in 130–135 C.E. already showed itself in the gospels, the Acts of the Apostles, and the Letter to the Hebrews. This created a retrospective apologetic that declared certain matters unthinkable for Judaism and dogma for Christianity. An exhaustive knowledge of the post-biblical writings by Jews, especially the later ones before the Mishnah rendered them redundant, reveals a surprising latitude of belief within Judaism. There was also a wide latitude among early Christian groups that is easily forgotten. The Christian movement, a rival claimant to Jewish loyalties, became unthinkable as a form of Judaism because of its increasing Graeco-Roman cultural component. In the opposite direction, it was Judaism and not paganism that provided the greatest attraction to Christians to return to or, if they were Gentiles, to start practicing.

The direction in which this discussion is going seems to suggest that some good can be derived from establishing how close Christianity was to Judaism in its earliest phases. What purpose exactly would be served if such an affinity were provable? These two ways of being religious are different. They have been so almost from the beginning of the corporate memory of either at the time of the separation. The learned and the simple in both traditions so wish to maintain the difference that it may appear mischievous to put the two in a relation that did not continue very long. Why go back to the fork in the road if it achieves nothing but revive old resentments?

The way forward seems the better way to go: a harmonious existence built on respect and nurtured by common action to heal society's ills. Hunger and homelessness, prejudice, and peace and armaments are public causes enough to draw on the ethical commitment of the two communities. A review of history not only appeals to very few but is seen by many as a way of ensuring that no practical measures will be taken. It is thought to be an academic exercise in the worst sense. Show us your deeds, the Jew says to the Christian. With far less right to make the demand, the Christian says the same to the Jew.

The reason the exploration contained in the following chapters should go forward is that religious hostilities flourish not only because antagonists do not know the traditions of the other but because they do not know their own. They rest secure in a double caricature, that of the religion which they see as the root of all their ills and that of the one they profess. Ignorance of where one's religious family has been, and why its commitments are as they are, is the chief reason the vacuum is filled with a fictitious reading of "the other." The prime benefit achieved by serious interreligious inquiry is a more secure hold on what one is committed to. This is not to say that looking at things as they were when a historic split was effected is the only fruitful way to proceed. It is, however, one that has merit. Buddhism coming forth from Hinduism, Puritan dissent from the established church, Conservative and Reform Judaism from European Orthodox Judaism: in every case it makes sense to ask what the issues were then and what they say to different traditions now. In brief, who are we religiously—whoever the "we" is—that we felt we had to leave the religious family that nurtured us, or dismiss from our company some of our number? Would we do it again? Could we do it again? There is nothing quite like this painful exercise to help discover who we are and whether we have sufficient grounds to go on in this way forever as we felt we had to at the time. If the answer has to be yes, can the separate existence be a matter of peace rather than harshness and enmity?

One important discovery in the Jewish-Christian situation might be that the Jesus of history, difficult as it is to reconstruct him, was a recognizable Jewish reformer whose utterances—however much edited by disciples—disclose him as a man of religious genius. That conclusion could either alienate Christians and Jews further or convince them that they can both claim him without validating the interpretation the other puts on him. Jews generally have no desire to claim Jesus as one of their own because of the pain to their people he symbolizes. If they were able to separate him from the faith tradition that centers on him, they might be able to see him as one of their great ones. Normally that is impossible. Christian affirmations of faith in the divine as well as human Jesus interfere with Jews' considering him on *any* terms. On the other hand, many Christians want to see Jesus in opposition to Judaism rather than in agreement with it. Jewish denials of the divine nature of Jesus interfere with Christians' considering him to be faithful to the Jewish beliefs and practices of his time.

There is another discovery that can come from dialogue. Christians read in their Scriptures the resistance to the gospel that its second- and third-generation proclaimers encountered. Some Christians attribute to "the Jews" the conscious resistance that this frustrated band first experienced. Unaware that all religious movements as described by their protagonists do the same, they read as history the record of sectarian struggle within a tradition. Seeing themselves there as "the Christians"—already a full-blown, non-Jewish group—they have no difficulty identifying with their fellow-religionists. Jews give the Christian Scriptures the same *prima facie* sort of reading, imposing the concept "anti-Semitic" on a literature that describes an internal struggle in a religious community whose real enemy is pagan political power. Reports on Christian origins from rabbinic sources might provide some perspective, but they might also only exacerbate the situation.

The point is that a polemical literature constitutes the only *monumenta* we have of Christian beginnings. It describes two tendencies or parties within a tradition, a land mass coming apart to form two continents. These tendencies would before too long be two religions. Their similarity in dissimilarity is their pain. This Humpty-Dumpty sundered beyond the power of all the horses and men of the great King to reassemble is almost impossible to envision. The inclination is to say, why bother? Too much acrimony has followed upon the initial fall. Besides, any semblance of primitive unity is irretrievable. But in the struggle to reconstruct history, some Jew or Christian is likely to say: "It is not as I was led to believe. My popular instructors (or my scholarly sources) had no inkling of a reading of the data like this one." If any were to discover themselves the victims of an interpretation of first-century happenings in a patristic (talmudic, reformation) pattern, much would be achieved. Learning what happened in history may seem to make a small difference, but it can make all the difference.

The major discovery is that what have been portrayed as diametric oppositions prove often differences of emphasis; that what was spoken of as inconceivable in Jewish or Christian circumstances proves to have had a home there over a long period; that patterns of grace and law and righteousness and hope of the final triumph of God have been the common possession of the two. They are not undiscoverable in the other, as was so repeatedly and erroneously said.

The danger of reading any documents in a new way is that an inappropriate, romantic reconstruction or an economic revisionism or a *Realpolitik* of antiquity may prevail. Once an ideology has begun to spin its web there is no end to the possibilities. In the present instance a person may be bent on productive dialogue and for that reason may try to avoid over-optimistic presupposition. The net result may be the reasonable hypothesis that matters were of a certain character for a brief period in a small part of the Roman empire. The coexistence thus discovered did not endure for long, however, being shortly succeeded by the angry counterclaims of the threateners and the threatened. But the hypothesis of the situation *in illo tempore* seems unassailable. What has been gained?

The will to uncover and understand the truth may lead to unfamiliar conclusions such as that, while according to the gospels Jesus attacked the scribes and Pharisees, he was actually one of them. Or that Stephen was a supporter of the Law and temple sacrifice; his stoning was on cultural or linguistic grounds but not religious. Or that Paul was set against certain confused believers in Jesus but had no quarrel with Jews outside of believing Christian circles. Having encountered someone in ecstatic vision who rechanneled his apocalyptic enthusiasm, he continued to direct it toward diaspora Gentiles. Scenarios such as these are numberless. The only question to be asked is, what is the evidence for them? Given the glaring omissions in the extant documents, how plausible is the reconstruction and how would the acceptance of one or more of these scenarios change us, our tradition, and our view of the other and their tradition?

The essays in this collection are revisionist only because the authors think that the evidence in hand does not lead to familiar conclusions. The authors are not bent on novelty for its own sake, nor out to twist first-century data to yield a benign twentieth-century result. They do think that ignorance of certain realities in Jesus' lifetime and Paul's, compounded by the desire of Jews and Christians ever since to maintain a mutually antagonistic stance, has kept even the world of scholarship from an honest look at the data. Learned Christians have persisted in anti-Jewish readings of their own sources. Learned Jews have followed the Christian lead when, in fact, the same hard look they give to other aspects of their peoplehood might have disclosed the unfair burden much "critical" study of the New Testament has placed on them. Christians have had the necessary tools but not the will to achieve a better reading. Jews have a sense of the terrible injustice but no great desire to put critical scholarship to work on certain of their own first-century materials which they find of little value. Nor do Jews wish to examine those Christian writings that have touched them deeply in such negative ways because of their long experience of Christian responses to such efforts. Few Jewish or Christian scholars have bothered to master the basic medium of the other's literature or language—biblical Hebrew yes, but not Aramaic or Greek—to be fully at ease in the elements of the problem.

If this seems to be written from a superior pose, it is a superiority to the determination of the last two centuries to read post-biblical and early Christian literature as if no continuity were involved, only a sharp break. The two destructions of Jerusalem, in 70 and 135, brought about a tremendous historical shift. So did the rise of the Jesus movement, however imperceptible it was to the bulk of Jews in its earlier stages. Not to know the precise social effects on Jewry of the double military repression in the land of Israel and elsewhere is a great handicap. Were it not for the huge lacuna of information, fragmentary data like the carving on the arch of Titus in the Roman forum and 1 Clement's reference to Peter and Paul, the mentions of Hillel and Shammai in the Mishnah and Justin's reconstruction of Trypho's part of the dialogue would not loom so large.

The Pauline correspondence, the gospels, and the other Christian materials exist. So do the Pseudepigrapha, the *Pirqe Avot*, and the other tractates of the Mishnah. But because the two religious communities have viewed them as absolutely distinct literatures, one of them adversarial, each has disregarded the other except in a polemical spirit. There are exceptions, of course, but by and large this observation is true.

A further complication is the sixteenth-century breach in Western Christianity that has led to reading Paul as if he had written in the grace controversy of the fifth. As a result, chapter 11 of the epistle to the Romans has a long Christian history of interpretation about the sovereignty of the divine predestinarian will and surprisingly little about the Jewish people. "Works of the Law" became the rabbinic *mitzvoth* and Catholic Masses for the dead indiscriminately, since the two were understood as identical denials of justifying faith that became "the Gospel." Neither Protestants nor Catholics have noted that Paul was saying important things to them about Jews and Judaism, things that could terminate their espousal of him as their champion of the Gentiles against his own people. It is a rare Jew who has explored Paul enough to conclude that he might have something to say to Jews about the Law in relation to God's care for them and for the Gentiles. It is a rare Christian who has studied Jewish literature sufficiently to understand the Jewish background of Paul.

Both sides have built their defensive walls high. Those whose writings, canonical and other, testify to their origins as a new religious tradition have not been open to the possibility that these could tell against their dearest prejudices. Those who find themselves described there as persecutors of a religious minority in their midst have not been open to learning whether their centuries of being the persecuted had any such prehistory. All new births bring pain to mother and child. But also joy. The joy in this case will not come with the mother's claiming the offspring, nor by the child's recognizing the mother as she truly is. That may take centuries. The joy will come in the short term from another quarter. It will derive from the knowledge that there has been more misunderstanding than understanding. Simple ignorance is a heavy burden to bear. When it is crass or supine (medieval language for the willingly adopted or passively allowed) it becomes intolerable. To be quit of this weight can bring a spring in the gait, a livelier approach to life for the few who are thus unburdened. It can bring a new respect for the religiously other who has been feared or despised for numerous wrong reasons.

The essays that follow may themselves be marked by error, thereby adding to the confusion. But the authors are convinced that they have a few things right. They believe that it is better to try to find a new road to truth, even if they stumble, than complacently to follow the old road which they know leads to error. Authentic history is potentially everyone's enemy. Ultimately it is a friend, but only to those who will accept its cauterizing of old wounds. The reflections that follow are written with the hope of increasing amity, not enmity. The physicians know that they above all need the healing.

PART I

A Jewish-Christian Dialogue on Jesus

Leonard Swidler   **Lewis John Eron**

1

Why Christians Need To Dialogue with Jews and Judaism about Jesus

LEONARD SWIDLER

There are several very important reasons why Christians need to be in dialogue with Jews and Judaism about Jesus. The most significant of them can be summed up in the brief statement that Jesus was a Jew.[1] It is a truism that whatever sort of Christianity a person claims to profess, that Christianity must somehow ultimately be based on Jesus of Nazareth (or *Yeshua*, as he was called in Hebrew by his own followers). Therefore, it is vital that Christians learn who and what Yeshua was. This means learning what a Jew and Judaism are—and that is best done in dialogue with Jews and Judaism. In such a move Christians will come to know better their roots, or rather their root, in the Jew Yeshua who was born of the Hebraic tradition and was related somehow to the early rabbinic Jewish tradition. The primitive Christian church had the same origins. Very soon, however, Hellenist Jewish elements entered into nascent Christianity and played a great role in its subsequent development. In the third quarter of the first century Gentile Greek and Syrian elements were added.

Christians also need to be in dialogue with Jews and Judaism for the same reasons they need to be in dialogue with all other religions and ideologies—in brief: (1) to gain an insight into reality that they are not able to attain from their own standpoint in the world; (2) to learn to know themselves more profoundly, as it were, in the mirror of their dialogue partner, and (3) to come to know and appreciate Jews for what they truly are, rather than to denigrate them for what Christians distortedly think they are.

The third point leads to another major reason why Christians need to be in dialogue with Jews and Judaism. Namely, there exists a need to explore the overwhelmingly negative history of the relations of Christians with Jews throughout most of the two thousand years they have in common. From the Christian side this history can be largely summed up in two words: anti-Judaism (hatred of Jews on religious grounds) and anti-semitism (hatred of Jews on ethnic and racial grounds)—a history of suspicion, denigration, oppression, hatred, robbery, rapine, murder, and genocide of Jews. The horrible paradox is that Christians claim to be the followers of Jesus, of Rabbi Yeshua, who was a Jew. They claim that he showed them how to live a human life, and therefore they try to imitate him. They speak—and, to be more personal, I should say *we* speak—of *imitatio Christi*. But when we Christians hate Jews, we hate what Yeshua was, a Jew. We hate, then, what we say we are trying to be, a kind of Jew, one who has been led to the one true God, the God of Abraham, Isaac, and Jacob, Sarah, Rebecca, and Rachel, through Rabbi Yeshua whom we call the Christ. Then we Christians hate the people Israel, that "good olive tree onto which [we] wild shoots have been grafted," as Paul described the Gentile Christian relationship to the Jewish people.

Thus, we Christians must reject anti-Judaism and anti-Semitism, not only on general humanitarian grounds, but also because they mean a hatred of those whom our Scriptures tell us are the chosen people of God (and Paul reminds us that God can never go back on the promises made to that people). We Christians must reject anti-Judaism and anti-Semitism because they mean hatred of the Jew Yeshua whom we Christians call Lord and say we love and imitate. Lastly, we Christians must reject anti-Judaism and anti-Semitism because they mean self-hatred. Instead of being *anti*-Semites, we Christians should be *philo*-Semites, for Yeshua, Jesus, was a Jew, and we Christians are his followers and members of his people, religiously if not ethnically.

In this Jewish-Christian dialogue we are going to concentrate on one figure who has been both a bond and a barrier between the Jewish and Christian traditions and peoples, the Jew Yeshua. Whole libraries have been written by Christians, and in the last hundred years a mounting number of books by Jews, on Yeshua the Jew.[2] The potential areas of interest are vast. Here, of course, we can focus on only a few topics. Even then, our remarks will be very limited. For my part, I wish to concentrate on three areas: 1) Yeshua's place in the Jewish life of his time; 2) his attitude toward the Law; and 3) his relationship to messiahship and how his followers interpreted that relationship in the subsequent development of christology.

First, it would be helpful, especially for Christians, to recall something about the meaning of the name of Jesus, for it will provide an insight into the Jewish tradition.

Jesus, we know, is simply a Latin form of the Greek *Iēsous.* Even "Iesous" itself is not originally a Greek name, but rather a Greek form of a Hebrew name, "Yehoshua" (the biblical "Yoshua") which means "YHWH [probably pronounced "Yahweh"] is salvation." There is no difficulty in understanding the movement from Yehoshua, which in colloquial parlance would sometimes be abbreviated as Yeshua or even Yeshu, into the Greek and Latin transliterations *Iēsous* and *Jesus*. However, in the movement of the name Yeshua from its original forms into the various languages used by Christians and others, unfortunately something important has been lost. To begin with, Jews no longer use the name Yeshua, nor indeed do Christians. (In fact, both the Hebrew and Greek forms as proper names disappeared from usage after the first century.)[3] As a consequence, both Christians and Jews automatically think of Jesus as the name of someone other than a Jew. That simple fact tends to cut Christians off from the taproot of their religion, the Hebrew-Jewish tradition. Simultaneously, on the other side it also tends to cut Jews off from a very important son of their tradition, one who has become the most influential Jew of all history, surpassing in historical impact even such giants as Moses, David, Marx, Freud, and Einstein.

Yeshua is made up of two parts. The first, "Ye," is an abbreviated form of the Hebrew proper name for God, "YHWH." The second, "shua," is the Hebrew word for salvation.[4] However, the word *salvation* is one that to a large extent has been significantly altered in the Christian tradition from its meaning in Israelite religion and its root meaning in Greek and Latin. For the most part it has been given a restricted meaning since the third century C.E. Since that time, Christians have come to understand salvation to signify that when believers in Jesus Christ die, they will go to heaven if they have remained faithful. However, that is not at all what the word basically means. In its late Latin form, *salvatio,* it comes from the root "salv[-u]" (the Greek form is "Sōterion/sōteria" from "sōs") meaning wholeness, health or well-being — hence, salutary and salubrious in English. A similar derivation is true of the Germanic word for salvation, *Heil,* which adjectivally also means whole, hale, healed, healthy. In fact, this is also where the English word *holy* comes from. Being holy means being whole, leading a whole, a full life. If we lead a whole, full life, we are holy; we attain salvation, wholeness.[5]

Yeshua, then, means YHWH is salvation, wholeness; and the name YHWH is the Hebrew proper name of the one and only God who created everything that exists. The concept of monotheism is so taken for granted today that we do not realize what an extraordinary breakthrough this insight was in the history of humankind. The immediate implications for how one related to all other human beings and all reality were massive. If one lived in a nation that had its own god or gods, and all other nations also had their own god or gods, then the ethical rules developed by one god's religion would not be applicable to those persons and things under other gods. Therefore, there was not one ethic that was valid for all human beings and for all the earth — until the insight developed that there was, in fact, one creator God of all human beings and all reality.

Thus, the very name Yeshua is an assertion that YHWH is the source of wholeness for all human beings, for all things. It is a name that carries the very heart of the great contribution of the Hebrew people to humanity: ethical monotheism. There were of course many Jewish men who were named Yeshua besides Yeshua of Nazareth. Nevertheless, there is a special appropriateness in the fact that Yeshua of Nazareth was given this name, for it is through him that billions of non-Jews came to the Jewish insight of ethical monotheism, came to YHWH, came to salvation, to wholeness.

A Response to Leonard Swidler from Lewis John Eron

I agree most fully with your understanding that the fundamental reason for a person to enter interreligious dialogue is to learn about the other and one's self. The purpose of dialogue is neither to convince nor convert. Its purpose is to provide the opportunity to learn.

Dialogue is not negotiation. In dialogue the participants do not trade beliefs or bargain dogmas. Rather they try to listen and share. In this light, I would like to respond to a number of the points you made:

(1) I assume that you want to call Jesus by the Hebraic form of the name, Yeshua, in order to remind Christians that he was a Jew. That is surely a good reason. Yet I feel that in the context of Jewish-Christian dialogue, a Christian's calling Jesus of Nazareth by the name Yeshua is more of an impediment to dialogue than an aid. Yeshua is the name for Jesus used by members of the so-called Jews for Jesus cults in their attempt to convert Jews to their form of Christianity. For contemporary Jews, then, the name Yeshua has negative connotations.

In addition, I do not believe that Jews ever forgot that Jesus of Nazareth was a Jew. They may have considered him to have been a bad Jew, a false messiah, a misguided magician, or many other things, but he was always considered Jewish. Jews may be surprised to learn that Jesus did not see himself as any more than a reformer of the Judaism of his age, but even when they pictured Jesus in a dark light, Jews remembered that Jesus was born a Jew.

(2) Your description of Christians as Jesus' "followers and members of his people, religiously if not ethnically," is also confusing in light of Jewish-Christian dialogue. Christian use of the concept of peoplehood lacks the deep historical, cultural, ethnic, and familial resonances in the Jewish use of the term. More helpful, I feel, is Paul van Buren's distinction between God's Holy People, the Jews, and God's Holy Church, the Christians. The closest theological equivalent to the Jewish concept *Am Yisrael*, "the People Israel" is the Greek term *ekklēsia*, "the Church."

(3) Although you seem to feel that it is a great loss to the Jews that they were "cut off from a very important son of their tradition, one who has become the most influential Jew of all history," I do not sense this loss.

For Christians, a loss of Jesus' Jewish roots can result in a possible loss of identity. The Jews, on the other hand, at worst suffer from the lack of familiarity with a figure who has great significance for many in Western civilization, though little in Judaism.

I believe that Judaism as a cultural and religious system has little to gain and much to lose by anything but a carefully nuanced homecoming of Jesus. On the one hand, I believe that Jews have little to learn ethically and theologically from Jesus who, himself, is well situated in the Pharisaic/early rabbinic tradition. Yet, on the other hand, I feel that we Jews can learn a great deal from Christians.

Although I feel that Christianity is a remarkable and serious religious tradition, I do not find Jesus particularly engaging. My basic problem in this dialogue is to find a way to be able to tell Christians that although I respect and admire their tradition, my interest in Jesus is of a historical nature.

Unlike most Jews who write on Jesus, I have a much more positive view of Christianity than I do of Jesus. Despite the harsh treatment Jews received at Christian hands, I am intrigued and impressed by the religious creativity shown in the development of the Christian church from late antiquity to the present.

(4) Finally, I am surprised that you included Karl Marx in your list of influential Jews. I know there are some Jews who claim anyone as Jewish who has some Jewish ancestry. Although Jewish ancestry may be one of the ways of entering the Jewish people, unless we want to accept the criteria of our enemies, being Jewish involves much more than having "Jewish blood."

Karl Marx, religiously and culturally, fits much better in the Christian camp. Although his father and mother were Jews who converted to Christianity, Marx had no connections to the Jewish tradition. He was a baptized and confirmed member of the Protestant church.

In fact, one of the great problems Jews, in general, and Jewish socialists, in particular, have with Marxism stems from Karl Marx's misunderstanding of Judaism as an example of bourgeois capitalism. Not only did he disregard the Jewish self-understanding of being a historical people, but he also expressed his opinions on Jews and Judaism in highly negative terms using the most virulent language.

By the strict application of Jewish law that defines a Jew as one either born of a Jewish mother or converted to Judaism, one could argue that Marx was a Jew. Yet his Jewish origins played no role in his upbringing except as a curse that he could not escape. In that way alone, Marx was a typical deracinated, nineteenth-century Jew.

NOTES

1. This point was made with crystal clarity over eighty years ago by Julius Wellhausen: "Jesus was not a Christian; he was a Jew." *Einleitung in die drei ersten Evangelien* (Berlin: Reimer, 1905), p. 113.

2. For Jewish scholars see, e.g., Schalom Ben-Chorin, *Bruder Jesus* (Munich: Paul List Verlag, 1967); David Flusser, *Jesus* (New York: Herder & Herder, 1969); Joseph Klausner, *Jesus of Nazareth* (London: Allen & Unwin, 1925); Pinchas Lapide, *Der Jude Jesus* (Zürich: Benziger, 1979), and many others in both English and German; Geza Vermes, *Jesus the Jew* (Philadelphia: Fortress Press, 1981).

3. See *"Iēsous"* in Gerhard Kittel, ed., *Theological Dictionary of the New Testament* (Grand Rapids, MI: Eerdmans, 1966), vol. III, pp. 284ff.

4. Whereas the root meaning of the Indo-European word for salvation is fullness, wholeness, the root meaning of the Semitic word used here, "shua," is that of capaciousness, openness. Salvation in its Semitic root means the opposite of being in straits; it means being free in wide open space. Thus it is close to, though not precisely the same as, the Indo-European root meaning.

5. The Jewish scholar Geza Vermes confirms this Semitic understanding of salvation as being current with Yeshua and his contemporaries when he points out that they linked together physical and spiritual health: "In the somewhat elastic, but extraordinarily perceptive religious terminology of Jesus and the spiritual men of his age, 'to heal,' 'to expel demons,' and 'to forgive sins' were interchangeable synonyms," *Jesus and the World of Judaism* (Philadelphia: Fortress Press, 1984), p. 10.

2

The Problem of a Jew
Talking to a Christian about Jesus

LEWIS JOHN ERON

There is something very strange, if not wrong, when a Jew discusses Jesus of Nazareth for a predominately Christian audience as part of a Jewish-Christian dialogue. The role and function of the historical Jesus and the proclaimed Christ is a central Christian issue, not a Jewish one. It turns out that Jesus, his teachings, and his disciples did not, for better or worse, find their place in the tradition and history of the people Israel. Rather, they survived in the bosom of a collection of Gentiles who became known as the Church. Yet Jesus, as man and as Christ, has been the point of contact and, all too often, the point of conflict in the almost two-thousand-year-long relationship of the Church and the Synagogue.

Jesus' almost completely insignificant role within the Jewish tradition has appeared scandalous to his faithful and believing followers. Loyal Christians, for whom Jesus is the center of their lives and faith, have been bewildered, threatened, and angered by the Jews' refusal to accept Jesus. This factor provided the theological underpinnings for the sad history of the Christian world's disputes with Jews and persecutions of Jews. These disputes and persecutions answered, at least in part, Christians' need for self-confirmation as God's chosen people in light of the perceived threat to that hope suggested by the continuity of Jewish life.[1]

Jews, challenged by Christian claims for Jesus, remembered Jesus through garbled historical traditions that were preserved and transmitted as part of a polemical defense of Judaism.[2] Attempting to understand Christian theological claims for Christ, primarily to structure the ways Jews were to interact with the Christian world, Jewish lawyers and philosophers struggled to describe the ways in which trinitarian Christianity could be seen as a monotheistic faith.[3] Subject to Christian persecution and lacking the political and economic power base to defend themselves successfully, pre-modern Jews developed strong negative views of Christianity and its founder. These views still influence popular Jewish understandings of Jesus and Christianity.

In the last two hundred years and, particularly, in the last forty years, the historical relationship of Jews and Christians has undergone fundamental changes. Since the Enlightenment and Jewish emancipation from the ghettos of central Europe almost two hundred years ago, Jews were no longer a separate estate within a medieval state, but potential citizens of a modern state. The Jews' ability to assimilate into the life of modern states depended, naturally, on how the state and society defined citizenship and membership.

In a nation that de-emphasized ethnic heritage and religious affiliation as a condition of membership in the society, such as the United States in the latter half of the twentieth century, the Jews did very well. In a nation in which ethnic and racial heritage was essential for membership, such as Nazi Germany in the 1930s and 40s, the Jews suffered a disastrous fate. Overall in Europe and North America, the status of Jews in the modern period varied. They were never totally excluded but, on the other hand, were never unequivocally accepted.

The Enlightenment and Jewish emancipation began the process of integrating the Jews as individuals into Christian society. The Holocaust and the subsequent establishment of the State of Israel completed that process by integrating the Jews as a people not only into the Western world but into the entire world.

Today, Jewish interest in Jesus of Nazareth is significant for Jewish-Christian interrelations and dialogue in three areas: (1) the position of the Jews and their cultural relationship to Western civilization; (2) the Holocaust and Christian responsibility; and (3) the meeting of Jews and Christians in dialogue.

In the first area, the relevant issue is whether Judaism is to be considered integral to Western culture or is to be considered an exotic culture of an ethnic and religious minority.

Jaroslav Pelikan, the prominent professor of Church history at Yale University, begins his thoughtful book, *Jesus Through the Centuries: His Place in the History of Culture*, with the telling statement:

> Regardless of what anyone may personally think or believe about him, Jesus of Nazareth has been the dominant figure in the history of Western culture for almost twenty centuries. If it were possible, with some sort of super-magnet, to pull up out of that history, every scrap of metal bearing at least a trace of his name, how much would be left?[4]

Although this is a difficult question to consider, it is clear that, to Pelikan at least, the Jews would be left, as he left them out of his description of

Western culture. For the Jews, whose culture has flourished for almost twenty centuries in the lands of the West under both the Cross and Crescent, Jesus of Nazareth has been, at worst, a symbol of oppression and, at best, a historical footnote. Even after the Emancipation of the Jews, when they came running willy-nilly out of the ghettos and Städtels of central and Eastern Europe into the mainstream of European/Christian culture, Jesus of Nazareth did not become a central issue of Jewish concern.

Jewish involvement with Jesus was based primarily on the apologetic task of defending their tradition.[5] Yet even a cursory glance at Jewish writings from the Enlightenment onward shows that concern with Jesus of Nazareth is at best marginal in the broad array of Jewish interests. Jews, like their Christian contemporaries, have continually struggled with the implications of the revolutionary developments in science, technology, economics, psychology, sociology, and history for their tradition.[6]

For me, the underlying issue is whether or not the Jewish endeavor is to be considered part of Western culture. However this question is answered, it challenges the underlying assumption — expressed by Pelikan, who is not in any fashion antagonistic to Jews and Judaism — that Western culture is necessarily Christian culture. If Jewish civilization is acknowledged as part of Western culture, one admits that the terms Christian culture and Western culture cannot be used synonymously. Christianity was but one possible product of the amalgamation of the Hebraic and Hellenistic worlds that occurred in the last few centuries B.C.E. If Jewish civilization is considered not part of Western culture, only the centrality of Christianity and its founding figure, Jesus of Nazareth, appears to stand. The Jews and their culture remain a hidden challenge.

They can only be understood as the eternal *doppelgänger* to the predominant Christian culture of the West. Jewish culture is the threatening yet unseen ghost whose very presence challenges the assumption that Jesus of Nazareth is necessarily the central figure of Western culture. Jewish culture growing out of the same soil as Christian culture, reacting to the same historical events and cultural developments, existing side by side in the same lands, remains as the hidden challenger.

However, Judaism's challenge to the claim that Jesus of Nazareth is central to Western culture can be reduced to the extent that one can demonstrate the importance of Jesus to Judaism. The closer Jesus and his teachings come to represent the kernel of Jewish teachings, the more diffuse the challenge.

Since the Enlightenment, such an approach has found followers among Jews and Christians. For Christians, it domesticates the Jews. The more closely Jesus is tied to Jewish sources, the more useful rabbinic materials prove in the exegesis of the New Testament. As the continuity between Jesus and post-biblical Judaism appears stronger, Judaism becomes less threatening to the Christian sympathetic to Judaism. In addition, a close connection between Jesus and post-biblical and rabbinic Judaism provides these Christians a way of feeling part of Israel's endeavor without the rejection of Israel.

For Jews, such an approach to Jesus has been advantageous, for it enables them all the more easily to enter the Christian world. Jews are thus able to proclaim a high regard for Jesus of Nazareth, the perceived central figure in this world, and they can stress the compatibility of Judaism and Christianity.

The popularity of this approach is clearly marked in the common usage of the expression "Judaeo-Christian ethics." In contemporary American English, at least, the use of this term provides the vocabulary for the inclusion of Jews and Catholics into the social religion of a nation that had previously considered itself exclusively Protestant.

It is painful to fault people of good will. After nearly eighteen hundred years of Christianity's defining itself in opposition to Judaism, this modern and predominantly post-World War II shift in Christian self-awareness is in many ways welcome.

The point of view has surely been useful to Jews as they have tried to find a place for themselves in the Christian world. The implicit criticism of Christianity in this Jewish acceptance of Jesus, so clearly noted by Nancy Fuchs-Kreimer in an unpublished paper related to her doctoral work on Jewish views of Paul, has, however, been for the most part not noticed by Christians.[7] A Jewish Jesus could be used by Jews as part of an apologetic polemic against Christianity.

A high appreciation of Jesus, the loyal Jewish religious reformer, is balanced by a condemnation of Paul as a disloyal Jew who misunderstood the teachings of his professed master and founded a new religion. Jesus could be presented positively, but Christianity could still be seen negatively. The willingness of liberal Christians to apply a historical critical analysis to New Testament materials added to a general Protestant devaluation of Church tradition, clouding a large part of the Christian perception of this side of Jesus' homecoming.[8]

In this light, the concern with the Jewishness of Jesus takes on a negative aspect. For Jews, it allows their social integration into the predominant but ultimately intolerant society. For Christians, it makes Jews and Judaism safe.

The second area of significance pertains to the study of the Holocaust. This issue goes beyond determining to what extent traditional Christian anti-Judaism can be seen as a contributing factor to the Nazis' extermination of the Jews. It is concerned with which ways and on whose terms Christianity will develop a new understanding and acceptance of Judaism.

The history of intergroup relations in general and intra-Christian conflict in specific do little to support the hope that a renewed Christian understanding of the Jewishness of Jesus will necessarily make the world safer for Jews. Other factors, primarily those of economic and political power, play more important roles in the interaction between groups than religious and ideological ones. Christian theological anti-Judaism should not be seen as the sole cause of persecutions of the Jews. Were that the case, one could not explain the flourishing of Jewish life and culture in Christianized lands. Rather, it provided an ideological basis for the oppression of the Jewish minority when other factors came into play.[9]

Although the post-Holocaust encounter between Jews and Christians has sharpened Christian awareness of the theological roots of modern anti-Semitism, the resolution of whatever problems this awareness may cause in Christian theology needs to be done by Christians.[10] Jews cannot write theology for Christians; nor do we, who live after the Holocaust, have the authority to forgive (or perhaps, even, condemn) the Church and its members for the suffering that may have arisen from its theological anti-Judaism. That power rests in those who suffered and died.

Rosemary Ruether appears to be correct in indicating the close relationship between classical Christologies and anti-Semitism. The Reform Jewish scholar Eugene Borowitz, in his review of contemporary Christologies indicates, however, that on the whole today's liberal, post-liberal and even traditionalist Christologies avoid the theological anti-Judaism that supports anti-Semitism. At best, one of the traditional excuses for the persecution of Jews may be in the process of being eliminated.[11]

Although these two reasons for increased interest in Jewish understandings of Jesus arise out of the interrelationship of Judaism and Christianity, they are not necessarily grounded in the experience of dialogue. The way Jews and Christians understand Jesus and his relationship to Judaism have definite social and theological payoffs.

The third area of significance grows directly out of the dialogic encounter. In a dialogue a Jew can talk to a Christian about Jesus not because of Jesus' importance or lack of importance to Judaism but because of Jesus' importance to Christianity and the Christian. It is out of respect for the Christian partner that the Jew carefully enters into dialogue over Jesus.

It is obvious that a Jewish-Christian dialogue centering on Jesus of Nazareth is only part of a dialogue. I, as a Jew, cannot and do not enter the dialogue with the same concern and intensity as my Christian partner. Naturally, I need not be a passive partner in this dialogue. I can surely respond to statements and comment on what is being said. The centuries-long interrelationship between Judaism and Christianity, as well as the Jewish roots of Jesus and most of his earliest followers, should permit me to explore in some limited sense the theological as well as historical implications of the life, teachings and influence of Jesus of Nazareth. Jesus of Nazareth, however, is not my topic.

A similar, although not entirely congruent, problem would occur if we chose the Talmud and talmudic tradition as the focus of our dialogue. This work and tradition is central to Jewish life and culture but is incidental to Christianity. To be sure, Christians might find talmudic thought useful in studying the early years of their tradition, for they were also the early years of rabbinic Judaism, but their approach to the subject would be historical. Of course, it would be helpful to clear up Christian misunderstandings of the Talmud, but that would involve education and not dialogue. The fact that the New Testament employs many of the same methods in interpreting the Hebrew Scriptures as does rabbinic literature, permits the Christian partner to expand his or her exploration. But it would still be only a partial dialogue.

A theoretical Jewish-Christian dialogue on the Talmud could easily be part of a more extensive dialogue on the role of a common tradition in Judaism and Christianity. However, there is no simple counterpart to Jesus within the Jewish tradition. The centrality of Jesus to Christian faith, as well as the centering in Jesus of most of the leadership archetypes of the Hebrew Scripture from the writings of the earliest Christians on, has no simple parallel within Judaism. Kingship, prophecy, sacrifice, redemption, priesthood, messianism, apocalypticism, discipleship, and so on are among the many topics that find their focus in Jesus in Christianity but have no such single focus within the Jewish tradition.

In addition, Jesus, particularly in the guise of the proclaimed Christ, becomes a way of access to God for Christians. This topic could open up a spiritual aspect of our dialogue. As Christians find God through Jesus, Jews find God through Torah. Investigating this aspect of the dialogue surely needs to bring the partners beyond the historical question of Jesus' understanding of the Law and into the deeper questions of how one approaches God. What is one to do or to believe? What does it mean if one considers God's word incarnate in a flesh-and-blood human or in a book? What does it mean that this book itself has a history and that it grew over time? How does the presence of God's word in a continuing Torah tradition in the Jewish tradition function with respect to Jesus in the Christian?

There is also a particular Jewish interest in Jesus as a historical figure. Some modern Jewish scholars and authors have taken an interest in Jesus in the same way that they have with Jewish figures, such as Elisha ben Abuya, Josephus, David Reubeni, various mystic teachers, and messianic pretenders. This reflects their search for new models of leadership in persons outside of the "normative" Jewish tradition during a period of radical change in the structure of Jewish personal and communal life.[12] As a Jew studying Jesus and the earliest Church in a Jewish context, I do not approach the issue as part of a primarily religious quest. Jesus and the writings of his apostles are for me examples of the broad span of Jewish religious and philosophic experiences of the first centuries B.C.E. and C.E. Jesus of Nazareth is of course interesting as the inspiration of a vast religious movement; so too is, for example, the more elusive Teacher of Righteousness of the Community of the Qumran scrolls. Jesus of Nazareth, a Jew of the first century, is for me—Lewis Eron, a Jew of the twentieth century—of interest and concern mainly insofar as I am interested in the history of my people in late antiquity. Jesus and his followers are a few of the many who attract my interest.

Yet it is important to remember that for an individual or an event to be of historical interest to me, as to many other contemporary Jews, it is to be of great importance. For all Jews since the rise of *Wissenschaft des Judentums* in the nineteenth century and, particularly, for Jews following the Conservative or Reconstructionist approaches, the people and events of Jewish history take on a central role in our understanding of Judaism and in our project of making Judaism viable in the present. If sensitively read from a Jewish perspective, the extensive record concerning Jesus that is preserved in the New Testament and early Christian writings holds out the promise of being a major source for a crucial but poorly documented period in Jewish history.[13]

If through dialogue we can lower the walls of Jewish distrust of Christians, built over the centuries of oppression, it is possible that Jesus and his immediate followers will attain a new stature in Jewish circles as important witnesses to an exciting period in the life of the people Israel. For a charismatic preacher from the Galilee, this is no mean accomplishment.

A Response to Lewis John Eron from Leonard Swidler

I would like to reflect a little from a specifically Christian perspective on your introductory remarks from a Jewish perspective. In particular, I would like to address the question, Why an interreligious dialogue, and in particular a Jewish-Christian dialogue on Jesus?

You suggest that Jesus is of no more interest to you than the Teacher of Righteousness of Qumran because as a Jew you would find Jesus of interest "mainly insofar as I am interested in the history of my people in late antiquity." That indeed is a valid reason for your interest in Jesus, but, as you yourself later indicated, it is only one of several possible valid reasons for Jewish interest in Jesus.

Let me muse on some of those possible reasons other than the ones you commented on. For example: If Jesus is the foundation-stone of Christianity, and Christianity can properly be perceived as a kind of spiritual offspring of Israel, then there is valid reason for Jewish interest in Jesus, the foundation-stone of its offspring Christianity—deviant though that offspring may be perceived to be.

As you have pointed out, there has been something of a small tidal wave of positive Jewish interest in Jesus in recent decades. Not only have there been many Jewish articles and books written about Jesus; there have even been whole books written about all the Jewish books on Jesus.[14] Let me cite just a few of the scores of Jewish authors who have found valid positive reasons for Jewish interest in Jesus.

Professor Nicolas de Lange of Cambridge University wrote in 1979:

Jesus is the spiritual father of a vast race of righteous gentiles, who have voluntarily chosen to separate themselves, up to a point, from the gentile world and taken upon themselves not only the privileges but some (at least) of the burdens of the people of Israel. Through their faith, Jesus is alive today. . . . They are our younger brothers, and our fellow-workers in the same vineyard. Surely we must agree with the words of Franz Rosenzweig: "Before God, Jew and Christian both labor at the same task. He cannot dispense with either" [*The Star of Redemption*, p. 415].[15]

No less a revered Jewish figure than Rabbi Leo Baeck wrote a book in the midst of the Nazi horror, entitled *Das Evangelium als Urkunde der jüdischen Glaubensgeschichte* ("The Gospel as Document of the Jewish History of Faith, 1938"). In it he wrote:

In the ancient Gospel there stands before us a man with noble traits, who during tumultuous tension-filled days in the land of the Jews lived, helped, worked, endured and died, a man of the Jewish people, who walked in Jewish ways, in Jewish faith and hope. . . . We see in this ancient tradition a man before us who shows forth the form of Judaism in all the lines and features of his being, in which the pure essence of Judaism is so authentically, so clearly revealed, a man who, as what he was, could have come forth only from the soil of Judaism, and it is only from this soil that his disciples and followers could have been recruited as they were.[16]

He went on to say of the gospel, the heart of which is Jesus:

When this ancient tradition comes thus before our view, then this Gospel, which was originally Jewish, will become a book—and not a minor one—within Jewish literature. . . . It is thoroughly a Jewish book. . . . a Jewish book amidst Jewish books. Judaism may not pass it by, may not misperceive it, nor wish to hold back from it. Here too Judaism should take up its own, in order to know its own.[17]

On the negative side, since Christianity has been the source of so much Jewish pain throughout two millennia of anti-Semitism, there is here as well valid reason for Jewish interest in Jesus, in whose name so much of this pain was caused—especially if it turns out that he too was a life-long Jew and lover of Jews. That the Holocaust would not have occurred solely on the basis of Christian anti-Semitism, as you state, is clear enough. However, it is also true that it could not have occurred without it as a basis: Christian anti-Semitism was not a sufficient, but a necessary, cause of the Holocaust.

Further, even if anti-Semitism were non-existent, it has been and still is largely within a Christian-influenced culture, Western civilization, in which most Jews live. For this reason they can quite validly have a serious interest in Christianity—and its foundation-stone, Jesus. Western civilization can be understood as being in the main a result of three major cultural forces: Graeco-Roman, Judaeo-Christian, and Teutonic. In fact, however, the Judaic religion/culture flows into Western civilization through the gate of Jesus of Nazareth—of course, as he is interpreted by others; nevertheless, he is the central or foundational figure in that cultural force in Western civilization.

You suggest that the very existence of Jews in Western civilization challenges the Christian notion of the centrality of Jesus to that civilization. If, however, as I have just suggested, Jesus is seen as one of several foundational influences in the formation of Western civilization, and in fact the central figure through whom the Judaic influence entered that civilization, then it would seem sensible for Christians to be interested in, not threatened by, this continuing Judaic culture in which Christians participate in a particular way.

You are right, of course, to point out that many—and in the past, perhaps most—Christians have not reacted in a sensible way, but in fact have felt threatened and have acted with hostility. You then suggest that perhaps those contemporary Christians who are striving to show the nearness of Jesus to Judaism are really attempting to diffuse the threat or challenge Judaism poses to the centrality of Jesus. They in effect say: Since there is no great distance between Jesus and Judaism, the existence of Judaism does not threaten Jesus' centrality in Western civilization; rather, it provides a living religio-cultural context for it to be more fully understood.

I think that you are correct in this insight, but I would not view it in quite as negative a light as you seem to. For in this way, I believe, the tension between Christianity and Judaism is perceived more clearly to be what it really is—namely, a family debate on the best way to live a human, a "Jewish," life. Ay, there's the rub!—there is not so much the tension between Jesus and Judaism on how best to lead a human life, but between Judaism and how subsequent followers of Jesus have interpreted him.

In this connection you point out that "a Jewish Jesus could be used by Jews as part of an apologetic polemic against Christianity. . . . by a condemnation of Paul as a disloyal Jew who misunderstood the teachings of his professed master and founded a new religion." Again, you are certainly right; there has often been a perhaps too facile, though not incomprehensible, tendency of Jewish scholars to open up a gap between Jesus and Paul. Our dialogue with our colleagues in this book, in fact, is partly directed toward bridging that gap, if possible. How well we succeed remains to be seen.

Nevertheless, it is also true, as I will try to document and argue later, that a growing number of Christians are once again making that perennial reforming move of a "return to roots": The Jesus of history is the measure of what it means to be Christian. Paul, as well as Mark, Luke, the Council Fathers of Nicaea, Chalcedon, and Vatican II, and so on are all a help to Christians in becoming more fully Christian to the extent that they help them see more clearly what that Jesus of history thought, taught, and wrought and how it can apply to concrete life.

As it turns out, that Jesus was thoroughly Jewish—in his own particular way, just as Yohanan ben Zakkai and other rabbis were Jewish in their own particular ways—and hence, learning more about the Jewishness of Jesus in fact will lead Christians closer to their *fons*. That this move poses all sorts of challenges to contemporary Christianity is absolutely true, but those are challenges Christians themselves would have to face even if Judaism had ceased to exist. But since it has not, Christians can hope to look to sympathetic Jews for some insights in this regard in meeting their own Christian challenges. That is surely not all the dialogue with Jews can or should mean for Christians, but it is one very important element.

Much more could be discussed in detail, of course, on this subject of why there needs to be interreligious dialogue. The fundamental reason for entering into dialogue is to learn from our partners how they perceive reality so as to enrich our knowledge, which of course means that we will want to learn not only about our commonalities, but also our differences. But let this suffice as an initial response in our mini-dialogue on dialogue.

NOTES

1. Such a process has its sources in the New Testament and clearly develops in the patristic period. See: Rosemary R. Ruether, "The Negation of the Jews in the Church Fathers," *Faith and Fratricide* (New York: Seabury, 1974), pp. 117–82; David P. Efroymson, "The Patristic Connection," in *Antisemitism and the Foundations of Christianity*, edited by Alan Davies (Ramsey, NJ: Paulist Press, 1979), pp. 98–117. Expressions of anti-Judaism within the Church developed a life of their own. John Gager stresses that the expression of negative attitudes toward Judaism by the patristic authors does not necessarily reflect their encounter with Judaism and the Jewish people. Rather, accusations of Judaizing appear as part of the vocabulary of invective against their rivals employed by these writers in their struggle to articulate the orthodox faith. See: *The Origins of Anti-Semitism, The Attitudes Towards Judaism in Pagan and Christian Antiquity* (Oxford: Oxford University Press, 1983).

2. The rabbinic material concerning Jesus and the earliest Church can be found in Jacob Z. Lauterbach, "Jesus in the Talmud," *Rabbinic Essays* (New York: Ktav, 1973), pp. 473–570.

The *Toledot Yeshu* (History of Jesus) is the collection of traditional Jewish legends concerning Jesus. It is not a reliable historical source. Rather, it reflects the manner in which the Jews assimilated the information they acquired concerning Jesus, the Jew, from the Church. Pinchas Lapide recommends Samuel Krauss' study of this literature, *Das Leben Jesu nach jüdischen Quellen* (Berlin, 1892) as still the best treatment. See: *Israelis, Jews and Jesus* (Garden City, NY: Doubleday, 1979), p. 76.

3. On the development of the concept of *shittuf*, "association" as a means to understand Christianity's trinitarian beliefs and its veneration of saints by the rabbinic and medieval rabbis, see: David Novak, *The Image of the Non-Jew in Judaism*, Toronto Studies in Theology, Vol. 14 (Lewiston, NY: Edwin Mellen, 1983), pp. 130–48. The economic and social roots for the medieval development of the concept are found in Jacob Katz, *Exclusiveness and Tolerance* (Oxford: Oxford University Press, 1961), pp. 34–35.

4. Jaroslav Pelikan, *Jesus Through the Centuries: His Place in the History of Culture* (New Haven: Yale University Press, 1985; New York: Harper & Row, 1987), p. 1.

5. Moses Mendelssohn developed his picture of Jesus as a good man whose teachings were in line with those of the rabbis as part of his rejection of Johann Casper Lavater's impudent attempt to push Mendelssohn toward conversion to Christianity.

6. For a survey of modern and contemporary Jewish views on Jesus, see: Shalom Ben-Chorin, "The Image of Jesus in Modern Judaism," *Journal of Ecumenical Studies*, 11 (1974), pp. 401–430; Pinchas Lapide, *Israelis, Jews and Jesus* (Garden City, NY: Doubleday, 1979). Trude Weiss-Rosmarin's anthology, *Jewish Expressions on Jesus* (New York: Ktav, 1977) is a useful collection of essays on Jesus by leading modern Jewish scholars and thinkers. Donald A. Hagner's study of modern Jewish views of Jesus, *The Jewish Reclamations of Jesus* (Grand Rapids, MI: Zondervan, 1984), is useful but highly problematic because he judges these Jewish views from his conservative Protestant standpoint. Alan Mittleman argues effectively that modern Jewish views of Jesus reflect internal Jewish changes and developments. He stresses that by studying Jewish views of Jesus Christians can learn much more about the way contemporary Jews struggle for self-understanding than they can about Jesus. See: "Modern Jewish Views of Jesus—A Search for Self," in *Breaking Down the Wall,* edited by Leonard Swidler (Lanham, MD: University Press of America, 1987), pp. 161–70.

7. Nancy Fuchs-Kreimer, "Jesus, Bond or Barrier?" unpublished paper, National Conference of Christians and Jews Scholars Conference, April 1986 at the Reconstructionist Rabbinical College, Wyncote, PA.

8. The picture of Jesus and Paul in Leo Baeck's essay "Romantic Religion" and in Martin Buber's *Two Types of Faith* are good examples of this approach. See: Mittleman, "Modern Jewish Views of Jesus," p. 165. See also John T. Pawlikowski, *What Are They Saying About Christian-Jewish Relations?* (Mahwah, NJ: Paulist Press, 1980), pp. 69–92, for a summary of contemporary Jewish views on Jesus and Christianity.

9. John Gager in the conclusion to his book, *The Origins of Anti-Semitism*, pp. 267–68, claims that Hannah Arendt is wrong in seeing the heritage of Christian anti-Judaism as the major cause of the Nazi persecution of the Jews. He rather agrees with the Israeli historian, Uriel Tal, *Christians and Jews in Germany, Religion, Politics, and Ideology in the Second Reich* (Ithaca, NY: Cornell University Press, 1975) who perceives multiple sources for modern anti-Semitism. Tal described the co-existence of two forms of anti-Semitism. The first was traditional, Christian anti-Semitism, while the second was a modern, secular anti-Semitism, which, though opposed to Christianity, used traditional Christian anti-Semitism for its own purposes.

10. This is not to diminish the creative efforts of Christian post-Holocaust theologians and scholars, such as A. Roy Eckardt, Franz Mussner, Rosemary R.

Ruether, John T. Pawlikowski, Clemens Thoma, Paul van Buren, and others. Rather, it is to emphasize that from a Jewish point of view the validity of the Jewish experience is a separate issue from Christianity.

11. Ruether, *Faith and Fratricide*; Eugene B. Borowitz, *Contemporary Christologies: A Jewish Response* (Mahwah, NJ: Paulist Press, 1980), pp. 185–86.

John T. Pawlikowski in his book *Christ in the Light of the Christian-Jewish Dialogue* (Mahwah, NJ: Paulist Press, 1982) paints a less optimistic picture. In the third chapter, "Christology and Judaism in Current Systematic Theology," he reviews the positions of European theologians, focusing on the Protestant theologians Wolfhart Pannenberg and Jürgen Moltmann, and the Catholic theologians Hans Küng Edward Schillebeeckx, and Latin American liberation theologians José Míguez Bonino, Jon Sobrino, and Leonardo Boff.

Pawlikowski argues that new Christian theological understandings of the continuing validity of Judaism after the Easter event arising out of the experience of Jewish-Christian dialogue still have not penetrated the Christian theological mainstream, represented by the leading European Protestant and Catholic theologians. In addition, he claims that "among the Latin American liberationists there has been even less impact. Several of the former have in fact only reinvigorated the longstanding stereotypes of Judaism by trying to define the freedom message of the Gospels in direct opposition to the imagined oppression of the Jewish Torah system," p. 75. Pawlikowski concludes that at present "Christology continues to suffer from a deep anti-Judaic malady," p. 75.

12. This concern is seen most sharply in such novels as Sholem Asch's *The Nazarene* on Jesus, Milton Steinberg's *As a Driven Leaf* on Elisha ben Abuya, Max Brod's *King of the Jews* on David Reubeni, and Lion Feuchtwanger's trilogy on the life of Josephus.

Gershom Sholem's historical research into the sources of Jewish mysticism served to open up areas of Jewish history and thought disdained by earlier scholars.

13. The deeper issue for Jews is the role of historical research for contemporary Jewish life. The crucial question is how one builds a living tradition when one's primary sources are the results of critical historical research and texts understood critically as documents with their own history. While all four religious movements within contemporary North American Judaism deal with the issues of historical development, the Reform movement's roots in philosophy and theology and the Orthodox movement's roots in the internal development of the Jewish legal tradition protect them from the full strength of the issue.

Both Conservative Judaism and Reconstructionist Judaism are founded on historical-developmental concepts of Judaism. Conservative Judaism, growing out of a history-of-ideas background, has maintained a stronger commitment to Jewish law and legal development (*halakhah*) than the smaller Reconstructionist movement whose roots are in social history and the sociology of religion. Thus, for Reconstructionists this major hermeneutical problem is even more complicated because we claim to employ as our canon not a fixed literature, biblical and rabbinic, but the life experience of the Jewish people over time. Historical knowledge and method become central. Through the proper study of the Jewish past, our hope is that we will be able to suggest and to test behaviors we believe will promote the continued flourishing of Jewish life and culture. In this perspective, the historical figure of Jesus of Nazareth, along with the community of his followers, becomes important as a possible model (either positive or negative) for Jewish leadership and community. The failure of the community of Jesus' followers to take root in the Judaism of their time is equally significant.

Although I attempt to approach the subject of Jesus of Nazareth with the tools of a historian, my interest in that bit of Jewish history, as in Jewish history in general, is to strengthen contemporary Jewish life. I strive to present honest history but I am simultaneously committed to find within that history a sense of personal transcendence that gives meaning to the life of the Jewish people.

14. See: Gösta Lindeskog, *Die Jesusfrage im neuzeitlichen Judentum* (Uppsala, 1938; 2nd ed., Darmstadt, 1973); Pinchas Lapide, *Ist das nicht Josephs Sohn? Jesus im heutigen Judentum* (Stuttgart-Munich: Calwer-Kösel, 1976).

15. Nicolas de Lange, "Who Is Jesus?" *Sidic*, 12,3 (1979), 13.

16. Cited in Pinchas Lapide, *Er Predigte in Ihren Synogogen* (Gütersloh: Gerd Mohn, 1980), p. 23.

17. Ibid., pp. 23f.

3

Yeshua's Place in the Jewish Life of His Time

LEONARD SWIDLER

YESHUA, PHARISEE-LIKE?

For almost two thousand years, most Christians have thought that Pharisaism and the subsequent Judaism said to have descended from it were *the* enemies of Yeshua and Christianity. Recent research, however, which has been mostly Jewish but also Christian, is calling this notion into serious question. We Christians have much to learn about ourselves from it.

A great deal of scholarly debate has been going on in recent years about just who and what the Pharisees were.[1] The scholarly search for the "true Pharisees" is being pursued with such intensity for largely two reasons: some Jews have recently understood the Pharisees to be the forerunners of the rabbis, and therefore an essential link in the development of post-70 C.E. Judaism (referred to somewhat tautologically as rabbinic Judaism). We Christians have also traditionally made this same link between Pharisaism and rabbinic Judaism and have further linked rabbinic Judaism with the highly negative picture of the Pharisees portrayed in the gospels as the polar opposites of Yeshua. Although the sorting out of the scholarly puzzle is by no means complete, much has already been accomplished, especially by way of clearly setting aside a number of distortions. Bearing in mind, therefore, the incompleteness and at times the tentativeness of present-day scholarship as well as its advances, let us proceed to look briefly at the emerging image(s) of the Pharisees and Yeshua's relationship to them.

In the area of Pharisaism one of the most penetrating scholars has been Ellis Rivkin, who is Jewish.[2] His argument is that the Pharisees represent a triad: "(1) The singular Father God so loved the individual that he (2) revealed, through Moses, his twofold Law which, if internalized and steadfastly adhered to, (3) would gain for such an individual eternal life for his soul and the resurrection of his body."[3] The second portion of the triad, the twofold Law, is made up of the written Law or Torah (the Scriptures) and the oral Torah (the rabbinic commentary and application of the written Torah).

John Pawlikowski, a Christian scholar, following the traditional path of linking closely the post-70 C.E. rabbis with the pre-70 C.E. Pharisees, but attributing the documented positive characteristics of the rabbis to the Pharisees as well, has written that through the use of the oral Torah process the Pharisees "deepened, humanized and universalized" the previous traditions. While the priests focused on the codification of the cultic legislation, the Pharisees, he states, concentrated on the "codification" of love, loyalty, and human compassion, making them incumbent upon all the people Israel; general propositions were now spelled out as specific religious and moral duties to be lived out by all Jews. "Hospitality to travelers, visiting the sick of all religious groups, dowering the indigent bride, universal education for all males, attending the dead to the grave and helping to bring peace to those for whom it was absent" had never clearly been religious obligations in the Hebrew Scriptures, though they were implied in its spirit. "The rabbis fashioned these concerns into new commandments, or 'mitzvot.' "[4]

Christians have often depicted Yeshua's intimacy with God his Father or his insistence on the interior spirit of prayer and morality as something new and opposed to the way of the Pharisees. The research of Rivkin leads him to argue that the opposite is true. The source of the attractive power of the Pharisees, he finds, was the relationship they established between the one God and the singular individual: "The Father God cared about *you*; He was concerned about *you*. He watched over *you*; He loved *you*; and loved *you* so much that He wished *your* unique self to live forever." To the Pharisees,

> The Heavenly Father was ever present. One could talk to Him, plead with Him, cry out to Him, pray to Him—person to Person, individual to Individual, heart to Heart, soul to Soul. It was the establishment of this personal relationship, an inner experience, that accounts for the manifest power of Pharisaism to live on. . . . *Internalization* is the only road to salvation.[5]

Pawlikowski writes in similar fashion that with the Pharisees "a sense of a new intimacy between God and the human person was beginning to dawn. He had now become the Father of each and every person."[6]

The image of the Pharisees that emerges from this research is that they were a group of lay scholar-teachers[7] who first appeared in history about a century and a half before the birth of Yeshua, developed the above teachings and practices, used proof-texting from the Bible as a technique, and became authoritative in the life of the Jews during the reign of Queen Alexandra (76-67 B.C.E.), long before Yeshua's day. Clearly this was a revolution, for Moses gave no authority over the Torah and the religious life to any lay scholar class; nor indeed did the Bible use proof-texting as a technique — that was a peculiarly Pharisaic-rabbinic development. Following the death of Queen Alexandra the influence of the Pharisees appeared to retreat, though by no means disappear. After the destruction of Jerusalem in 70 C.E. they emerged as evidently influential in the areas around the Christian churches for which Mark and Matthew wrote (the use of the term *Pharisee* in Luke and John requires further careful examination), so that the quality of their importance in Matthew's milieu in particular (c. 85 C.E.) will be at least partly reflective of that period rather than solely of the time of Yeshua.

Keeping this differentiation in mind, it is clear that the New Testament offers irrefutable proof of the first century C.E. influence of the Pharisees. In Matthew, chapter 23, which excoriates the Pharisees violently, Yeshua is nevertheless recorded to have said the following: "The scribes and Pharisees sit on Moses' seat; so practice and observe whatever they tell you" (Mt. 23:2f.). Yeshua says: "Unless your righteousness exceeds that of the scribes and Pharisees, you will never enter the kingdom of heaven"(Mt. 5:20). The context of the second statement has Yeshua saying that he came to carry out the Torah (5:17), that it indeed will be completely carried out (5:18), that to teach the violation of the Torah is bad, and its vindication good (5:19). Hence, the Pharisaic reverence for the Torah is to be emulated — and surpassed — by his followers (5:20).

This picture of the Pharisees sounds dramatically the opposite of what Christians have had projected for themselves. Indeed, it appears extraordinarily like the image of Yeshua and later of that of his followers. Rivkin perceives the same thing, for after speaking of the Pharisaic triad he describes Yeshua as being nurtured on the twofold Torah:

> The grand faith of the Pharisees in the Triad was inscribed within his conscience. God was indeed the loving and caring Father. God had revealed ... the twofold Law ... [and] promised that everyone who served with love and loyalty would enjoy eternal life and resurrection. For Jesus, as for the Pharisees, the ultimate reality was within, not without.[8]

As noted, it is argued by Rivkin that the custom of biblical proof-texting — including that of Christians — was originally a Pharisaic technique;[9] it is found only in the early (Pharisaic)-rabbinic (*tannaitic*) materials of the Mishnah and Tosefta[10] and so forth, *not* in the Hebrew Bible nor even in the apocryphal or pseudepigraphical writings. However, Rivkin continues, these "Pharisaic" forms underlie the gospels, the Acts of the Apostles, and the epistles of Paul. Paul, for example, constantly cited Scripture in the

"Pharisaic" manner. When Yeshua wished to prove that God had made a covenant with Abraham before Abraham was circumcised, he clinched his argument with a conclusive proof text from Scriptures (cf. Rom. 4:1–12). The Sadducees were refuted with a proof text (Mk. 12:12–27), and Yeshua justified the expulsion of the money changers from the Temple with a proof text (Mk. 11:17–18). "Indeed, wherever one turns within the Gospels, one is offered proof text after proof text—a vivid testimony to how utterly normative this Pharisaic original had become."[11]

The authoritative position and attitude of the Pharisees emerging from this line of thought is stunningly like that which numerous Christian scholars have claimed exclusively for Yeshua: Moses never granted a scholar class any authority over God's Law. Authority such as this had been given to prophets and priests, but not to scholars. And yet nowhere in the Mishnah—recall that Rivkin maintains the traditional link between the rabbis and the Pharisees—is the *halakhah* (the concrete application of the Torah) expounded by either a prophetic or a priestly class. *Halakhah* is never introduced with the prophetic formula, "Thus says the Lord." Nor do we find in the Mishnah the priesthood as a class exercising any authority that is not on sufferance of the scholar class. In addition, the Mishnah is the repository exclusively of the teachings of a scholar class. Since these teachings are presented as authoritative and binding, and since they are teachings that, for the most part, are not written down in the Pentateuch, "they testify to a system of *authority that is self-assumed, self-asserted, and self-validated*."[12] Therefore, when Yeshua said things like "You have heard it said, but I say to you . . ." he was simply treading the (Pharisaic)-rabbinic path. In fact, Phillip Sigal has given abundant references to similar rabbinic sayings.

> The form with which Jesus presents his strongest halakhic remarks, "I say unto you," (Mt. 5:22, 25, 32, 34, 39, 44) should not be regarded as evidence of anything more than proto-rabbinic insistence upon one's own view even when it contradicts and abolishes earlier teaching. . . . It is self-evident that people "marveled" at Manahem b. Sungai (T. Ed. 3:1) as they did at Jesus (Mt. 7:28).[13]

The ministry of Jesus, if carefully reviewed, reveals many parallels between him and the proto-rabbinic (Pharisaic) movement. Yeshua is often seen in the process of teaching his oral Torah, reinterpreting the Hebrew Scriptures in a manner in line with the social setting in which he found himself. Yeshua's emphasis on teaching falls into the general pattern of the authentic rabbi. Though Yeshua himself gave no clear indication of the type of institutional arrangements he wished his disciples to make after his death, the example of the early Jerusalem and Galilean churches, which can be presumed to reflect his teachings in at least a general way, shows great similarities to the synagogue model advocated by the proto-rabbis (Pharisees). Yeshua likewise participated in Pharisaic-type fellowship meals, instituting the Christian Eucharist at the final one he attended. In the area of doctrine the resemblance continues: emphasis on love, on the *Shema* (monotheism prayer), on the themes summarized in the Beatitudes and on the Resurrection indicates the presence of a strong Pharisaic spirit in the life of Jesus. In particular, Jesus' stress on his intimate link with the Father picks up on a central feature of Pharisaic thought.

Consequently, it is not at all surprising that Pawlikowski, a Catholic, concludes that it would not be wrong "to consider Jesus as a part of the general Pharisaic movement, even though in many areas he held a distinctive viewpoint."[14] E. P. Sanders, a Protestant scholar, is somewhat more cautious, but nevertheless moves in the same direction when he states, "I am one of a growing number of scholars who doubt that there were any substantial points of opposition between Jesus and the Pharisees."[15] The Jewish scholar Geza Vermes comments: "Not that there appears to have been any fundamental disagreement between Jesus and the Pharisees on any basic issue. . . . the conflict between Jesus of Galilee and the Pharisees of his time would, in normal circumstances, merely have resembled the in-fighting of factions belonging to the same religious body."

In terms of influencing preaching and teaching in the Catholic Church, and indirectly other Christian churches as well, it is extremely important that practically all of the above-described research and reasoning on the Pharisees, including the positive as well as the negative relationship between them and Yeshua (and Paul as well), has been adopted by the Vatican Commission for Religious Relations with the Jews in its June 24, 1985, "Notes on the Correct Way To Present the Jews and Judaism in Preaching and Catechism in the Roman Catholic Church," as found in paragraphs 16–19. For example, the Commission states: "It may also be stressed that, if Jesus shows himself severe towards the Pharisees, it is because he is closer to them than to other contemporary Jewish groups."

Recently, Rabbi Harvey Falk has painstakingly argued for a nuancing of the claim of Yeshua's closeness to the Pharisees, stating that Yeshua stood with a particular school or "house" of Pharisees, the House of Hillel (Bet Hillel), rather than their opponents Bet Shammai.[16] It has long been generally contended by Christian scholars that in a number of disputes between Yeshua and Pharisees or Sadducees Yeshua defends the Pharisaic position of Bet Hillel. It has likewise been briefly alluded to by some Christian scholars "that it was Pharisaism, and that of the Shammaite kind, that dominated first-century Judaism,"[17] and that "it was perhaps only after the fall of Jerusalem that the Hillelites gained the ascendancy."[18] Despite a somewhat uncritical handling of New Testament materials, Falk thoroughly analyzes the rabbinic materials (though he unfortunately does not deal critically with the dating problems) and argues that Bet Shammai was dominant in Judaism from about 30 B.C.E. to 70 C.E. (among other causes might be the fact that Hillel died around 10 C.E. but Shammai only around 30 C.E.), "and that the murderous Zealots, often represented in the priesthood in Jerusalem, were followers of Bet Shammai. . . . [and] demonstrate that the Shammaites were responsible for handing Jesus over to the Romans for the crucifixion, and that their decision was in violation of Jewish law."[19] Falk in addition claims that the various criticisms of and attacks on the Pharisees by Jesus are in fact attacks specifically on the narrow-minded Pharisaism of Bet Shammai, that Jesus was trying to bring Judaism back to the generous-hearted Pharisaism of Bet Hillel, who taught his followers to be "one who loves peace, pursues peace, loves mankind, and draws them [Gentiles] nigh to the Torah."[20]

For example, Bet Hillel taught that Gentiles who live righteously—who observe the Noahide Commandments—will merit a share in the World to Come. Bet Shammai taught that they would not.[21] Perhaps the so-called Judaizers that Paul opposed in Acts 15, and who were described by Luke in unnuanced fashion as "Pharisees" (Acts 15:5), were of Bet Shammai: "But some men came down from Judea and were teaching the brethren, 'Unless you are circumcised according to the custom of Moses, you cannot be saved' " (Acts 15:1). Because after 70 C.E. subsequent Judaism rejected Bet Shammai in favor of Bet Hillel, the following conclusion is drawn:

> The Talmud states explicitly, a Jew who follows the teachings of Bet Shammai "deserves death." Hence, there is no basis for Christian enmity toward the Jews of today because of the actions of certain individuals who lived in the first century. We do not identify with them nor with their teachings. A Heavenly Voice settled the matter toward the close of the first century: "The Halakhah is as Bet Hillel [teaches]." [22]

The most recent and perhaps most insightful and exciting research on this matter is the book by the Jewish scholar Rabbi Phillip Sigal (1986)—unfortunately a posthumous work. Sigal exhibits extraordinary scholarly expertise in New Testament, rabbinic, and other Jewish materials.

Sigal argues that the Pharisees of the gospels are *not* the predecessors of the post-70 rabbis, from whom come the rabbinic writings and who are the clear "founders" of present-day rabbinic Judaism. Instead, the Greek term *Pharisaioi*, from the Hebrew *perushim*, meant largely what it said literally, "the separatists": "The *Pharisaioi* in controversy with Jesus in Matthew are *perushim*, pietistic sectarian Jews of various circles whose identity is still not clear to us. . . . who were rigid in their halakhah, 'strict constructionists' in their hermeneutics and exegesis, and were therefore at serious odds with Jesus."[23] Sigal refers to the predecessors of the rabbis—who came into existence as a clear group after the destruction of Jerusalem in 70 C.E. and who gathered around Yohanan ben Zakkai in the Palestinian village of Yavneh—as "proto-rabbis." In the Gospel of Matthew "the term *nomikos* [expert in the law] refers to a proto-rabbi. As over against a Sadducee, he too may be taken as a *parush* in colloquial idiom,"[24] but in reality he is quite distinct from the *perushim*.

The argument presented by Harvey Falk is that the Pharisee opponents of Yeshua in the gospels were in fact Shammaites, who were basically repudiated by the post-70 rabbis, followers of Hillel (to whom Yeshua was *similar*); therefore, they were not the forerunners of present-day rabbinic Judaism. A somewhat similar position is held by Sigal, but he argues that the pre-70 predecessors of the rabbis were neither Hillelites nor Shammaites, but belonged to no school or "house" (*bet*) as such. Moreover, because Sigel sees the proto-rabbis as operating much more as individuals in their interpretation of the rules of conduct, the *halakhah*, than the various pre-70 schools and groups, he can claim on the basis of his evidence and argument that Yeshua is not merely *like* or *near* the proto-rabbis. Instead,

> he acted on principles that were not acceptable to *perushim* but were either already part of or destined to become part of proto-rabbinic and rabbinic Judaism. He was therefore an early proto-rabbi of the tannaitic era and taught halakhah accordingly. He was neither a Sadducee nor a Pharisee, neither a Hillelite nor a Shammaite. He employed freedom of interpretation and authority in conformity with the fashion of proto-rabbinic Judaism.[25]

Sigal even goes so far as to strongly suggest a personal link between Yeshua and the post-70 rabbis of Yavneh by claiming that the founder of Yavneh and "rabbinism," Yohanan ben Zakkai, was not only a contemporary of Yeshua, but since he spent twenty years in Galilee, including before and during the time of Yeshua's public ministry, he probably was a colleague of Yeshua:

> Jesus was first a disciple and then a colleague of proto-rabbis in Galilee. The most celebrated of those was Yohanan b. Zakkai. My conjecture is that Jesus and Yohanan were the same age and ultimately were colleagues in Galilee. Jesus would have been a mature disciple and colleague of proto-rabbis during the decade 20–30 when Yohanan b. Zakkai was in Galilee and Jesus was in his formative period. Both probably studied at both the schools of Hillel and Shammai and both took independent directions. . . . During Yohanan's period of leadership at Yavneh, no action was taken against Christians.[26]

Hillel's and Shammai's deaths are placed around the year 10 C.E. and 30 C.E., respectively, and the birth of Yeshua around 4 B.C.E. Assuming that these dates are reasonably accurate, it is even possible that Yeshua sat at the feet of either Hillel or Shammai themselves or both, especially when one recalls that Jewish lads came of age religiously and otherwise at the age of twelve. The fact that Yeshua was already steeped in religious learning by that age is recorded in Luke 2:40–52, where it is said that Yeshua was filled with wisdom and that he spent three days with the rabbis, discussing religious matters with them and astonishing them with his answers. (*Didaskalōn*, "teachers," which is the term Luke uses here, is of course what *rabbi* came to mean and is doubtless the Greek translation for *rabbi* used throughout the gospels in general.) In any case, it would seem that Yeshua most likely studied with the rabbis during his youth in Galilee, as did also Yohanan ben Zakkai. It would appear very unlikely that two such brilliant rabbinic students living and working in the same confined area of Galilee would not have learned of each other's teachings. Still further, it does indeed seem quite likely that they would have sought each other out for extended discussion, as Sigal suggests. Of this, to be sure, we have no documentary proof, and so we are left with likelihood.

Sigal finds the reason for the expulsion of the followers of Rabbi Yeshua from Judaism not as being Yeshua's, or his followers', attitude toward the Law, or even because of theology in the early decades: "At no time during the first five decades after the crucifixion were Christian Judaism and pre-rabbinic Judaism wholly incompatible." But rather, "Post-70 Jews were antagonistic to the returned Christians at Jerusalem [they were "peace-people," like Yohanan ben Zakkai, who also fled the Roman war in the capital] and to the expansion and success of their movement [e.g., Saul's persecution of the followers of Yeshua, Acts 8:3]."[27] Whatever the cause for the antagonism, Sigal finishes his book with the following pregnant conclusion: "Had Christian Jews not been expelled from the synagogues after 90 A.D., but remained a segment of Judaism, it is well within the realm of possibility that Jesus would have secured a place in the proto-rabbinic pantheon."[28]

YESHUA, A GALILEAN HASID?

Here note should also be taken of the assertion by the Jewish scholar Geza Vermes that "the person of Jesus is to be seen as part of first-century charismatic Judaism and as the paramount example of the early Hasidim or Devout."[29] His argument is detailed and documented, but let an earlier description of the Hasidim by another scholar, Shmuel Safrai, suffice to illustrate the extraordinary parallels between them and Yeshua:

> Prominent in their doctrine is the importance attributed to good deeds in public life (redemption of captives, the digging of cisterns for the benefit of wayfarers, the restoration of lost property, the consolation of mourners, the giving of alms etc.). . . . The Hasidim trust in God and sublime providence, are confident that it is not the snake but the sin that is fatal, and behave accordingly in actual practice, in full faith in God *even in cases in which such behavior opposes the accepted ruling.*

Their confidence in providence and in the salvation resulting from right behavior, and even in the miracles which were to be revealed to them, stands in the numerous anecdotes told of Honi the Circlemaker, R. Hanina ben Dosa, Phineas ben Ya'ir and other Hasidim. They appeal to God as if commanding Him to make rain fall [conversely with Yeshua: calming of the storm, Mk. 4:49]. . . . Among all the austerities practiced by the Hasidim there is no trace of austerity in *halakhoth* concerning ritual purity, a subject which burst all bounds in Judaism. In effect, the only tradition which concerns subjects of purity accuses them of failing on a clearly explained passage of the Pentateuch which in itself is one of the principal sources for rulings on purity [Yeshua too was often accused of violating purity laws].[30]

What can be said then of the relationship of these Hasidim—including Yeshua, if indeed, as it appears, he can be called one of them—to the Pharisees? Safrai offers an interesting speculation that places the Hasidim eventually within—albeit somewhat uneasily—the society of the Pharisees and rabbis (according to the gospels, Yeshua was addressed as "rabbi") who developed their own literary traditions and interpretations of the Law (*halakhah*)—as did Yeshua: "As to the use of the concept 'Hasid' . . . as time went on, and perhaps as early as the end of the Hasmonaean period [63 B.C.E.], this concept became confined to a certain defined group within the society of the Pharisees and rabbis; this group had a literary tradition and its own halakhic practices."[31]

Vermes' position is reinforced by Phillip Sigal, who speaks of Yeshua not only as a proto-rabbi but also as a charismatic, Hasid-like figure: Yeshua, Sigal says, was a *hakham* [a sage, a term Sigal identifies with proto-rabbi] who had become spiritually converted and transformed into a charismatic prophet-figure. "Like a prophet he preached fearlessly of awesome things, but like the *hakham* he taught halakhah along with his aggadic preaching. In this function he employed the freedom of interpretation, the independent authority and methodology that was the style of proto-rabbinism."[32]

SUMMARY

Hence, perhaps the best way to understand Yeshua within the context of the Judaism of his time is as a wandering, wonder-working teacher (*rabbi*), a sage (*hakham*), from Galilee, a Galilean *Hasid*, who in many ways was similar to Hillel (whose teaching eventually came to prevail generally over Shammai's in rabbinic Judaism), and whom some scholars would also see as having had a close relationship to the Pharisees centered in Jerusalem (whom he nevertheless criticized and who in turn criticized him). Sigal sees him as a Galilean *Hasid*, a *hakham* and a proto-rabbi, who, like Yohanan ben Zakkai both before and after 70, severely criticized the *Phar-*

isaioi, the *perushim* (whom Sigal does not identify as the predecessors of rabbinic Judaism, even though at times a loose use of the term *Pharisaioi* by the gospels and Josephus might include some proto-rabbis). I am convinced that Sigal provides the most accurate and comprehensive description of Yeshua's place in the Jewish life of his time.

IMPLICATIONS FOR JEWS AND CHRISTIANS

One of the immediate implications of this research, if it is valid, is that Yeshua, far from being in intense opposition to the forerunners of the Yavneh rabbis and subsequent rabbinic Judaism, was very like them, close to them, one of them, perhaps even in his youth a colleague of the founder of rabbinic Judaism, Yohanan ben Zakkai. Rather than perceiving Yeshua as breaking away from Judaism, as we Christians from an early period have been wont to do, we should be inclined to link him closely with the Judaism of his day. We should see him as an important—indeed, along with Yohanan ben Zakkai—a pioneering figure in the development of Judaism in continuity with its biblical past and rabbinic future. This link was apparently broken by the way his disciples proclaimed him and definitively by post-90 historical developments. In view of this research, then, if and as it is sustained in the future, Christians will need to rethink their relationship with Judaism, in the founding period of Christianity at least.

A Response to Leonard Swidler from Lewis John Eron

I am in general agreement with your understanding of Jesus' place in the Jewish world of his time. My real problem is with the Jewish scholars whose work you cite. I feel that both Rabbi Harvey Falk and Rabbi Phillip Sigal are not reliable.

I do not want to enter a battle of authorities, but, in both cases, good will does not make up for a lack of critical scholarship. I will discuss Phillip Sigal briefly in my next response and express some of my reservations concerning Rabbi Falk's work in my presentation on this topic.

Part of the problem in our enterprise can be seen in Falk's work. In 1982 he published an important article in the *Journal of Ecumenical Studies* on Rabbi Jacob Emden's views on Christianity. Rabbi Jacob Emden (1697–1776), the last major pre-Emancipation figure in German Judaism and an older contemporary of Moses Mendelssohn, had a surprisingly open and positive understanding of Christianity and its founder. Emden's insight was the impetus behind Rabbi Falk's investigation. Falk wanted to defend Emden's position by an historical argument.

This is where, in my opinion, Rabbi Falk made a wrong turn. His work shows a mastery of traditional talmudic sources and he identifies many striking parallels between the teachings of Jesus and later rabbinic material. Unfortunately, Rabbi Falk did not apply modern critical scholarship to his treatment of the New Testament, early Judaism, or the rabbinic literature. He is, therefore, unable to support his insights, attractive as they may be. I do not want to fault Falk on what he did not do. Rather, I point to his work as an illustration of what needs to be done.

Had he written on Jacob Emden's understanding of Christianity rather than trying to defend the master, he could have written an ultimately more important, although surely not as popular, work. If he could have supplied the social, historical, and halakhic background to Jacob Emden's all too brief letter, he would have given us a valuable insight into Jewish-Christian relations in Germany at the very dawn of the modern era.

Such a work could have also provided Jews, particularly traditionalist Jews, with a theological and halakhic argument for involvement in Jewish-Christian dialogue. On the whole, Orthodox Jews are reluctant to enter into Jewish-Christian dialogue. Twenty years ago, the leading halakhic authority for Modern/Centralist Orthodox Jews, Rabbi Joseph Soloveichik, in one of his few written pieces, took a strong stand against participation in interreligious dialogue. On the one hand, he saw a place for Jewish cooperation with non-Jews in "secular" activities. On the other hand, he (mis)understood dialogue on an academic and theological level as negotiation and felt that it was therefore inappropriate for people of faith. Today, as the Orthodox Jewish community moves more and more to the right, those Orthodox Jews who are involved in dialogue risk alienation from the bulk of their community.

I could not write a work that would encourage Orthodox Jews to participate in Jewish-Christian dialogue. My position in the liberal Jewish camp as a Reconstructionist rabbi would quite understandably and justifiably render my arguments unconvincing. Unfortunately, even scholars and thinkers such as Pinchas Lapide and Irving Greenberg, although they identify themselves as Orthodox Jews, do not speak out of an Orthodox consensus. A scholarly insider able and willing to speak to the Orthodox community in their idiom might have a better chance of being heard.

In any case, I can see how Rabbi Falk's book might be attractive to a considerably theologically more conservative Christian scholar than yourself and a more traditional Jew than myself. Perhaps his traditionalist treatment of his sources might accomplish the task I have just outlined. In this way, his book might be of help in dialogue for more traditionally minded Christians and Jews than ourselves. Jewish-Christian dialogue in general, however, would have been better served if he had taken another tack.

NOTES

1. See: Louis Finkelstein, *The Pharisees*, 2 vols. (Philadelphia: Jewish Publication Society, 1962); R. Travers Herford, *The Aim and Method of Pharisaism*, repub-

lished as *The Pharisees* (Boston: Beacon Press, 1962); Asher Finkel, *The Pharisees and the Teacher of Nazareth* (Leiden: Brill, 1964); Jacob Neusner, *The Rabbinic Traditions about the Pharisees before 70*, 3 vols. (Leiden: Brill, 1971); John Bowker, *Jesus and the Pharisees* (London: Cambridge University Press, 1973). For updating articles see: Michael Cook, "Jesus and the Pharisees: The Problem as It Stands Today," *Journal of Ecumenical Studies*, 15,3 (Summer 1978), pp. 441–460; Leonard Swidler, "The Pharisees in Recent Catholic Writing," *Horizons*, 10,2 (Fall 1983), pp. 267–287; Lewis Eron, "Implications of Recent Research on the Pharisees for Jewish-Christian Dialogue," in Leonard Swidler, ed., *Breaking Down the Wall* (Lanham, MD: University Press of America, 1987), pp. 131–160.

2. Ellis Rivkin, *A Hidden Revolution* (Nashville, TN: Abingdon, 1978). The method Rivkin uses is to analyze separately the three bodies of early literature that deal with the Pharisees: The New Testament, late first century C.E.; the Jewish historian Josephus, late first century C.E.; early rabbinic writings, e.g., Mishnah, codified late second century, but including materials going back to 200 B.C.E. His conclusion is that they all come out with fundamentally the same image of the Pharisees.

Up until recently almost all Christian scholars have been simply ignorant of rabbinic literature. Even now many are reluctant to admit its helpfulness in understanding the New Testament. Often Christians have been so bent on insisting on Yeshua's difference from his contemporary fellow Jews that they discount the validity of Mishnaic materials when they produce rabbinic parallels to teachings or actions of Yeshua. Without doubt much work remains to be done on the form-critical analysis and dating of these rabbinic writings (Jacob Neusner and his students have been hard at work on the task for years). Still, if the Mishnah, or even the two Talmuds (codified at the end of the fourth and fifth centuries respectively), attribute a teaching to a predecessor or contemporary of Yeshua, the logical assumption should be to accept its accuracy until some counterevidence challenges it. This sort of rabbinic documentation would not, of course, be the strongest possible documentary evidence, for the later redactors of the Mishnah and Talmuds reshaped the cited material for their contemporary purposes. Nevertheless, it would be stronger than the simple a priori assumption that it is not valid merely because it appears in a later codified document. It is clear, I believe, that the burden of proof is on the "rejectionist" Christian scholar, not the one who carefully uses rabbinic documents.

A Catholic scholar of the targumic literature, Martin McNamara, who has made a study of its relevance to the New Testament, not only says much the same but goes further:

> We are still left with the delicate task of how to approach rabbinic material for New Testament studies. Authors, as already noted, differ on the point and most probably will continue to do so. A legitimate, and probably wise approach would appear to be the following: accept rabbinic tradition of New Testament times and earlier, and regard both as being in the same spirit. Even if a given formulation of rabbinic tradition may be later, it is to be presumed as being in the spirit of earlier Pharisaism. We may freely have recourse to the rabbinic tradition for New Testament studies because of this. ... The problem of dating will always remain with us in the use of this material, and the efforts being made to refine our methodology in its use

must continue. But the problems in assigning an exact date to individual pieces of rabbinic tradition are amply offset by the realization that the tradition as a whole has every appearance of continuing the form of Judaism with which Christ and his followers had the closest contact [*Palestinian Judaism and the New Testament* (Wilmington DE: Michael Glazier, 1984), pp. 177, 204].

Geza Vermes, a Jewish scholar, as an expert in both the Jewish literature and the New Testament, categorically supports this position: "Rabbinic literature, skillfully handled, is still the richest source for the interpretation of the original gospel message, and the most precious aid to the quest for the historical Jesus." *Jesus and the World of Judaism* (Philadelphia: Fortress Press, 1984), p. 125.

3. Rivkin, *A Hidden Revolution*, p. 293.

4. John T. Pawlikowski, *Christ in the Light of the Christian-Jewish Dialogue* (Mahwah, NJ: Paulist Press, 1982), p. 82.

5. Rivkin, *A Hidden Revolution*, p. 310. Joachim Jeremias, a Protestant scholar, in a number of places has argued that Yeshua's addressing God as *Abba*, Father, was unique and indicated an extraordinarily intimate relationship between Yeshua and God. However, as Rivkin argues, to address God as Father was already something traditionally Pharisaic. Of course God was referred to as Father in the older Hebrew Bible numerous times. In addition, God is addressed as Our Father, *Avinu*, in Jewish, i.e., Pharisaic-rabbinic, prayers, carefully traced back to the years 10–40 c.e. by Louis Finkelstein, *Phariseeism in the Making* (New York: Ktav, 1972), pp. 259f.

There is also evidence that the ancient hasidim—devout Jews living in Palestine before the birth of Yeshua—"spent an hour (in recollection before praying) in order to direct their hearts towards their Father in heaven," from m. Ber. 5:1. There is even evidence that precisely the child's term of endearment for father, *Abba*, was used by the first-century Palestinian Jew Hanan to refer to God in prayer: "When the world was in need of rain, the rabbis used to send school-children to him, who seized the train of his cloak and said to him, *Abba, Abba*, give us rain! He said to God: Lord of the universe, render a service to those who cannot distinguish between the *Abba* who gives rain and the *Abba* who does not." b.Ta'an. 23b.

Since here the structure of the whole story is formed around the fact that Hanan referred to *God* in prayer with the same term for father (*Abba*) used by the children to address him, Hanan, the use of the term *Abba* could not be a retrojection into the story from the time of the codification of the Talmud. And Hanan was a grandson of Honi the Circle-maker, who we know was an adult before Jerusalem fell to Pompey in 63 B.C.E. See Geza Vermes, *Jesus the Jew* (Philadelphia: Fortress Press, 1973), pp. 72, 210f. So, the events of this story probably occurred some years before the birth of Yeshua.

Vermes added to the arguments against Jeremias' "*Abba*" claim in a later book:

Jeremias . . . understood Jesus to have addressed God as "Dad" or "Daddy," but apart from the *a priori* improbability and incongruousness of the theory, there seems to be no linguistic support for it. Young children speaking Aramaic addressed their parents as *abba* or *imma* but it was not the only context in which *abba* would be employed. By the time of Jesus, the determined form of the noun, *abba* (= "the father,"), signified also "my father"; "*my* father," though still attested in Qumran and biblical Aramaic, had largely disappeared as an idiom from the Galilean dialect. Again, *abba* could be used in solemn, far from childish, situations such as the fictional altercation between the patriarchs Judah and Joseph reported in the Palestinian Targum, when the furious Judah threatens the governor of Egypt (his unrecognized brother) saying: "I swear by the life of the head of *abba* (= my father) as you swear by the life of the head of Pharaoh, your master, that if I draw my sword from the scabbard, I will not return it there until the land of Egypt is filled with the slain," [*Jesus and the World of Judaism*, p. 42].

Although Georg Schelbert in "Sprachgeschichtliches zu 'abba' " (Pierre Casetti *et al.*, eds., *Mélanges Dominique Barthélemy*. Orbis Biblicus et Orientalis, 38 [Fribourg: Éditions Universitaires Fribourg, 1981], pp. 395–447), confirms that "the word play with *'abba'* certainly belongs to the original form of the tradition" of the gospel story being analyzed, he argues that it is not possible to be certain that the text as we have it is verbatim from before the time of Jesus. Nevertheless, as a result of his thoroughgoing analysis of all the pertinent Aramaic texts and inscriptions, he concludes that "In the Aramaic language of the time of Jesus, there was absolutely no other word [than *Abba*] available if Jesus wished to speak of or address God as father. Naturally such speaking of and addressing thereby would lose its special character, for it is then indeed the only possible form!" (p. 396). He notes that Jeremias' claim of "special character" for the use by Yeshua—and worldwide popularization of that claim—was not only unwarranted but that this error was also recognized by others (e.g., such recognized scholars as H. Conzelmann, D. Flusser, E. Käsemann, E. Hänchen), and later even partly by Jeremias himself, although "the consequences were really not drawn in his text," nor were the contradictory opinions of the other scholars "really taken account of" (p. 396). Moreover, Schelbert shows in great detail that the Mishnah "without any doubt manifests an extremely intimate relationship to God as 'Father in heaven' " (p. 419).

6. Pawlikowski, *Christ in the Light*, p. 88.

7. Jacob Neusner in his three-volume work *The Rabbinic Traditions about the Pharisees Before 70* argues that the Pharisees were essentially *haberim*, a small pacifist party concerned with purity. Rivkin rejects this, as does also E. P. Sanders: "His [Neusner's] analysis of the rabbinic texts is unpersuasive and is made especially dubious by the evidence from Josephus," E. P. Sanders, *Jesus and Judaism* (Philadelphia: Fortress Press, 1985), p. 188.

8. Rivkin, *A Hidden Revolution*, p. 303.

9. Rivkin finds that in the rabbinic writings, all of which were codified after the writing of the gospels, the rabbis used the proof-texting method. Because he understands the Pharisees as the predecessors of the rabbis, he attributes this practice to them. The only first-century "Jewish" document other than the New Testament (wherein Yeshua and Paul do indeed proof-text), however, that evidences the practice of proof-texting are the Dead Sea scrolls of the Qumranites. Thus, perhaps it would be safer to say that the technique of proof-texting was widely practiced in pre-70 Judaism, which of course included the Pharisees, but not claim that the Pharisees invented the practice.

10. "Mishnah" means teaching that is recited orally (as does also the Arabic term "Qur'an"), coming from "shani," "to repeat." The Aramaic root "teni" has the same meaning, and therefore the teachers of this material are known as "Tan-

naim." The "Tosefta" is a collection of halakhic teaching omitted from the 200 C.E. edition of the Mishnah and edited probably shortly afterwards; the term means "supplement." The Palestinian Talmud (the term means "instruction"), by far the shorter of the two Talmuds, was edited around the year 400 C.E., the Babylonian Talmud around 500 C.E. The Talmud consists of quotations of the Mishnah and commentary known as "Gemara," coming from the root "gamar," "to complete." The rabbis responsible for the "Gemara" are known as "Amoraim," meaning "interpreters."

11. Rivkin, *A Hidden Revolution*, pp. 273f.

12. Ibid., p. 232; italics added.

13. Phillip Sigal, *The Halakhah of Jesus of Nazareth According to the Gospel of Matthew* (Lanham, MD: University Press of America, 1986), pp. 81f.

14. Ibid., p. 92.

15. Sanders, *Jesus*, p. 264.

16. Harvey Falk, *Jesus the Pharisee* (Mahwah, NJ: Paulist Press, 1985).

17. W. D. Davies, *Paul and Rabbinic Judaism* (London: SPCK, 1970), p. 54.

18. George Foot Moore, *Judaism in the First Centuries of the Christian Era* (Cambridge: Harvard University Press, 1972), vol. 1, p. 81.

19. Falk, *Jesus the Pharisee*, pp. 8f.

20. m.Avot 1:12.

21. Cf. Gerd Theissen, *Sociology of Early Palestinian Christianity* (Philadelphia: Fortress Press, 1977), p. 83: "The result was that in the first century A.D. they [the Pharisees] split into two schools. . . . Thus the Shammaites required strict separation from the Gentiles. In eighteen halakhoth, there were prohibitions against various Gentile foods, the Greek language, Gentile testimony, Gentile gifts, sons and daughters-in-law (j.Shab.3c 49ff.). They even used force against the Hillelites to carry through these intensified norms (j.Shab.3c 34ff.). Only after the catastrophe of A.D. 70 did the more moderate Hillelites succeed in gaining the upper hand."

22. Falk, *Jesus the Pharisee*, p. 158.

23. Sigal, *Halakhah of Jesus*, pp. 9, 4.

24. Ibid., p. 163.

25. Ibid., p. 9.

26. Ibid., pp. 248ff.

27. Ibid., pp. 7f.

28. Ibid., p. 159.

29. Vermes, *Jesus the Jew*, p. 79.

30. S. Safrai, "Teaching the Pietists in Mishnaic Literature," *The Journal of Jewish Studies*, XVI, 1–2 (1965), 32f.

31. Ibid., p. 33.

32. Sigal, *The Halakhah of Jesus*, p. 154.

4

Jesus' Place in the Jewish Life of His Time

LEWIS JOHN ERON

The issue of Jesus' place within the Jewish life of his time can be approached from two basic perspectives: (1) What Jesus had in common with the Judaisms of his day; and (2) How Jesus differs from the Judaisms of his day. From my Jewish viewpoint, these two perspectives reflect the Christian theological issue of Jesus' simultaneous participation in humanity and divinity cast in historical terms. The more, it seems to me, a Christian is intrigued by Jesus' humanity, the more important Jesus within Judaism becomes. On the other hand, the more a Christian is attracted to Jesus' divinity, the more important the distinctiveness of Jesus becomes.

For Jews, the theological issues are even more subtle. The basic issue is how one can appreciate Christianity as a religious and cultural tradition that is as authentic for its followers as Judaism is for Jews. Both perspectives can be used to authenticate as well as depreciate Christianity.

Approaching the issue from the first perspective, one has to deal with two fundamental issues. The first is that Jesus' immediate followers revered him as a teacher and spiritual figure otherwise unattested to in Jewish literature of the period. The second is that in less than a generation after Jesus' death, nascent Christianity, the Jesus movement, had broken the ethnic and cultural boundaries of the Jewish people and began to spread among the Gentiles. Simply put, one cannot domesticate Jesus so completely within Judaism as not to be able to explain the rapid growth and branching off of the Jesus movement in any other fashion but by accusing his followers of duplicity and guile.

Approaching the issue from the second perspective is equally problematic. Concentrating on what makes Jesus unique denies the clear commonalities between Judaism and the image of Jesus preserved by the early

47

church. Such a viewpoint also clouds the similarities between Judaism and Christianity.

As a Reconstructionist Jew, with Reconstructionism's almost total stress on the human side of revelation, I find many of the theological issues obviated. Put briefly, I understand revelation as the human discovery in human affairs of divinity and the transmission of this discovery in societal structures. For me, revelation is not God's handing down of something to humanity but rather humanity's discovery of some aspect of life that brings it closer to divinity. This leads me to frame the underlying theological issues in ways that allow Christians to find authentic contact with the divine through Jesus of Nazareth without the need to place Jesus in any special position within the Jewish tradition.

My studies of the New Testament and early Christianity have taught me that a simple reading of the gospels does not bring one to the teachings of the Jesus of history. At best, one comes to the image of Jesus contained in the traditions revered and preserved by the various communities of early Christians to whom the gospels and other early Christian writings were addressed. What I find intellectually exciting in the study of early Christianity is how these Christians, the earliest mostly of Jewish origin and later more of Gentile origin, found divinity through Jesus of Nazareth's life and teachings. In order to trace this development, it is important to attempt to develop a picture of Jesus within his Jewish background.

On the other hand, my academic area is not New Testament but the closely related field of Jewish Apocrypha and pseudepigraphic literature. Therefore, though I am informed concerning the Judaism of Jesus' day, I am not as expert in the literature that provides the vast bulk of material on Jesus, the New Testament. I am well aware of the methodological pitfalls in studying the gospels, and I know I must walk carefully to avoid falling into a trap.

The discussion of Jesus' place within the Judaism of his times often centers on his relationship with the Pharisees.[1] This is natural for a number of reasons. First, in the gospel accounts of Jesus' ministry, the Pharisees appear as the Jewish party with which Jesus most often stands in dispute. It must be noted, however, that the gospels' passion narratives identify the Sadducees and the priestly party as Jesus' antagonists. Second, our sources offer more information concerning the Pharisees than any other Jewish party of the period. Unfortunately, the sources are generally late and can be easily shown to be tendentious. Third, the Rabbis claimed the Pharisees as their predecessors. Attempts, therefore, to show Jesus' affinities with or differences from Judaism centered on the similarities or dissimilarities of Jesus' teaching with those of the Pharisees and their rabbinic followers.

Yet we know very little about the Pharisees. Whatever can be said about the Pharisees and their successors, the Rabbis of the Mishnah, it is clear, as E. P. Sanders has recently and carefully demonstrated, that they were not the legalistic, narrow-minded hypocrites pictured in the gospel accounts. The need of the early Christian communities for self-definition led to the strong polemic against Judaism that is seen in the condemnation of the Pharisees. This anti-Jewish polemic appears even today in otherwise respectable Christian theology and scholarship.[2]

Jesus most likely was not a Pharisee. Neither the Jewish nor Christian traditions place him in their camp. He is not remembered within the rabbinic tradition as one of the pre-70 C.E. Pharisaic sages whom the post-70 C.E. rabbis understood as their predecessors. His followers, perhaps retrojecting their conflicts with their Jewish contemporaries, picture their master, Jesus, more often in conflict with the Pharisees than in agreement.

For them, Jesus' differences from the Pharisees were most important. The fact that Jesus was not strictly a Pharisee in his teaching and approach to the Jewish tradition made his teachings distinctive. His distinctiveness led him out of the chain of Jewish tradition and gave his followers a sense that they were bearers of something new.

It is difficult to describe clearly the ways in which Jesus either joined with or separated from the Pharisees. Jewish and Christian scholars have identified many similarities between Jesus' teaching and those of the rabbis as they have noted Jesus' similarities with other Jewish groups of his time.

Yet, Jesus does not seem to have rejected many of the major points of first-century C.E. Pharisaism, as they can be reconstructed. Both Jesus and the Pharisees were concerned with making God immanent and immediate. He followed the rabbinic concept of building a fence around the Law when, for example, he forbade oath taking. Like them, he stressed a strict sexual morality. Like them, he taught in parables. His suggested form of prayer, the "Our Father," is similar to rabbinic forms of prayer.[3]

In two important areas Jesus held religious positions very close to those held by his Pharisaic contemporaries and their rabbinic successors. These are seen in (1) his attempt to provide a sense of the immanence of God and (2) his stress on the double commandment of love of God and love of one's fellow.

Ellis Rivkin stresses that the commitment of the Pharisees to the twofold law demonstrated their belief in God's love for the individual believer. According to Rivkin, the Pharisees held the fundamental beliefs that (1) the singular father God so loved the individual that he (2) revealed, through Moses, his twofold Law that, if internalized and steadfastly adhered to, (3) would gain for such an individual eternal life for his or her soul and resurrection of the body. These beliefs form the ideological basis for Western religion. Early Christianity adapted this triad for its own use by replacing the internalization of the revealed twofold Law with the internalization of Jesus revealed as Christ.[4]

Jacob Neusner argues convincingly that the Pharisaic concern with purity was part of a program to extend the experience of holiness from the Temple precinct throughout all of Israel. The Pharisees attempted to "democratize" the Temple purity by applying it to everyday life.[5]

Although Jesus attacks the Pharisees for an obsession with ritual purity (Mt. 23; Lk. 11:37–54), a concern for purity and purity customs appears in the gospel accounts. Foot-washing and baptism play an important role in the life of the followers of Jesus. In John 13:10, for example, Jesus relates baptism directly to purification.

The Pharisees and the later rabbis would have had no problem with Jesus' answer to their question, in Mt. 23:35, of which commandment of the Law is the greatest. For Pharisaic and later rabbinic Judaism as well as for Jesus, love of one's fellow is second only in importance to love of God. Hillel (first century C.E.) used the "golden rule" to summarize the Law to respond to the request of the potential proselyte (b. Shab 31a). Antigonus of Soko (first century C.E.) taught that one should serve God out of love and not for the sake of reward (m. Avot 1.3). Rabbi Eleazar ben Azariah (second century C.E.) insisted that Yom Kippur does not enable one to be forgiven for sins against God until one secures forgiveness from one's fellows (m.Yoma 8:9).

Although the double commandment of love of God and love of humanity appears in Jewish literature from at least the first century B.C.E. (Jubilees 20:9; Testament of Issachar 5:2; Testament of Benjamin 3:3; Testament of Daniel 5:3), the two commandments first appear together in rabbinic literature in a debate between two second-century C.E. sages, Ben Azzai and Rabbi Akiba. In a discussion with Rabbi Akiba, debating the issue of the most important commandment, Ben Azzai rejected Akiba's claim that love of one's neighbor (Lev. 19:18) is the most important. He argued that the obscure passage of Gen. 5:1–2 ("This is the record of Adam's line. When God created the human, He made him in the likeness of God; male and female He created them") is more important presumably, for it demonstrates that love for one's fellow is also love for the God in whose image he was created (Sifra 89b).

Unlike the Pharisaic sages who were teachers and interpreters of Jewish law and tradition, Jesus' primary public face was as a wandering miracle worker and preacher. He taught a stark ethic and preached repentance in the presence of the soon-to-arrive Dominion of God.

As will be noted below, Geza Vermes discusses the similarity of Jesus to other Jewish miracle workers from the Galilee, such as Honi the Circle Maker and Hanina ben Dosa. Although even early rabbinic material preserves legends concerning these popular figures, they are not integrated into rabbinic Judaism until late in the rabbinic period.[6]

Jesus, perhaps, came into conflict with the Pharisees because of the eschatological stress given to his teaching. Yet it should be remembered that eschatological expectation played an important role in all varieties of Palestinian Judaism in the pre-70 C.E. period. It is only after the catastrophic revolts against Rome in the first and second centuries that the rabbis de-emphasized immediate eschatological speculation. Yet even rabbis of the Mishnah maintained messianic expectation. Part of the Mishnah's platform appears to be a reform program for the conduct of the priesthood in the restored Temple. The Mishnah itself contains a short apocalypse in m.Sota 9.15. Prayers for the restoration of the Temple and the arrival of the messianic figure play an important role in Jewish liturgy.

It is hard to determine Jesus' relationship with the radical political revolutionaries of his time although it is clear that the Romans and certain of their Jewish collaborators saw Jesus as a subversive.[7] If Jesus was associated with the insurgents or was a sympathizer, this could have been a source of tension in his relations with the Pharisees as well as the Sadducees. This is not to claim that either the Pharisees or Sadducees were collaborators. Rather, their programs for Jewish cultural and religious autonomy were different and allowed for some accommodation.

Followers of all the movements within first-century Judaism participated in the Great Revolt against Rome (64–70 c.e.). The severe differences in their programs led, unfortunately, to vicious infighting that weakened the Jewish war effort.

It is also possible that Jesus' lifestyle as a mendicant preacher was seen as socially disruptive. It may even be the case that his or his disciples' claim that he might be the Messiah was the source of antagonism. All that can be known for sure was that his disciples found Jesus to be a distinctive teacher whose teachings led them away from the broad stream of first-century Judaism.

The desire of certain scholars, such as the Orthodox Rabbi Harvey Falk, to identify the Pharisaic opponents of Jesus with followers of the School of Shammai is attractive but misleading.[8] Its attractiveness lies in the fact that it allows for the historicity of the gospel accounts as well as demonstrates the correctness of the rabbinic Judaism of the Mishnaic period, which saw itself as heir of the opposing, less rigorous School of Hillel. In this reading of the material, Jesus did not oppose the good Pharisees, the School of Hillel, but like the Hillelites, Jesus vigorously opposed the narrow-minded followers of the School of Shammai.

Such identification is misleading since our accounts of the debates between the Schools of Shammai and Hillel are late and cannot be trusted to give reliable information about the two Pharisaic traditions. As these accounts stand today they present the major points of debate in a stylized, orderly fashion that reflects a carefully considered editorial plan. The safe statement is to say that it appears that there were two early Pharisaic schools of thought. The one that survived, the School of Hillel, characterized its opponent, the School of Shammai, as being narrow, hard, rigorous, and unforgiving. There is no way of determining if this were truly the case.

Furthermore, at times Jesus seems to side with the stricter reading of the Law attributed to Shammai and his school. Like the Shammaites, he appears to have a low opinion of converting Gentiles to Judaism. Among the woes of the Pharisees in Mt. 23 is the accusation that they engage in an overseas mission to Gentiles (v. 15). Jesus, himself, directed his disciples to avoid the Gentile and Samaritan towns in the land of Israel and go, instead, to "the lost sheep of Israel" (Mt. 10:6).

Jesus' teaching concerning divorce—restricting it altogether in Mk. 10:11–12 and Lk. 16:18 and allowing it only in the case of some sexual misbehavior in Mt. 5:31–32; 19:9—is closer to that of the School of Shammai than to the School of Hillel (m.Git. 9.10).

In a much more scholarly fashion, Phillip Sigal attempts to make a similar distinction.[9] Arguing that the Rabbis, who were guided by the principle of love and mercy, replaced rather than succeeded the Pharisees (whom he described as strict and fanatic), Sigal places Jesus in the company of the founders of the rabbinic movement, his "proto-rabbis." Although Sigal seems correct in noting that rabbinic material does not make the connection between the Rabbis and the Pharisees as clearly as most scholars have assumed it does, it is curious that Sigal identifies Jesus with the pre-70 C.E. heroes of the post-70 C.E. rabbinic movement.

For both Falk and Sigal, Jesus of Nazareth is brought home to Judaism as at least sympathetic to what later became rabbinic Judaism. Such an approach presents not only the difficult problem of answering the historical question of why the Jesus movement so early split from the Jewish group with which its master had the greatest affinities, but also the theological question of the validity of the Jesus movement as it moved away from its good, rabbinic, Jewish founder.

Although many of the moral and legal teachings ascribed to Jesus by the authors of the New Testament are not out of line with that which was taught by first century C.E. Jews as well as by the slightly later rabbis, the very early creedal and hymnal materials embedded in the New Testament demonstrate that Jesus' followers related to him differently than other Jews did to their rabbis and teachers.

The difficulty in placing Jesus within his Jewish context is that for most Jews of his time and later he was unremarkable, but for a few Jews of his time, he was crucial. This difference most likely rests in the way he affected his immediate followers and has probably very little to do with what he taught or what he did.

A Response to Lewis John Eron from Leonard Swidler

It is clear from our two statements that we are in large agreement on the place of Jesus in the Jewish life of his time, including in the conclusion that he was very close to, though not a member of, the Pharisees, who customarily have been thought of as the predecessors of rabbinic Judaism. It is within this context of general agreement that I would like to comment on your remark that "the fact that Jesus was not strictly a Pharisee in his teaching and approach to the Jewish tradition made his teachings distinctive," and that this "distinctiveness led him out of the chain of Jewish tradition." You would seem here to identify the pre-70 Pharisaic tradition and the "Jewish," presumably "post-70 rabbinic Jewish (?)," tradition. I would like to suggest a possible nuance.

Although it is true that the two did *de facto* flow one into the other, it would, of course, be an unhistorical anachronism to retroject a post-70 development upon the Judaism of the time of Jesus. At that earlier time there were, as you also have indicated, several contending understandings of how one should lead an authentic Jewish life, among which the Pharisaic was prominent but by no means alone (indeed, as George Foot Moore, W. D. Davies, and, most recently, Rabbi Harvey Falk argue, it may well have been largely that form of Pharisaism that was subsequently largely rejected by post-70 rabbinic Judaism, namely, Bet Shammai).

Although Jesus ran fatally afoul of the Roman-appointed Jewish authorities, there is every evidence that his followers both during his lifetime and the immediately following decades understood themselves as true members of the Jewish household, attending the Temple and synagogue regularly and following the Torah in all its prescriptions.

It is only with the Roman destruction of the Jewish homeland and all the contending ways of being Jewish save that of the Bet Hillel Pharisees (who thereafter ceased being called Pharisees and gradually became known as rabbis) and the followers of the "Way" of Rabbi Yeshua (who gradually became known as Christians) that the situation changed radically. It was only then, in that polarized crisis situation, that the terms *Jew* and *Judaism* began to be attributed solely to the spiritual descendants of the rabbis other than Yeshua, Jesus. (The fact that after 70 the followers of Jesus soon were to be found more and more among Gentiles rather than ethnic Jews made such a terminological and conceptual shift increasingly likely.)

Hence, I would suggest that it might be more accurate to say that the fact that Jesus took a more "Reform" approach to the Torah than that of the dominant Pharisaic school of his day (Bet Shammai) made it *possible* that he would be perceived by later Jews and Christians as being "led out of the chain of Jewish tradition," as you put it. However, by itself this "distinctive" approach did not *necessitate* his being so perceived. That *de facto* development needed other added historical factors to become a reality.

I would also like briefly to join in your discussion with Rabbis Harvey Falk and Phillip Sigal. You see a flaw in Falk's too easily trusting the post-70 rabbis' (and hence, Bet Hillel descendants') description of pre-70 Bet Shammai; the "winners" tend to paint the "losers" in too distinctive a fashion. However, is it not enough for Falk's case to grant that there must have been a significant difference between the two schools and that Bet Shammai was the conservative, "strict constructionist" one? That the latter may well have been overdrawn in narrow terms would not undermine the basic argument of Falk.

You also criticize Falk, and rightly so, when you point out that Jesus did not in fact always take the side of Bet Hillel, although in general he certainly was on the "liberal" side. The two cases you cite, about Jesus' attitude toward the Gentiles and toward divorce, are indeed most probably authentically Jesuanic just because they do run counter to the general image of him as portrayed in the gospels—the tendency of the early Church and the evangelists would have been to "round off" those atypical extrusions rather than be the source of them.

In fact, such relatively moderate "aberrations" on the part of Jesus strengthen the argument of Phillip Sigal that Jesus was one of the so-called proto-rabbis (the true predecessors of rabbinic Judaism, he contends) who were ultimately quite independent in their religious decisions. Nevertheless, Jesus does appear to have been vastly closer to Bet Hillel than Bet Shammai, and it was in fact the former that replaced the latter in dominance in subsequent Judaism—placing Jesus and the foundation of later rabbinic Judaism largely in fundamental agreement, as Falk argued. Sigal, of course, draws a similar final conclusion, although he links Jesus with later rabbinic Judaism through the proto-rabbis rather than through Bet Hillel.

In either case, the conclusion raises the critical problems you insightfully point out, namely, why did "the Jesus movement so early split from the Jewish group with which its master had the greatest affinities," and also, what of "the validity of the Jesus movement as it moved away from its good, rabbinic, Jewish founder?"

This is indeed a critical issue, one which I attempt to address directly and in some detail in my next two sections. However, let me say here that I agree completely with the first part of your solution—the more important part—though not with the latter. You write: "This difference [of Jesus from other Jewish teachers of his time] most likely rests in the way he affected his immediate followers and has probably very little to do with what he taught or what he did." The fact that Jesus probably only "taught" for a single year, and then mostly in "backwater" Galilee, and that he was then executed—not at all an "in" thing for teachers, messiahs or any kind of Jewish leader—meant that his personality could not have been effectively brought to bear on more than a modest number of, mostly uninfluential, Jews during his lifetime. Those he did affect (and I argue later that what he "taught and did" were essential parts of how he affected people), however, obviously were so "turned on" that after some time, particularly after 70, claims began to be made for him that made him appear to be "out of the chain of Jewish tradition." But more of this later.

NOTES

1. See note 1 of Swidler's section, "Yeshua's Place in the Jewish Life of His Time."

2. E. P. Sanders, *Paul and Palestinian Judaism* (Philadelphia: Fortress Press, 1977).

3. Samuel Tobias Lachs, *A Rabbinic Commentary on the New Testament: The Gospels of Matthew, Mark and Luke* (Hoboken, NJ: Ktav, 1987) is a recent and suggestive attempt to use material from the Apocrypha/ Pseudepigrapha and from the corpus of rabbinic literature to elucidate the synoptic gospels and their picture of Jesus.

4. Ellis Rivkin, *A Hidden Revolution* (Nashville, TN: Abingdon, 1978).

5. A concise version of Neusner's approach to the study of Pharisaism can be found in his *From Politics to Piety* (Englewood Cliffs, NJ: Prentice Hall, 1973).

6. Geza Vermes, *Jesus the Jew* (Philadelphia: Fortress Press, 1973). Vermes argues that Jesus should be placed in the context of Galilean charismatic Judaism, pp. 58–82.

7. S. G. F. Brandon, *Jesus and the Zealots* (Manchester: Manchester University Press, 1967), argued strongly for placing Jesus within the movement of the zealots. Few scholars today would hold that Jesus was a revolutionary.

8. Harvey Falk, *Jesus the Pharisee* (Mahwah, NJ: Paulist Press, 1985).

9. Phillip Sigal, *The Halakhah of Jesus of Nazareth According to the Gospel of Matthew* (Lanham, MD: University Press of America, 1987).

5

Yeshua: A Torah-True Jew?

LEONARD SWIDLER

From a very early time Christians have tended to depict Yeshua as having made the Law no longer binding, as having left the Law behind along with Judaism, both of which had a purpose only in preparing the way for and bringing forth the Messiah. Since he had come, however, both were superseded. While Judaism held onto the Law, which led to death, Christianity followed the gospel and grace, which led to life. It was almost as if Kipling were anticipated: "Law is Law and Gospel is Gospel, and ne'er the twain shall meet." It was with this club of the "death-dealing Law" that Christians have bludgeoned Jews since New Testament days. Therefore, it is essential to Christian self-knowledge and to the relationship between the two religions that the record be set straight on the attitude of Yeshua, the "founder" of Christianity, toward the Law.

First, it should be recalled that although the Hebrew term *Torah* was translated by the Septuagint as *nomos*, Law, Torah in fact has a much wider meaning, namely, "instruction" on how to lead a proper, full, Jewish, human, life. Hence, when the term *nomos* appears in the New Testament it almost invariably means Torah, although in some instances it might also include the "oral Torah," or *halakhah*—the rules of conduct as interpreted and derived from the written Torah by the rabbis, or proto-rabbis, including Yeshua.

Halakhah, the Hebrew term meaning the "way" or "walk," which in rabbinic writing came to mean the decision on the correct way to act in a specific case, does not as such turn up in the gospels, but the reality to which it refers is often recorded, as when Yeshua asserted that a particular way was appropriate for applying the Torah in a life circumstance. It is interesting to note, however, that the equivalent of *halakhah* in Greek, *hodos*, does appear in the Acts of the Apostles when this writing describes the practices of the followers of Yeshua: "I worship the God of our fathers according to the Way (*hodos*)" (Acts 24:14). In this sense of a decision about the correct way to apply the Torah, God's instruction, to concrete life Rabbi Phillip Sigal speaks of the *halakhah* of Yeshua—and I do the same here.

To start, it must be recalled that Yeshua was a Jew and an observant one. That is, he was committed to the keeping of the Law in the way that seemed best to him. Because he was a "rabbi" he taught others to do likewise. In short, he did not come to dispense with or do away with the Torah, the Law. Rather, he came to carry it out.

This blunt a statement might well have been a shock to most past Christians, and to many today, but it has the growing support of contemporary Christian and Jewish scholars. Pinchas Lapide, an Orthodox Israeli Jewish scholar, says of Yeshua that he "never and nowhere broke the Law of Moses, the Torah of Moses, nor did he in any way provoke its infringement—it is entirely false to say that he did. . . . This Jesus was as faithful to the Law as I would hope to be. I even suspect that Jesus was more faithful to the Law than I am—and I am an Orthodox Jew."[1]

Franz Mussner, a Catholic New Testament scholar, argues that one should not read the Yeshua tradition in the gospels *a priori* in the light of the Pauline justification teaching, which grew out of the reflection on the saving significance of the death and resurrection of Yeshua. Rather, one should not hesitate to view the affirmation of the Law in Mt. 5:19 (Lk. 16:17) as coming from Yeshua. Indeed, "The Jewishness of Jesus is especially reflected in it."[2]

The matter is put this way by another Israeli Orthodox Jewish scholar: Yeshua was "a Torah-true Jew."[3] Still another states: "Jesus remained steadfast to the old *Torah*: till his dying day he continued to observe the ceremonial laws like a true Pharisaic Jew."[4] The same idea is expressed by a Jewish professor of rabbinics at Cambridge University: "Nor can I accept that Jesus' purpose was to do away with Judaism as he found it. He had his criticisms, to be sure, but he wanted to perfect the law of Moses, not to annul it. The Christian hostility to this law strikes me as a betrayal of Jesus' teaching."[5] Johann Maier, a scholar of judaistics, has argued similarly:

> There is no evidence that Jesus had intended a suspension of the Torah. Rather, he was perceived as so devout that the Pharisees even displayed a positive interest in him and viewed him as worthy of traveling around with. Likewise, the Jewish-Christian community saw no reason to give up the Torah either in theory or practice. . . . In no individual concrete case—either in relation to the Sabbath healing, or in ritual purity practice, or in the question of divorce—is there a fundamental conflict with "the Law."[6]

The Lutheran New Testament scholar Julius Wellhausen is equally strong in insisting that Yeshua was not a Christian, but a Jew: "He did not preach a new faith, but taught humans to do the will of God; and in his opinion, as also in that of the Jews, the will of God was to be found in the Law and in the other books of Scripture."[7] E. P. Sanders, a contemporary Protestant exegete, coolly rejects the view that Yeshua broke the Law: "Opinions range from this extreme all the way to another: there is no violation of the law at all or none worth much mention. In this case, one of the extremes must be judged to be correct: the second one."[8]

These and other scholars argue vigorously that those Christians who attempt to set up some sort of dichotomy between the Law and grace, as if Judaism were a religion only of Law and Christianity were a religion only of gospel, of grace—whatever else they might be, in this regard they are not followers of Yeshua. He clearly was committed to the keeping of the Law, the Torah, "as long as heaven and earth last!" He said: "Whoever breaks even the smallest of the commandments, and teaches others to do the same, will be least in the Reign of heaven" (Mt. 5:18f.). There is no intimation whatsoever of the abolishment of the Law in his words: "Do not think that I came to destroy the Law or the prophets; I came not to destroy but to carry out" (*plerōsai*, literally, to implement; Mt. 5:17-19).[9]

This is also true of the variant claim that Judaism is a religion of law and justice but that Christianity is a religion of love. It was made clear by Yeshua that there was no split between the two. They were, rather, one. His understanding of religion demanded one to follow the twofold command or law: to love God and neighbor. Of course, this was nothing new. Yeshua was simply quoting from the ancient Torah, Deut. 6:5, from a portion of the opening of the Jewish daily prayer, the *Sh*e*ma*: "Love the Lord your God with all your heart, with all your soul, and with all your strength," and Lev. 19:18: "Love your neighbor as you love yourself." Indeed, the linking together of these two commandments and the summing up of the Law in them was not something new or special to Yeshua. Luke 10:25–28 records that it was an "expert in the law" (*nomikos*) in the crowd who spoke of the twofold command of love; Yeshua merely agreed with him.

Furthermore, perhaps two hundred years before Yeshua was born other Jewish writers stated much the same sentiments. They can be found in various of the Pseudepigrapha (noncanonical Jewish writings in Greek): "Love the Lord and the neighbor" (Testament of Issachar 5:2); "I loved the Lord and every human being with my whole heart" (ibid., 7:6); "Love the Lord in your whole life and one another with a sincere heart" (Testament of Daniel 5:3); "Fear the Lord and love the neighbor" (Testament of Benjamin 3:3); "And he commanded them to keep to the way of God, do justice, and everyone love his/her neighbor" (Jubilees 20:9); "Love one another my sons as brothers, as one loves oneself. . . . You should love one another as yourselves" (ibid., 36:4–6).

The very same summing up of the Law, Torah, in the double command-ment of love was expressed by a Jewish contemporary of Yeshua, Philo of

Alexandria (c. 20 B.C.E.–50 C.E.). In his tractate "Concerning Individual Commandments," II, 63, he wrote: "There are, so to speak, two fundamental teachings to which the numberless individual teachings and statements are subordinated: in reference to God the commandment of honoring God and piety, in reference to humanity that of the love of humanity (*philanthrōpia*) and justice."

Phillip Sigal remarks that "the rabbi par excellence of the first century, Akiba, far from denying that the love command is a significant criterion by which all action should be measured, insisted upon it." Sigal provides the rabbinic references, as well as several other supporting rabbinical citations, in addition to those given above.[10]

In summary: these are not the words of a religion that is defective in love. Indeed, Yeshua did stress Torah and love—but in this he drew upon the Jewish tradition.

What of those who would make of Christianity a religion that was concerned not with works but with faith (with "faith alone") and who regard Judaism as a religion of "works of righteousness"? Whatever they may be, in this they are not followers of Yeshua. According to Yeshua, those who are saved, who will enter into the Reign of God, are not those who claim they have faith, who cry out "Lord, Lord!" but they are those who *do* corporal works of mercy. Such acts include feeding the hungry, clothing the naked, housing the homeless, and caring for the sick and imprisoned.

Yeshua, according to Matthew, commended the good, saying: "For I was hungry and you gave me food; I was thirsty and you gave me drink; I was a stranger and you made me welcome; naked and you clothed me, sick and you visited me, in prison and you came to see me" (Mt. 25:35–36). This is paralleled, however, both in the earlier Hebrew Bible and in later rabbinic writings. R. Hama, son of R. Hanina (a third-century Palestinian rabbi) said one should imitate God: "as he clothes the naked (Gen. 3:21) . . . so you too must clothe the naked. The Holy One . . . visited the sick (Gen. 18:1), so you too must visit the sick. The Holy One . . . comforted the mourners . . . (Gen. 25:11) so you too must comfort the mourners. The Holy One . . . buried the dead (Dt. 34:6), so you too must bury the dead."[11]

James wrote: "Faith without works is dead" (Jas. 2:17). It should be noted, however, that the teaching of Yeshua and James is not a polarizing "either-or" but a comprehensive "both-and." "His faith and his actions worked together" (Jas. 2:22). This is very old Jewish teaching, as is exemplified in the words of the prophet Habakkuk: "The just *live* by faith" (Hab. 2:4). Faith, *emunah*, trust in God, and the works that naturally flow from this sustaining trust and commitment, together are what characterize the just man and woman, the Jew, and hence also the follower of Yeshua.

In short, Yeshua, as a faithful Jew, was committed to affirming and keeping the Torah.

Very similar to Hillel and Shammai before him, Yeshua developed his own way of how to interpret and apply the Torah to life—not at all a simple matter, as the dozens of volumes of the Talmud indicate. Much of Yeshua's Torah interpretation, his *halakhoth*, can be found embedded in the gospels, though perhaps often in redacted form—though so are the other rabbis' *halakhoth* redacted in the Talmud. In interpreting and applying the Torah, Yeshua thus followed good rabbinic practice. He in no way thereby moved outside Judaism, despite what might be considered by some Jews his "liberal" handling of the Torah. He was in this manner much more like Hillel than Shammai.

The author of our version of the Gospel according to Matthew wrote perhaps around 85 C.E. with great polemic against the Pharisees (and probably also the post-70 rabbis) and their interpretation of the Torah, *halakhah*. Hence, he had every reason to neglect, suppress, significantly change, or at least to nuance Yeshua's strong commitment, quoted above (Mt. 5:17–19), to the keeping of the Torah. He did not, however. The Yeshuanic tradition of adhering to the Torah apparently was still so strong more than half a century after the death of Yeshua that he did not dare distort it. Regardless how "liberal" an interpretation of the Torah Yeshua may have been perceived as teaching in order to fulfill "the spirit" rather than just "the letter" of the Torah (as Paul expressed it: "in the spirit, not in the letter," *en pneumati, ou grammati*; Rom. 2:29), it is undeniable that he was immovably firm on the "carrying out" of all of the Torah—till the end of the age.[12]

Perhaps the most definitive argument to prove that Yeshua had not stood in opposition to the Torah is put forth by E. P. Sanders, one of the few Christian New Testament scholars who know the Jewish materials, including the rabbinic. From the New Testament we know that from the very beginning, immediately after the passion and resurrection events, the Jewish followers of Yeshua were expected to continue to follow the Torah, and that they did. Whether or not the Gentile followers who came later were expected to was the subject of a great dispute between Peter and Paul and others. Both facts exhibit clear proof that Yeshua had *not* in his lifetime signaled opposition to the Torah. Sanders, in explaining that sometimes Yeshua took a more stringent stand than that required by a passage in the Torah—e.g., regarding the divorce of women by men—speaks of Yeshua's affirming the Torah and moving beyond it, and in that limited, negative sense finding it not adequate.[13]

The Catholic New Testament scholar Franz Mussner has a perceptive remark in this regard:

> One could describe Jesus of Nazareth, precisely in what concerns his understanding of the "fulfilling" of the Law, as a "Reform Jew," but of course as the most influential and most radical Reform Jew Judaism has ever produced. There has, however, always been a place for a "Reform Judaism" within Judaism. With his criticism concerning the concrete realization of the life according to the Law Jesus has not

fallen outside the framework of Judaism—as precisely the Jewish scholars of the life of Jesus emphasize.[14]

In order to deal with the Law, the Torah, Yeshua had to apply it to everyday life. He had to fashion concrete rules of conduct, called *halakhot*. As Phillip Sigal phrases it, Yeshua was "a proto-rabbinic halakhist as well as a charismatic prophet."[15] If he applied the Law to concrete life, it would, of course, be apparent that Yeshua was in favor of the Law. But a traditional Christian move here has been to point out that he abrogated parts of the Law, indeed even the written Torah—something a rabbi would never do! As Sigal points out, however, "the abrogation of specific precepts of the written Torah is not unusual for Jesus' milieu." He notes that the tannaitic rabbi R. Nathan stated that when "one must act for the Lord, annulment of provisions is allowed. He maintains this in reference to either Torah, the written or the interpretative . . . no 'law' is absolute. What stands above all is the will of God,"[16] which is applied through the interpretative wisdom of the rabbi. An example of the many such rabbinic abrogations of parts of the written Torah is the rescinding of the trial by ordeal of the suspected adulterous wife (Num. 5:11–31) by the contemporary of Yeshua, Rabbi Yohanan ben Zakkai.[17]

An example often offered by Christian scholars of Yeshua's "sovereign abrogation" of a central written Torah obligation which set him outside the rabbinic tradition is Yeshua's statement found in Mark 2:27: "The sabbath was made for human beings, not human beings for the sabbath." A very close paraphrase, however, is also found in an early rabbinic writing: "The sabbath is committed to you; you are not committed to the sabbath" (Mekilta *Shab.* 1). Sigal argues, in fact, that, "During his brief ministry Jesus was a proto-rabbi whose views influenced his contemporaries and possibly entered tannaitic literature as the views of others. . . . A classic example of a view enunciated by Jesus which is attributed to later tanna R. Simon B. Menasia" is the Mekilta statement about the sabbath.[18] Both ways, Yeshua in this regard was in the center of the rabbinic tradition; he was either being paralleled or plagiarized.

Sometimes seeming almost desperate to make Yeshua different, to separate him from Judaism, Christian scholars point out that a number of times Yeshua cites the Torah and then says, "but I say to you"—*egō de legō hymin*—arguing that as an ordinary rabbi he could not do such a thing in contradiction to the word of God; he must have divine sovereignty over the Torah. Here again, a lack of knowledge of the rabbinic materials has betrayed such Christian scholars. This sort of language used by Yeshua "should not be regarded as evidence of anything more than proto-rabbinic insistence upon one's own view even when it contradicts and abolishes earlier teaching. It is found used by the first-second century sage, R. Simon b. Yohai, at t. Sot. 6:6–11. . . . It is self-evident that people 'marveled' at

Menahem b. Sungai (T. Ed. 3:1) as they did at Jesus (Mt. 7:28)."[19]
In another place Sigal states clearly:

A major characteristic of this proto-rabbinic development, however,
was the assumption of religious authority by individuals. These
individuals, by force of personality and learning, were capable of
changing previous halakhah, unsettling tradition and inaugurating
new trends. . . . It is this diversity which in great measure is the key
to our understanding of the Matthean Jesus.[20]

Hence, far from being different because of his strong teaching style in
regard to Torah, Yeshua fitted very well into his intellectual and cultural
environment. Of course later, after 70 c.e., the custom developed of decid-
ing on the correct way, the *halakhah*, by a majority vote among the rabbis —
but that was not yet the case before 70 when Yeshua taught.

Another strong teacher of Torah, who also abrogated the written Torah,
was Yeshua's contemporary Yohanan ben Zakkai. As noted before, he
spent twenty years in Galilee, studied with Hillel and Shammai, was a
forceful, independent and original thinker, and in a significant way
"founded" a new religion, or rather, forged a new direction in Judaism. In
these aspects Yohanan and Yeshua were much alike. Sigal, with sufficient
warrant, has speculated that Yohanan and Yeshua knew each other. They
might well have been at first fellow students of the schools of Hillel and
Shammai and then colleagues, and hence could very well have held halakhic
discussions together. Furthermore, when it is recalled that Yohanan ben
Zakkai became the leader of the Hillelite school — to which Yeshua was in
many regards very close — and made that interpretation of Torah dominant
in all subsequent Judaism, it would seem to make much more sense to view
Yeshua as very much "in" rather than "out" of the mainstream of pre-70
Judaism.

Geza Vermes remarks on the striking similarity between Yeshua and
the Qumran Teacher of Righteousness. Like Yeshua,

The Teacher of Righteousness . . . served as transmitter and interpreter of the divine mysteries, of God's definitive revelation. Like
Jesus, he was surrounded by faithful disciples who continued to
adhere to, and practice, his doctrines after his death. . . . Like Jesus'
followers, they organized themselves into a separate, self-contained
body of the chosen, some of them living like the Jerusalem church
out of a common purse and shunning private ownership of property.

Unlike the Qumran sectaries, however, who "closed the doors of their
community to all except Jews,"[21] the followers of Yeshua, after much soul-
searching, decided to admit non-Jews to their company without requiring
them first to become Jews.

What was special, then, about the teaching of Yeshua? Indeed, was there anything at all special? As noted before, the great commandments of love were already in the Judaic heritage. The idea of freedom from the Law was something that Paul, not Yeshua, expressed (and then only for the Gentile followers of Yeshua, not the Jewish; see Rom. 9–11). But certainly there was something special about the teaching of Yeshua. To begin, the specific extraordinary constellation of teachings is a mark of his creative genius. David Flusser, a Jewish New Testament scholar, has pointed out that although one may fundamentally be able to reproduce the gospel out of citations from the many volumes of rabbinic writings, one would first have to have the gospels available. Moreover, as noted, given the fact that the interpretation and application of the Torah was greatly in flux at the time of Yeshua, Yeshua's own interpretation "according to the spirit" was just that, his own, even though it lay in the direction of his great predecessor, Hillel.

Yeshua, however, was not satisfied with teaching that the whole of the Torah should be carried out according to its spirit. He moved beyond it in holding out the ideal of a self-emptying (*kenotic,* as Paul said in Phil. 2:6) love for one's friends, one's neighbors, and even one's enemies—as seen especially in the Sermon on the Mount (Mt. 5ff.). The subsequent Rabbis had a phrase for halakhic decisions that went beyond the demands of the Torah, *lifnim meshurat ha din* ("beyond the requirements of the court"). Vermes notes: "Proto-rabbis sometimes encouraged going beyond the strict requirement of law or the literal reading of a text. In this way they inspired some to sacrifice their monetary or property right under law in order to extend equity to others. This is how we are to understand Mt. 5:40 ['And if anyone sue you at law and take away your coat, let him have your cloak as well.']."[22]

What was most special about Yeshua, however, was that he *lived* not only according to the Torah, but also according to his supererogatory kenotic ideal, *lifnim meshurat ha din* — even to the point of agonizingly dying for the sake of his friends: "Greater love than this has no one, but that he gives his life for his friends" (that is, for those loved by him, *tōn philōn autou*, Jn. 15:13). Geza Vermes states: "the heart of Jesus' message" was its "stress on interiority and supererogation."[23]

Hence, what apparently struck many of Yeshua's contemporaries about him and made them his disciples must have been his inner wisdom and love, which shone through his teaching the fulfillment of the whole Torah according to its spirit. He set forth an ideal of kenotic love that went beyond it, and lived and died accordingly in his *whole* person. It was what Yeshua "thought, taught, and wrought," that whole, that life (and death), that made him special—for many, a human transparency of the divine.

Obviously for Yeshua it was not a question of living by the Law, the Torah, *or* the spirit. Rather, by living (and dying) the whole Law (Torah) according to its spirit, he thought, taught and wrought a life that was open to and showed forth the Source and Goal of the Torah—YHWH: "Be perfect as your heavenly Father is perfect." It was not freedom *from* the Law but freedom *through* the Law *and beyond* to kenotic love, *lifnim meshurat hadin*. Augustine put it: "Love, and do what you will," "*Ama, et fac quod vis*," for your love will lead you not contrary to the Law, but to it, and beyond.

Nevertheless, the living and dying according to the Torah and beyond did not in any way place Yeshua outside of Judaism. This kenotic love was described by the Rabbis with the biblical term *hesed*, often simply translated as "loving kindness." A *hasid* is someone whose life is centered on *hesed*, one whose philosophy of life is not to be "content with a minimum standard of conduct but to go beyond the letter of the law."[24] Hence, as Yeshua urged his followers to be "perfect as your heavenly Father is perfect," so the later Rabbis often described God as practicing *hesed*, as being a *hasid*.[25] When advocating living in kenotic love, in *hesed*, Yeshua also spoke of living in the spirit, of sending the holy spirit, and urged others to learn from his humility. Observe the following striking rabbinic parallels: "A life led in the spirit of *hesed* was, moreover, thought to be the harbinger of the holy spirit (Shekalim 9b)."[26] "Holiness leads to humility; humility to the fear of sin; the fear of sin to the holy spirit; the holy spirit to the resurrection of the dead. But *hasiduth* [the practice of *hesed*] is greater than all these!"[27] Mordecai Paldiel, a contemporary Jewish scholar, summarizes his description of a *hasid* in a way that for a Christian is extraordinarily reminiscent of Yeshua's kenotic love and reference to the two great commandments of love:

> A *hasid* is, then, a person who practices *hesed* in his or her daily life — in our parlance, a higher ethic. This, according to Jacobs, implies a disposition combining an intensity of love for God and the human being — a complete devotion to the former and an unqualified benevolence to the latter. ... As the Talmud points out, it is fitting for those who practice *hesed* to seek out the poor (Shabbat 104a).[28]

Geza Vermes similarly stresses Yeshua's *hesed* and theocentric qualities, which here interestingly contrast with Paul's christocentrism: "Jesus' *hasiduth*, his *theocentric* devoutness, has been overlaid by the ramifications of Paul's *christocentric* spirituality. His opinion of human nature, unlike that of Jesus, was deeply pessimistic."[29]

Hence, in teaching and living his life in fulfilling the Torah and beyond in kenotic love, in *hesed*, the *hasid*, proto-rabbi Yeshua indeed lived a special, extraordinary life, the like of which his followers never before, or since, experienced, but in this he was quintessentially Jewish.

Consequently, Vermes sees Yeshua not as a barrier but a bond between Christians and Jews — and all human beings:

In this so-called post-Christian era, when Christ as a divine form seems to ever-increasing numbers not to correspond, either to the age's notion of reality, or to the exigencies of the contemporary human predicament, is it not possible that Jesus the healer, teacher and helper may yet be invited to emerge from the shadows of his long exile? And not by Christians alone? "If, above all, his lesson on reciprocal, loving and direct relation with the Father in heaven is recalled and found universally valid, may not the sons of God on earth stand a better chance of ensuring that the ideal of human brotherhood becomes something more than a pipe-dream?"[30]

A Response to Leonard Swidler from Lewis John Eron

It is helpful to destroy the false and polemical dichotomy between Judaism as a religion of law and Christianity as a religion of grace. You have clearly shown that what many took as Jesus' distinctive message is really quite commonplace in rabbinic Judaism. It would be surprising were it otherwise.

A commitment to God's *Torah/Nomos/*"Law" is ubiquitous to early Judaism and Christianity. The debate centers not on whether or not God has a law that we should attempt to follow but rather on which group correctly promulgates and follows that law as God intended it to be promulgated and followed.

The discussion of Jesus as a "Torah-true" Jew is complicated, not simplified, by talking about Jesus' *halakhah*. The term *halakhah* has a specific range of meanings within rabbinic Judaism, the earliest writings of which date two centuries later than Jesus. Although the rabbinic tradition contains material from the time of Jesus and earlier, it is exceedingly difficult to attempt to discuss the meaning of the term *halakhah* in the first century.

The Hebrew word *halakhah* does not appear in the Hebrew Scriptures, although its grammatical form is well attested in the Bible. It is, therefore, likely that it could have existed. Whether or not it would have been used to refer to Israelite legal practice is impossible to determine. Its meaning could have been much closer to the basic meaning of its verbal root h-l-k, "to go." The related Aramaic form, *hilkheta*, has as one of its meanings the noun "step."

The use of the term *halakhah* to refer to the established patterned behavior of Jewish life has its source in the biblical concept of "walking in God's laws" (Ex. 16:4; Lev. 18:4; Deut. 8:6; 30:16). This concept remains current in the time of Jesus. It appears in the writings of the Qumran community. In 1QS (The Manual of Discipline) 9:12, the "man of understanding's" devotion to the rules of the community is described as his "walking in them." The verbal noun *halakhah* also appears in the Qumran writings.

There it has the general sense of "walking" or of "going" (1QS 1:25; 3:9) in connection with God's precepts.

Even if one wants to use the term *halakhah* to refer to Jewish law in the time of Jesus, one has to remember that there was not one Jewish law, *halakhah*. A perplexing problem for students of this period is to understand the relationship between the form and contents of presentations of Jewish law in such diverse sources as Philo, Josephus, Jubilees, the Qumran writings, and later rabbinic legislation. There are both striking similarities and marked differences.

Although Phillip Sigal has identified certain clear parallels between rabbinic usage and the way Matthew's Gospel presents some of Jesus' legislation, he does not establish that Jesus taught in such a manner. Jesus may very well have. On the other hand, it is important to remember that Matthew, of all the gospel writers, presents Jesus as the eschatological teacher, the "scribe of the Dominion of Heaven." It would be surprising for Matthew not to stress the similarities between Jesus and the developing rabbinic tradition of his time.

It is particularly risky to accept Sigal as an authority. In many ways his reading of Matthew's Jesus seems intuitively correct. The parallels in the form of legal presentation between Jesus and the rabbis that Sigal notes are convincing. Unfortunately, his treatment of the specifics of rabbinic *halakhah* and their relationship with Jesus' teachings is flawed. In addition, his argument that Jesus was in close contact with the leading rabbinic figures of his day better fits the genre of the historical novel than academic history.

There is no good reason to assume that Jesus met Yohanan ben Zakkai and if they did meet that they spoke about things of a religious nature. If these two "kindred spirits" met, they may as peers have enjoyed speaking of more mundane matters. It is equally plausible that if they had met they would not have liked each other. We do not know and we cannot know.

It is more likely that early Jewish Christianity developed without any contact with the heroes of Pharisaic/rabbinic Judaism. The rabbinic tradition does not take note of any such early contact. The traditions concerning Jesus in the Talmud are late and do not provide any reliable information about Jesus. Although the New Testament reports close contact between Jesus and his followers with members of various groups in first-century C.E. Judaism, on the whole these people are either anonymous or are otherwise unknown. The only identifiable rabbinic figure mentioned in the New Testament is Rabban Gamaliel the Elder (Acts 22:3), and he is mentioned in connection with Paul, not Jesus.

The Greek term *hodos*, "way," may not be the Christian equivalent of the rabbinic term *halakhah*. It is clear that in the passage you cited—Paul's accusation and defense before the Procurator Felix (Acts 24)—Paul's Jewish accusers understood Paul's *hodos* as being sectarian. It is the path of the Nazarenes (24:4, 14).

The use of the term *hodos*, "the Way," to refer to the Christian movement appears in the New Testament only in the Book of Acts. Rather than seeing the term *hodos* as the Greek form of the still relatively rare and hard-to-define Hebrew term *halakhah*, it seems to me to be more helpful to look at its usage in the Septuagint, the Greek translation of the Hebrew Scriptures. There it most often is the translation of the Hebrew word *derech*, "way," as in the phrase "the way of the righteous." This phrase and its counterpart, "the way of the wicked," appear most often in the Psalms and the Wisdom Literature such as the Book of Proverbs.

In light of Luke-Acts' interest in and dependence on Paul, it is likely that the Christian "Way" is not an alternative halakhic system but rather refers to the *derech tzadiqim, hē hodos tōn dikaiōn*, the Way of the Righteous. The Christian community is the community of the righteous and its way is the way of the righteous.

For an early Christian community to hold such a self-understanding is not surprising in light of what is known about the contemporaneous Qumran community's self-understanding of their role as the *"B'nei Or,"* or the "Children of Light." Since Luke-Acts portrays the early Christians as being persecuted by the greater Jewish community, the dichotomy between the expressed "Way of the Righteous" and the implied "Way of the Wicked" makes sense.

It should be remembered that the conflict recorded by the author of Luke-Acts is an *internal* Jewish conflict. Paul and his followers and his converts are in dispute with other members of the still predominantly Jewish Jesus Movement and with members of other Jewish groups. The author of Luke-Acts uses this internal Jewish conflict to justify his program of Gentile mission. The Jews and Jerusalem rejected Jesus and his teachings, therefore Paul, the hero of Acts, directs his mission to the Gentiles and to Rome.

One further point: as difficult as it is to place Jesus within the Jewish world of his time, it is misleading to try to place Jesus within our contemporary Jewish spectrum. The title you use for this section, "Yeshua: A Torah-True Jew," is not helpful in this regard. The expression "Torah-true" has been used by the Orthodox Jewish community since the last century to distinguish themselves from the reformers. Contemporary Jews have often pictured Jesus in terms of their ideal form of Judaism. Claude Montefiore, a leading English Reform Jewish historian and thinker from the first half of this century, pictured Jesus as a Reform Jew. Orthodox Jewish scholars such as Lapide and Flusser describe Jesus as an observant, "Torah-true," Orthodox Jew.

Though Jesus wanted to reform Judaism, he was not and could not have been a Reform Jew. Reform Judaism, as we know it today, is a movement that developed out of the unique situation of Jews in Europe and North America in the nineteenth and twentieth centuries. Likewise, even if Jesus had been meticulous in his observance of Pharisaic (or proto-rabbinic) practices, one cannot describe him as Orthodox. Orthodoxy in the Jewish world today implies a self-conscious, that is, post-Enlightenment/Emancipation, commitment to the regulation of Jewish practices as described in the sixteenth-century code of Jewish law, the *Shulchan Aruch*, and as interpreted by later authorities.

All we can safely say is that Jesus ben Joseph, the teacher from Nazareth, was not an antinomian. He cherished the Jewish tradition and taught his disciples to follow it. Although in certain respects his teachings may have been distinctive, in their form and for the most part in their content they were in line with the Pharisaic/proto-rabbinic understanding of the law, as far as we can reconstruct it.

NOTES

1. Pinchas Lapide and Hans Küng, "Is Jesus a Bond or Barrier? A Jewish-Christian Dialogue," *Journal of Ecumenical Studies,* 14 (1977), p. 473, a translation of Hans Küng and Pinchas Lapide, *Jesus im Widerstreit, Ein jüdisch-christlicher Dialog* (Stuttgart/Munich: Calwer-Kösel, 1976), p. 26.

2. Franz Mussner, *Traktat über die Juden* (Munich: Kösel, 1979); English translation, *Tractate on the Jews,* by Leonard Swidler (Philadelphia: Fortress Press, 1984), p. 118.

3. David Flusser, *Jesus in Selbstzeugnissen und Bilddokumenten* (Reinbeck, 1968), p. 43.

4. Joseph Klausner, *Jesus of Nazareth* (Macmillan: New York, 1925), p. 275.

5. Nicolas de Lange, "Who Is Jesus?" *Sidic,* 12, 3 (1979), p. 12.

6. Johann Maier, "Jesus von Nazareth und sein Verhältnis zum Judentum aus der Sicht eines Judaisten," in Willehad Paul Eckert and Hans Hermann Henrix, eds., *Jesu Jude-Sein als Zugang zum Judentum,* 2nd ed. (Aachen: Einhard, 1980), p. 95.

7. Wellhausen, *Einleitung,* p. 113.

8. E. P. Sanders, *Jesus and Judaism* (Philadelphia: Fortress Press, 1985), p. 264.

9. A word can have many meanings; the one intended can be known only in relation to its context, as was in this case again pointed out by Gerhard Delling: "The meaning of *plēroō* cannot be deduced . . . it must be based on the context. . . . According to Mt. 5:17a this [mission of Yeshua] is primarily fulfillment of the Law and prophets. . . . Jesus does not merely affirm that He will maintain them. As He sees it, His task is to actualize the will of God made known in the OT." Gerhard Kittel, *Theological Dictionary of the New Testament* (Grand Rapids, MI: Eerdmans, 1968), VI, pp. 293ff. For a thorough discussion of the meaning of *plērōsai* and the attitude of Yeshua toward the Law see Mussner, *Traktat über die Juden,* pp. 185–93; *Tractate on the Jews,* pp. 115–21.

10. Phillip Sigal, *The Halakhah of Jesus of Nazareth According to the Gospel of Matthew* (Lanham, MD: University Press of America, 1987), p. 18.

11. Geza Vermes, *Jesus and the World of Judaism* (Philadelphia: Fortress Press, 1984) p. 168.

12. I am particularly indebted to Pinchas Lapide for this understanding of Matthew's treatment of the attitude of Yeshua toward the Law (Torah) and his supererogatory ideal; conversation in Frankfurt, July 8, 1985.

13. E. P. Sanders, *Jesus and Judaism,* pp. 330; 263ff.
14. Mussner, *Tractate on the Jews,* p. 121.
15. Sigal, *The Halakhah of Jesus,* p. 6.
16. Ibid., p. 16.
17. m.Sota, 9,9.
18. Sigal, *The Halakhah of Jesus,* p. 159.
19. Ibid., pp. 81f; the form of the citation is Signal's.
20. Ibid., p. 79.
21. Vermes, *Jesus and the World of Judaism,* p. 68.
22. Ibid. Geza Vermes remarked on the one hand that

Jesus . . . more than once expressly urges obedience to the purely ritual and cultic precepts in sayings all the more historically credible in that they are peripheral to the gospel narrative and actually run counter to the essential antinomianism of Gentile Christianity,

but then adds that

the chief distinction of Jesus' piety lies in his extraordinary emphasis on the real inner religious significance of the commandments. . . . Philo and Josephus did the same. So did many of the rabbis, and the Qumran sectaries. . . . Interiority, purity of intention, played a greater part in Jesus' thought . . . because of his natural bias towards the individual and personal rather than the collective (*Jesus and the World of Judaism,* p. 47).

23. Ibid., p. 55.
24. Louis Jacobs, "The Concept of Hasid in the Biblical and Rabbinic Literature," *Journal of Jewish Studies,* vol. 8 (1957).
25. Vermes, *Jesus and the World of Judaism,* p. 52.
26. Cf. e.g. *Yalkut Shimoni*, Erev, 873, and Sifre, Erev, 49.
27. b. Avod. Zar., 20b.
28. Mordecai Paldiel, "*Hesed* and the Holocaust," *Journal of Ecumenical Studies,* 23, 1 (Winter 1986), p. 97.
29. Vermes, *Jesus and the World of Judaism,* p. 56.
30. Ibid., p. 57.

6

Jesus: A Torah-True Jew?

LEWIS JOHN ERON

Jesus' attitude to *Torah*, loosely translated as "the Law," allows some insight as to where Jesus might be placed within the collection of sects, groups, and parties that constituted first-century C.E. Judaism. Yet we must remember that the concern with exactly what the role of the Torah, the Law, was may not have been as central an issue for Jesus and his disciples as it became in later Christianity.

The major problem we have in understanding Jesus' attitudes to the Law—or better, the Torah—is that we are not at all certain how the term *Law* or *Torah* was understood in the first few centuries B.C.E. and the first few centuries C.E. At best, it seems that the issue of what was the Law, the Torah, was as complex in the pluralistic Judaism of the first century C.E. as it is in the pluralistic Judaism of the twentieth century C.E.

Going beyond the obvious statement that the Hebrew word *Torah* is only poorly reproduced by the Greek term *nomos*, one cannot claim that early Christians misunderstood what Torah meant to Jews because they saw it only in Greek categories. The term *nomos* is itself not so tightly defined as to be restricted to law as a body of rules and regulations established by a legitimate legislating authority. In Stoicism, for example, *nomos* refers to the power of an individual's reason to live in harmony with this order.

In Jewish circles the definition of Torah was vigorously debated. It seems that the Sadducees understood Torah as the laws of the Pentateuch. The Pharisees, on the other hand, argued for a twofold law consisting of the written Pentateuchal Law and oral tradition. The community of the Qumran scrolls demanded obedience to the Law not only as it appeared in Scripture but also in their own writings. There was a tradition in both Judah and in the diaspora that saw the Law, the Torah, as the embodiment of wisdom. Philo argued against those who allegorized the Law to the extent that they no longer followed it. Josephus discusses the Law as the sound, well-founded and reasonable principles of Jewish life established from ancient times by God through Moses the Law-giver.

Christians often misunderstand the Law, the Torah, by placing it in an artificial dichotomy with faith. This interpretation results from a powerful Augustinian and Lutheran misreading of Paul. Jews, similarly, often err in making the traditional but misleading distinction between *Midrash Aggadah* (homiletical, moral interpretation) and *Midrash Halakhah* (legal interpretation) as if to the rabbis of old they were two separate activities in the study of Torah.

These are some of the problems involved in asking about Jesus' attitudes toward the Law. We are not sure what the Law was in the first century C.E., and our view of the Law is distorted by the weight of centuries of misreadings. Compounding this problem is the fact that our sources are the highly subjective readings of Jesus' life preserved in the gospels and to a lesser extent in other early Christian literature. The various communities of followers of Jesus who produced the gospel accounts of their teacher's life drew freely on the facts of his life and his teachings. They carefully crafted religious works in a biographical form that produced various images of Jesus to answer the spiritual and social needs of their communities.[1]

This is not to accuse these early Christian groups of duplicity. It should be obvious that not everything Jesus taught and did in the Galilee in the first third of the first century C.E. should have been of interest to early Christian groups who lived a generation or two removed from their founder, living throughout the Land of Israel and the eastern Mediterranean littoral. The spiritual and theological needs of these groups after the destruction of Jerusalem and the entrance of large numbers of Gentiles into at least some of the communities of followers of Jesus led them to preserve and interpret those acts and teachings of Jesus that responded to these needs. Their memory of Jesus was selective.

Furthermore, the early Christians employed as well the interpretative method developed in Judaism, known by its Hebrew name as *midrash*. Midrash can be understood as a process of reading a text considered to be the authoritative word of God through the lens of a specific event and/or special concern that may or may not be explicitly referred to in the text. In the relationship between the original text and the focusing event and/or concern, the meaning of the original text is expanded and the significance of the focusing event and/or concern is underscored.[2]

In many ways one can understand the use by the earliest Christians of what were for them scriptural concepts and images in picturing Jesus as a midrashic process. The Hebrew Scriptures, the Bible of both the Jews and the earliest Christians, of course did not refer directly to Jesus of Nazareth. Rather, the life and teachings of Jesus served as the lens through which all his followers would subsequently read their scriptural heritage.

Likewise, events in the lives of the earliest Christian communities led them to read the life and teachings of Jesus in a special way. Jesus is at least expressly in John's Gospel described as the "word" of God. Thus, the record of Jesus of Nazareth preserved in the New Testament and other early Christian writings is not only a midrash on the Hebrew Bible but it is, as well, a midrash on the life of Jesus himself.

In the specific area of Jesus and the Law, we can expect the New Testament to present various pictures of Jesus' understanding of and relationship to the Law. Only through careful study of the material may one be able to gather some insights into Jesus' own positions.

Certain Jewish scholars, such as Pinchas Lapide, have argued that Jesus was a Law-abiding Jew. Lapide's statement, for example, that Jesus never and nowhere broke the Law of Moses is an irenic overstatement. If what Lapide means is that Jesus never set himself up against the Law as a regulating norm of Jewish life, then I must agree with him. If, on the other hand, Lapide claims that Jesus was not only meticulous in his observance of the Law but adhered to the interpretation of the Law of the Pharisaic schools as well, then it is clear that Lapide is overstating the case.[3]

Even in the most Jewish of the gospels, the Gospel according to Matthew, Jesus is pictured as provoking the scribes and the Pharisees by, at least, selective disobedience of the Law. Jesus' disciples pick and eat grain on the Sabbath and Jesus miraculously cures a man with a withered arm on the Sabbath (Mt. 12:1–14). Jesus also disregards the purity customs of the Pharisees (Mt. 15:1–20). Whether or not one agrees with the homiletical point he is making, this is a clear and deliberate violation of ancient custom and law, at least as it was understood by some groups in ancient Israel.[4]

Instead of trying to defend Jesus as an Orthodox Jew—whatever that means in a first-century context—it is better to try to look at his particular relationship to the Law. Jesus' attitude toward the Law may reflect his Galilean background. Like others in the tradition of the miracle-working, popular teachers in the Galilee (such as Honi the Circle-maker and Hanina ben Dosa), Jesus exhibits a disregard for the laws of ritual purity. Geza Vermes argues that Hanina, for example, owned goats against the ruling found later in the Mishnah (b.Taan. 25a; m.B. Qam. 7:7).[5]

Even Jesus' meticulousness is paralleled by the pious of old, the *hasidim*. Hanina was known to have begun his Sabbath observance earlier than the others. He was also particularly careful in paying his tithes (y. Ber. 7c; y. Dem. 22a). Geza Vermes points out that such idiosyncratic observance could only come into conflict with a movement within the Jewish legal tradition that aimed to establish a common order of behavior.[6]

Morton Smith attempts to place Jesus' teachings and, more importantly, his acts in the context of miracle workers, healers, and magicians of the Hellenistic Near East. He points out that Jesus neither presented himself as a legal authority with a consistent legal theory, nor was he remembered by his disciples as such a figure. According to Smith, Jesus' legal rulings were "mostly *ad hoc*, in attempts to answer objections that arose primarily from his and his disciples' libertine practices."[7]

Smith argues that the acceptance of, as well as the objections to, Jesus recorded in the New Testament pertain to his miracles and healings and not to his legal rulings. About half the legal questions put to Jesus, Smith claims, were attempts to embarrass him. The rest seem to have been developed by his followers in order to ground their later teachings in those of their master.[8]

Jesus' attitude toward the Law must be understood in his relationship to Jewish eschatological expectations. Although it is not clear whether or not Jesus saw himself as the messianic figure, it is clear that he taught with the expectation that the Dominion of Heaven was close at hand. If anything, one can expect Jesus to have taken a rigorous rather than a lenient approach to the Law and personal ethics.

Gerd Theissen understands earliest Christianity as a Jewish renewal movement and describes its leaders as wandering charismatic teachers. According to Theissen, Jesus, at least as he was perceived by his earliest followers, taught a strict personal ethic that suited the lifestyle demands of wandering preachers. He preached an asceticism that enabled his followers to be free to travel without strong ties to property or family. This asceticism also reduced their threat to the stability of the communities of sympathizers who would host them.[9]

In general, one of a group's possible responses to crisis is to intensify the norms of behavior that set the boundaries of the group. Theissen points out the sense of crisis in first-century C.E. Judaism and briefly describes how the various Jewish groups responded to crisis by stressing a tightening of the norms of behavior and demanding a stronger adherence to traditional customs and beliefs. The Pharisees stressed the twofold law (the written Torah and the unwritten oral tradition), the Sadducees stressed the traditional Temple worship, and the Essenes stressed a purified priesthood and Temple in light of their eschatological expectations.

I see Jesus' attitude toward the Law as colored as well by the eschatological nature of his preaching. The rapidly approaching Dominion of Heaven puts everything, including the Law, into perspective. One has to achieve a high level of personal piety and moral purity before the in-breaking of the messianic period. Hyper-observance as well as selective disobedience should mark the period just before the End of Days. Jesus' insistence on hyper-observance can be seen in the instructions given during the Sermon on the Mount. He insists that he came not to end the Law and the Prophets but to complete them. Not one iota or tittle will disappear from the Law until the End of Time. The scribes and Pharisees set the minimal standards of Law observance for entrance into the Dominion of Heaven. Jesus' disciples are told to be more observant, more meticulous. As Moses issued laws from Sinai, Jesus addresses the crowds below and stresses a personal and sexual morality stricter than demanded by the traditional Law.

On the other hand, Jesus' authority as the eschatological teacher is stressed by his ability to assert his power over the Law. The gospels report his healings on the Sabbath as well as his gathering of grain in the field on the Sabbath to demonstrate how Jesus took control of the Law. Jesus' condemnation of the hypocrisy of the scribes and the Pharisees is no more to be seen as a condemnation of the Law itself than the prophetic critique of the sacrificial system is a condemnation of sacrificial worship per se. It is not the Law itself that is wrong. It is people who abuse the Law for their own purposes.

The New Testament does not provide clear evidence of the method in which Jesus understood Torah. One cannot argue, for example, from Romans 6 that Jesus taught that the Torah, the Law, should be fulfilled "according to the spirit." That is Paul's phrase, not Jesus'. Paul was addressing a different set of issues than Jesus did. The broad issue in Romans, particularly, is what it means for Gentiles as well as for Jews to be part of Israel's covenant now that it has been opened up to them by Jesus' death and resurrection. On the other hand, Jesus saw his ministry directed primarily to his fellow Jews.

Jesus' supererogatory, kenotic ideal does not seem to be integral to the teachings of Jesus, but rather appears as an early theological explanation of the life, death, and resurrection of Jesus as perceived by his followers. Though there can be little doubt that Jesus lived and taught the by then traditional Jewish teaching joining the love of God with the love of people, one cannot claim that kenosis, even as it appears in Philippians 2:5–8 and John 15:13, represents Jesus' teachings. It would be hard to demonstrate, I think, that Jesus saw his execution as an atoning sacrifice in the sense given to it by Paul. Jesus' attitude toward the Law reflects his expectation that the eschaton is about to arrive.

To this extent Jesus' teachings can be compared with those of the Qumran community. Like them, he preached a stricter, more meticulous level of observance. Like them, he suggested distinctive practices for his followers. Like them, he condemned his closest opponents as hypocrites and sinners. Unlike the people of Qumran, however, Jesus and his followers did not retire into the desert to wait for the end. Rather, they wandered through Israel preaching a distinctive approach to the Law. Unlike the Qumran community, Jesus' immediate opponents were not the priests and the Sadducean establishment, but the Pharisees, the teachers of the twofold law.

A Response to Lewis John Eron from Leonard Swidler

I would first like to reinforce your observation that at the time of Jesus the understanding of the Torah in Israel was vigorously debated; there was no consensus view. In fact, it seems to me that this description of yours is in reality even more accurate than your later remark that we are "not at all certain how the term Law, or Torah, was understood in the first centuries" before and after Jesus. I would suggest that we are much more certain now than ever before in that we now know that there was not one but several contending understandings. I would also want to stress your comment that Jesus' "condemnation of the hypocrisy of the Scribes and Pharisees is no more to be seen as a condemnation of the Law, itself, than the [Hebrew] prophetic critique of the sacrificial system is a condemnation of sacrificial worship per se." In brief, as you said, Jesus criticized the abuse, not the use, of the Torah.

On the other hand, you speak of Jesus' "power over the Law. ... how Jesus took control of the Law." You give two proof-texts in support, namely, "his gathering of grain in the field on the Sabbath" and his healings on the Sabbath. It is true that the synoptic gospels do have Jesus—in response to the complaint that his followers (*not* he himself) violated the Sabbath by rubbing the grain in their hands to eat—make the claim that he has control over the Sabbath. But this is clearly an addendum of the early Church, for at first Jesus rejects the complaint as invalid, and in good rabbinic, Pharisaic, fashion he gives a biblical argument to sustain his position that the Sabbath was indeed not violated by his followers.

Moreover, as has been carefully pointed out after a very detailed discussion and documentation by the Jewish scholar Pinchas Lapide:

> From our contemporary vantage point we are able to affirm that the exegesis of Jesus has won out in talmudic praxis, which at that time was still fluctuating in the process of developing into a written form. What during his lifetime still was disputed has long since become a rule of life—not least thanks to an understanding of the Torah that often is reminiscent of the exegetical manner of the Nazarene.[10]

In brief, the gospel-reported alleged violations of the Law by Jesus were only that—alleged by some Jews, but disputed by others—and the position taken by Jesus was subsequently largely sustained within the rabbinic tradition. Thus, as Jesus said, "The Sabbath is for human beings and not human beings for the Sabbath" (Mk. 2:27), so was it recorded in a later rabbinic writing that, "The Sabbath is committed to you; you are not committed to the Sabbath" (Mekilta 31.13,14). Hence, I would suggest that rather than say that Jesus was trying to "assert his power over the Law," it would perhaps be more accurate to say that he, like all other rabbis and Jewish groups, had his own principles of interpretation, which he exemplified here as well as elsewhere in his teaching.

As I indicated in my own statement, I am convinced that one of Jesus' key principles was that he sought to carry out what he perceived to be the purpose of the Torah, or as the Pharisee Paul put it, to interpret it *en pneumati* (Rom. 2:29), according to the spirit, in good Reform fashion — and it was in that fashion that each *iota* and *keraia* (Mt. 5:18) was to be carried out, or "fulfilled" (Mt. 5:17, *plērōsai*). Hence, I would again suggest that it is not the most accurate expression to speak of "Jesus' insistence on hyper-observance" or of "selective disobedience," but rather, the careful observance of the whole Torah in a way that would lead to the attaining of its goal, its "fulfillment," as he understood and taught it.

It is clear that Jesus did not follow the Torah to the complete satisfaction of at least some of the Pharisees as they are described in the gospels — quite possibly the stricter Bet Shammai, as discussed earlier. Nevertheless, it in a way is quite extraordinary how almost nothing that is attributed to Jesus in the gospels is really in contradiction to what later became fixed law in rabbinic Judaism; he probably has a better record in that regard than most, if not all, the pre-70 Bet Shammai rabbis. But then, given his closeness in attitude to Bet Hillel, this really is not so extraordinary.

It is true that the terms *en pneumati* and *kenōsis* are Paul's. However, my use of them to describe Jesus' attitude toward carrying out the Torah in the first instance, and Jesus' self-giving lifestyle in the second was simply a picking up of New Testament terms familiar to many Christians to describe what I believe are documented facts — not because Paul said so, but because they are documented in the gospels. I am, of course, in complete accord with you that Jesus did not see "his execution as an atoning sacrifice in the sense given to it by Paul," or the Letter to the Hebrews. These are later theological reflections on the part of some, though not all, early Christians.

As a final comment, I would like to focus on your calling attention to the Jewish "traditional but misleading distinction between *Midrash Aggadah* (homiletical and moral interpretation) and *Midrash Halakhah* (legal interpretation)." It seems to me that most Christians — not Jesus though, for he was not a Christian — also accepted this understanding of the rabbinic tradition.

As a consequence, most Jews and Christians came to think of the Jewish Law as solely *halakhah* in an exclusive, formal sense, shorn now of its aggadic, moral "soul," if you will, thus moving it substantially in the direction of the legalism that Rabbi Yeshua and many of the rabbis recorded in the rabbinic literature bitterly complained about. Your calling attention to this unwarranted and deleterious separation helps greatly in setting Jesus more solidly back within the Jewish fold, and in making the Jewish understanding of the Torah much more humane and holistic.

NOTES

1. Howard Clark Kee, *Jesus in History: An Approach to the Study of the Gospels*, 2nd ed. (New York: Harcourt Brace Jovanovich, 1977) discusses the image of Jesus

as it appears in the four gospels and other ancient sources.

2. For an extensive discussion of the definition of midrash, see Gary Porton, "Defining Midrash," *The Study of Judaism I: Mishnah, Midrash, Siddur* (New York: Ktav, 1981), pp. 62ff.

3. Pinchas Lapide and Hans Küng, "Is Jesus a Bond or Barrier? A Jewish-Christian Dialogue," *Journal of Ecumenical Studies*, 14 (1977), p. 473, a translation of Hans Küng and Pinchas Lapide, *Jesus im Widerstreit. Ein jüdisch-christlicher Dialog* (Stuttgart/Munich: Calwer-Kösel, 1976), p. 26.

4. In his discussion of Mk. 7:15, Gerard Sloyan notes that in regard to dietary laws, at least, Jesus generally appears to have followed such laws, although at times he was sharply critical of ritual observance if moral precepts were not observed. Jesus' approach to dietary laws seems to provide the background to the earliest Church's feeling that Jesus set it free from the Law. "Faith and Law: An Essay Toward Jewish-Christian Dialogue," *Journal of Ecumenical Studies*, 18 (1981), pp. 95–100.

5. Geza Vermes, *Jesus the Jew* (Philadelphia: Fortress Press, 1981), pp. 80–82.

6. Ibid.

7. Morton Smith, *Jesus the Magician* (New York: Harper & Row, 1978), p. 23.

8. Ibid.

9. Gerd Theissen, *Sociology of Early Palestinian Christianity* (Philadelphia: Fortress Press, 1977).

10. Pinchas Lapide, *Er predigte in ihren Synogogen* (Gütersloh: Gerd Mohn, 1980), p. 30.

7

Yeshua: Messiah? Christ? Human? Divine?

LEONARD SWIDLER

In my first three statements I argued that Yeshua can most appropriately be understood as a devout Galilean rabbi of the first century who had a profound impact on his Jewish followers—without falling outside the framework of the Judaism of his time. Clearly that impact did not stop there, but rather continued through space and time, not so much like expanding ripples but more like an expanding tidal wave in subsequent history. It seems clear that Yeshua did not understand himself religiously as anything other than a Jew; nor did his initial followers. That was an age of extraordinary tension, with a sense of the imminence of extraordinary events, of apocalypticism. The Jews seethed under Roman occupation and as a consequence there was in the air the expectation of a great liberator, of one "anointed" (*Meshiach*) by God, the Messiah (in Greek, *Christos*).

The term *Christ*, of course, is simply a Europeanized version of a Greek translation of a Hebrew title. It was applied to a number of Jews during that apocalyptic period shortly before, during, and after the lifetime of Yeshua, including to Yeshua of Nazareth. It was one of many titles that were given to Yeshua by his followers, one which he almost certainly never used of himself,[1] but rather one that was attributed to him, possibly during his lifetime, by some of his followers. There is, however, a special irony in this attribution's having received such prominence, for he was later clearly recognized by his disciples not to be the sort of Messiah that was expected by his enthusiastic Jewish partisans. The Messiah, the Christ, expected by Peter and the other disciples, was first thought to be a Jewish royal figure in David's mold who would eject the Roman occupiers of the land of Israel and re-establish kingship in Israel. Obviously, this did not happen, and hence most Jews had no grounds for assuming that Yeshua was the promised Messiah.

Most probably not all of his followers were set on seeing him as the promised Messiah, but viewed him in other ways, for example, as a prophet or teacher (rabbi). However, those who did think of him as the promised Messiah were ready to admit after his crucifixion that they were mistaken. This is clearly seen, for example, in Luke's Gospel where two of Yeshua's followers on the way to Emmaus spoke of him as "a prophet" and, after referring to his crucifixion, added in disappointment, "but our own hope had been that he would be the one to set Israel free" (Luke 24:21).

However, after the resurrection experience some of Yeshua's followers apparently slowly began to decide not to abandon the term *Messiah* but to transform it, to read it in a different sense. Gradually the term *Messiah* or *Christ* became the preferred title for him, often functioning as a kind of surname. This, however, took some time and it was not until later in the first century that the followers of Yeshua were referred to as "Christians." As the Acts of the Apostles reports, the term first used was followers of "the way" (*hodos*, in Greek)—that is, the way to lead a whole, holy life, a Jewish life, which had been taught and exemplified by Yeshua of Nazareth.

Clearly not all Jews of that time were persuaded to fall in with this line of thought, just as not all Jews of that time became Hillelites, Shammaites, Essenes, or followed any other authentically Jewish schools. Nevertheless, even though among the various claimant schools there was much contention about how to be authentically Jewish, all of these schools were considered to be Jewish—including that which followed the way of Yeshua and claimed he was the Messiah, the Christ, in a transformed, spiritualized sense. Naming Yeshua the *Christos* in this transformed sense would not have been an insurmountable problem for the majority of Jews of that time, even though they might not have been convinced of the validity of the claim. It was the claim of being a crucified Messiah that proved to be a barrier.

The ontological notion of Yeshua's divinity posed an insurmountable barrier for most Jews in later times, but as the notion was expressed in the New Testament it need not have been so, as a variety of high titles given to an "expected one" in post-biblical apocalyptic writing attests. The major division between "Christians" and "Jews" of the early period was due to the fact that the claim of Yeshua's messiahship was not accompanied by what most Jews thought would be the signs of "the days of the Messiah." The question of whether the splitting of Christianity off from Judaism occurred as a result of the development of the "high Christology" of the John community or whether Christology was enabled to go from there into high orbit only after the split that occurred for other reasons (i.e., because of the Jewish "nationalism" suggested earlier by Phillip Sigal) does not admit of a clear answer and may never, given the evidence available to us. However, the early development of Christology, namely, what the subsequent followers of Yeshua made of him, does merit serious attention for those who are trying to understand the roles he plays as a bond or barrier between present-day Judaism and Christianity.

THE YESHUA OF HISTORY

For Christians, there were two major ways that Yeshua was thought to be the way to "salvation," and "deliverance from the power of sin and death" to a whole, holy human life. One was to follow and imitate what Yeshua taught and lived, and the other was to "be saved" by what Yeshua the Christ did for those who believed in him as raised up from the dead. In shorthand, the former could be called the "teaching Yeshua" or the "Yeshua of history," and the latter the "taught Christ" or the "Christ of faith."

With the help particularly of the historical-critical method, but also of other critical scholarly methods, such as literary criticism, we are now able to perceive the major outlines of the actual teachings of Yeshua. Of course, this perception will continue to be refined, but the essential elements are reasonably certain. We must keep in mind that it was only in the beginning of the nineteenth century that a sense of history as we now understand it developed in any civilization. One result was that Christian thinkers and scholars began the search for the "historical Jesus," the Yeshua of Nazareth who lay behind the many conflicting things said about him over the past two thousand years. Until that time, his teachings, contained in the gospels, were known as those of all the figures of antiquity are known: as transmitted by his disciples.

In the early part of this century, with the development of certain critical tools, it was perceived that the sources of our image of the historical Yeshua—the gospels—were not primarily historical documents. Instead of being four different modern biographies, they are rather four separate faith statements based on historical reminiscences. The gospels communicated what different early followers of Yeshua understood and believed to be of the greatest importance about him—his teachings and actions, and his final "exaltation in glory." For a number of decades beginning about 1918— although the tendency went back to S. H. Reimarus (d. 1768)—there was great skepticism among New Testament scholars concerning the possibility of getting behind the "Christ of faith" to the "Jesus of history."

Fortunately that astringent phase is now largely over, and it is now possible to state with confidence: "It is today a broadly held consensus that, although because of the nature of the sources it is impossible to produce a biography of Jesus, the description of the irreplaceable fundamental characteristics of his proclamation, his action and his fate, on the other hand, is very much possible."[2] This statement of a Catholic systematic theologian, Hans Küng, quite accurately reflects the view and work of a growing number of New Testament exegetical scholars, Catholic, Protestant, and Jewish. One of them, a Protestant, E. P. Sanders, refers to the works of ten of his most prestigious colleagues, including Martin Hengel, Paul Winter, Joachim Jeremias, Eduard Schweizer, C. H. Dodd, and Geza Vermes. Sanders states that "the dominant view today seems to be that we can know pretty well what Jesus was out to accomplish, that we can know a lot about what he said, and that those two things make sense in the world of first-century Judaism."[3] The Jewish scholar Geza Vermes argues that "we can manage to perceive his ideas, the *ipsissimus sensus*, even without the actual words in which they were formulated."[4]

It is precisely that Yeshua of history, then—the one who lived in the land of Israel two thousand years ago—who can clarify for contemporary Christians what must be the touchstone for all "reactions to" (that is, all "doctrines" about) him, including the various ones found in the New Testament itself.[5] Moreover, it may be objected that the image of the historical Yeshua produced by the help of the historical method is simply a contemporary "image" and can have no more claim of allegiance by Christians than any other "image" of Yeshua, as, for example, that of Paul, who never knew Yeshua, or a Gnostic Christian, or the Council of Chalcedon (451 C.E.). But this is a mistaken objection. To be sure, there is nothing in any living person's mind that is not an "image." However, there is a critical—indeed, a fundamental—difference between the image formed of a person from the words and actions of the person himself or herself and the image formed from what *someone else thinks* of that person.

Of course, I am aware of the grave difficulties of arriving at an authoritative, clear image of the historical Yeshua. However, to the extent that we Christians can do so, we must. *That* image of Yeshua must be our standard. Certainly, no one can ever arrive at a completely "objective" image of Yeshua—or anyone or anything else. Every fact is relativized by the perceiver. It is likewise true that we can come to a fuller grasp of a fact if we have perceptions of it from several different standpoints. However, it is the original datum, the *Urtatsache*, that we are trying to grasp so that we can somehow relate it to ourselves. This latter element, of course, again relativizes the original fact (i.e., puts it in relation to us), but it is the *Urtatsache* that we are trying to grasp and relate to ourselves. Today we know that we can never fully grasp this original fact as it originally existed—just as in modern physics we now realize that to pass light or electrons or whatever it may be through an object so as to "observe" it already changes it. Yet, with the now chastened knowledge that we can never attain a completely "objective" image of anything, we can always strive to come closer, as with the Parmenidian continuum. It is precisely this that I and a growing number of Christian thinkers believe we should do in regard to the historical figure of Yeshua.

Then, it seems to me that, with due modesty and openness, the best image of the historical Yeshua we are able to attain at a given moment has priority over all explanations as to his meaning. Even though we learn it only through others, *what Yeshua thought, taught and wrought is the Yesh-*

uanic, *if not the "Christian," gospel.* Edward Schillebeeckx makes a similar claim: "The constant factor in Christianity is that Christians determine the final or ultimate meaning of their concrete history by reference to Jesus of Nazareth."[6] Things are said to be Christian "with the same proviso that they are judged to conform to the yardstick of this historical reality that is Jesus himself."[7]

Every person stands in a particular historical context and place in the world so that all perceptions are fundamentally influenced by that fact, including perceptions of historical-critical images. Awareness of this limitation will allow a person to avoid naive absolute certitude on the one hand and total skepticism on the other. Moreover, as we become aware that human language is both a liberating and a limiting instrument, we will be able to proceed with modesty as well as with security, always being open to new evidence, insights, perspectives, and, hence, change. However, all this proper modesty is appropriate not only for the image of the historical Yeshua that is derived from the "primary data," but also, and all the more so, for all images of the "reactions to," or doctrines about, him.

What, then, does a contemporary Christian do with the historical fact that in the development of Christianity the "teaching Yeshua" quickly became the "taught Christ," even within the time of the writing of the New Testament? Obviously the resurrection experience was a transforming one for the followers of Yeshua. Regardless of how one understands the New Testament reports of him as risen, it is clear that the resurrection experience had a profound impact on the followers of Yeshua: They began to perceive things about him that they had not been conscious of when they were with him. It was clear, however, that the Yeshua they knew was not transformed into some kind of magic figure or totem for them. Instead, in the resurrection experience the followers of Yeshua felt first of all inwardly confirmed in their pre-crucifixion experience of the encounter with what they perceived to be the divine through Yeshua, through what he thought, taught, and wrought.

THE TEACHING YESHUA, NOT THE TAUGHT CHRIST

The Christian New Testament scholar Thomas William Manson remarked as follows: "We are so accustomed, and rightly, to make Jesus the object of religion that we become apt to forget that in our earliest records he is portrayed not as the object of religion, but as a religious man."[8]

Thus, in teaching about Yeshua his followers attempted to teach what they had learned from him. What they learned from Yeshua, however, could not be limited to what he put into words (what Yeshua "taught"); they obviously were deeply struck by his inner self, which appeared to them to be so full of wisdom and effective love (what Yeshua "thought"), and how this seemed to them to exude into his every action (what Yeshua "wrought"). This is evident in the synoptic reporting. It was Yeshua's whole person that was the source of this utterly transforming "learning experience" for his followers. Moreover, this transformation was so profound and so pervasive that, rather than being shattered by the shattering of Yeshua on the cross (its agony proved to be the crucible in which their "enlightenment" and love were purified, strengthened, transformed), they were enabled, as it were, in Pauline symbolic language, to go down into the tomb with him and rise with the reconfirmation of their pre-crucifixion experience of him. Put in other words, their experience of him was true and authentic; after all, he really was—is!—the source of true life; he lives on! Hence, the "taught Yeshua" (i.e., the taught or proclaimed Christ) was first of all the fullest way to hand on the "teaching Yeshua" (that is, what he thought, taught and wrought in his whole person). Thus, it appears to many Christian thinkers that any move to understand the proclaimed Christ as someone, something, other than the "teaching Yeshua" can easily become problematic. Any attempt to understand the "proclaimed Christ" in contrast to the "teaching Yeshua," to what he "thought, taught, and wrought" in his whole person, would be to play false not only with Yeshua but also his first disciples.

The Gospel of Luke's theology is even clearer in its insistence that it is primarily what Yeshua *preached*, rather than Yeshua himself, that should be preached by Christians. Joseph G. Kelly, a Catholic Scripture scholar, notes that according to Luke,

> Jesus always points not to himself but to God. As a result, the preacher cannot become the preached. . . . The disciples are not called upon to preach the person of Jesus. What they must do is preach the message of Jesus. . . . Jesus shows Christians the Way and Christians see themselves on the Way.

Hence, Kelly says, what Christians must now preach is the Way that Yeshua preached; that is, repentance and the forgiveness of sins—or release (*aphesis*, liberation, Lk. 4:18). For Luke, however, Kelly maintains that

> Jesus is not the Way. The Way is what Jesus taught must be done. The message is not Jesus, but release [liberation]. Jesus did not glorify himself, but lived in such a way as to give glory to God. This resulted in God's glorifying Jesus. Jesus did not proclaim himself but said that his person and life made God known.

Kelly adds that

> Every time that the reign breaks in at a moment of release, one can glimpse God. God is the end and the goal. One of the ways to

find God is to follow the Way of Jesus, but Jesus' Way is not the only way."[9]

From the beginning, most Christians have understood the historical Yeshua—what he thought, taught, and wrought—to be centrally important. For the most part it has been argued that a particular teaching about Yeshua was right, or orthodox, because it ultimately fit with the historical Yeshua who lived two thousand years ago. It is true that some teachings were directly based only on some later *traditio*, but then the claim was at least implicit that such a procedure was a sure way to link up with the real, historical Yeshua. Few Christians would be willing to affirm the statements about Jesus Christ in the Council of Nicaea (325 C.E.) or Constantinople (381 C.E.) if they did not think that these statements could be predicated of the historical Yeshua of Nazareth. The problem that historically conscious scholars point to in this situation is that the "reactions to" the statements about Yeshua, whether past (*traditio*) or present (*magisterium*), tend too often to be the yardstick for understanding the historical Yeshua, when it should be the other way around.

A recent book that has a great deal to recommend it in its expansive and balanced view, written by the Catholic theologian William M. Thompson, alludes to the "historical Jesus" and rejects him as "a final norm of Christian revelation and theology." One reason presented for this rejection is that our knowledge of the Jesus of history "must ultimately rely upon the kerygma."[10] Of course the assertion is true, but that fact does not invalidate the claim that the historical Yeshua is the ultimate standard. Naturally, for us it is our apprehension of the historical Yeshua, derived from a critical analysis of the kerygmatic text, that *de facto* is our final norm. However, that is also true of the kerygmatic Yeshua, the "previously 'reacted to'" Yeshua—only one step still further removed from the historical Yeshua. Mark, Matthew, Paul, Chalcedon, and other sources all believed and averred that they were communicating something very important about the historical Yeshua. None of them wanted readers to accept what they wrote simply because they wrote it but because it told them something important about the real, historical Yeshua, that would lead them to live a full human, "saved" life.

For a later Christian to claim that those earlier statements and those *kērygmata* (preaching about, reactions to) of the historical Yeshua are the ultimate norms of what is authentically Christian is either to miss or to reject the very essence of what they were saying. Certainly, the gospels are the final documentary sources we have for our knowledge of Yeshua. However, the point to be noticed here is that they are "*docu*ments," i.e., "teachings," and teachings are of or about something and/or someone—in this case, Yeshua. "Documents" are merely the pointers to, images (*eidōla*) of, the historical reality referred to. To stop finally at the *eidōla* rather than move on toward that which *eidōla* point to is *(e)idō-latria*.

YESHUA, HUMAN AND DIVINE

What, then, of the Christological dogmatic formulas hammered out in the ancient ecumenical councils to which assent was demanded under pain of excommunication? If they are accepted, do they not wipe out any "low Christology" and require a specific "high Christology," namely, according to Chalcedon (451 C.E.), that Yeshua is "truly God and truly a human being" (*theon alethōs kai anthropon alethōs* in Greek and *Deum verum et hominem verum* in Latin)? Clearly an old style catechism-like "yes" or "no" answer is not appropriate. First, one must be clear about precisely what the Chalcedonian formula meant.

To do that, however, it is not sufficient to come to understand the meanings of the various terms and images used in that intellectual milieu, especially in this instance. This is because the authors were dealing in part with that which "goes beyond" our experience, the "trans-scendent." If understood literally, their language was non-sense; it spoke of a non-thing, or no-thing, for it spoke of Yeshua being a "limited unlimited," a "finite infinite." Obviously, however, the Council Fathers did not mean to say nothing—even deliberately paradoxical language does not intend to communicate literal non-sense, but attempts to point to some reality beyond the apparent non-sense of the contradictory terms juxtaposed. Here, then, the reader has the first task of discerning what meaning the authors were pointing to beyond and by way of the seeming non-sense of the juxtaposed mutually exclusive terms *homo* and *Deus*.[11]

To begin, there is no reason to assume that the way in which the ancient Christian authors expressed the meaning they were attempting to communicate was necessarily the best possible or the clearest. The fact that the ancient Christians had to go back into council time and again over the same basic question (Nicaea, 325; I Constantinople, 381; Ephesus, 431; Chalcedon, 451) amply demonstrates this point. It seems to me that these ancient Christians were trying to express in Greek philosophical, ontological terms the Christian experience of the overwhelming confluence of the human and divine in *Yeshua ha Notzri*.

Parenthetically, it should be remembered that the whole detailed creedal enterprise was something specifically Hellenistic. The ontological question was not one that excited the Semitic world. Jews tended to ask axiological rather than ontological questions: not questions of theory, but of doing ("What must I *do* to gain eternal life?" not "What must I *think* to gain eternal life?" was asked of Yeshua the Jew). This is reflected in the entire history and structure of Judaism; it is rather the *halakhah*, the rules of ethics, of just action,[12] and not the creed or doctrine that holds pride of place in Judaism. It was the Greek-thinking world (which had invented the discipline of philosophy and ontology, as the very words tell us) that placed highest priority on the ontological question, on, What must I *think*? And of course their answers were expressed in the largely "substantialist" Greek philosophical categories in which their questions were phrased.

If it can be granted that the Christians meeting at Chalcedon might not have communicated their meaning in the most helpful, clearest possible language, I would then want to move from that subjunctive to the indicative mood. I am convinced that they did not express themselves as clearly or as helpfully as possible for all ages to come. (Again, the very existence of several traditional, serially known and accepted creeds—e.g., "Apostles," Nicene, Athanasian, Chalcedonian—demonstrates the judged inadequacy at least in some regards of the previous creeds.)

It is within this context that I want to offer a suggestion that is intended not to reject the teaching of the Christian tradition as found in the Council of Chalcedon, and elsewhere, but in fact to discern more precisely and meaningfully to Christians today what it in fact was trying to express. In the late twentieth century most critically thinking Christians do not live in a world that perceives reality in the "substantialist" categories of the largely Platonist world of the Chalcedonian Fathers. Most Christians live in a post-Kant, post-Wittgenstein, post-Gadamer, etc. philosophical world that requires a probing of the *intentio* of the Council Fathers and a translation of it in contemporary thought categories. It is toward that end that the following endeavor is made. Its success will of course be variously judged, but the attempt cannot be responsibly avoided.

I would suggest that the meaning of the Council of Chalcedon would be better expressed by using adjectival rather than nominative forms. That is, instead of saying Yeshua is "truly God and truly a human being" (*Deum verum et hominem verum*), it would be clearer to say that Yeshua is "truly divine and truly human," *vere divinus et vere humanus*. Here the paradoxical quality of the first statement is retained in the second in that the two terms, divine and human, appear to go in opposite directions, but the juxtaposition of the two does not result in non-sense: it is *conceivable* that someone could in some way be truly divine and truly human. The question then is, In what way not only *might* this be, but in what way *was* this affirmed to be true of Yeshua?

There is no doubt but that not only in the earliest layers of the Christian "good news" Yeshua is portrayed as and understood to be truly human, but also that even the "highest" orthodox Christian Christological formulas (like that of Chalcedon) insisted on this portrayal. However, the followers of Yeshua, especially upon post-resurrection-event reflection, perceived God working in and through him in an extraordinary manner.[13] For them, God's self appeared to be manifested through Yeshua. It seemed to them that Yeshua was so completely open to all dimensions of reality, of being (as all human beings, as intellectual cognitive beings, also are *in principle*), that he was totally suffused with an inpouring of being in a "radical," that is, in a "to-the-roots," way. This "being" included the "Root," the *Source* of all being—in theistic language, God. Hence, one could meaningfully say that Yeshua was fully, truly divine. Because he was fully open to all being and the Source of being, there was no part of him that was not permeated with the Source of being.

At this point it would seem that many Hellenistic Christians made the linguistic move of saying that because Yeshua was permeated with the Source of being, with God, he therefore could also meaningfully be said to *be* truly God. I suggest, however, that linguistically that was a confusing rather than a clarifying move because such language inadvertently also indicates that God is coterminous with Yeshua.

That is: God is infinite and unlimited, whereas human beings, as well as all other beings, are finite and limited. However, to say that Yeshua *is* God is to say that Yeshua — a human being and therefore finite — *is* not-finite, infinite. Or, in other words: to form a sentence linking together with the nexus *is* the subject and predicate when both are nouns and both are exhaustive of their categories can only mean that the subject and predicate are coterminous. For example, if there is only one President of the United States, the statement that "George Bush (one and only one specific human being) is President" means that there is no George Bush that is not President and no President that is not George Bush; George Bush and President are limited to each other. Or: "Yeshua is God" means that there is no Yeshua that is not God and no God that is not Yeshua; Yeshua and God are limited to each other.

That, of course, was not what was intended, for Christians did not wish to imply that the unlimited God was limited to Yeshua. Therefore, to avoid this unintended non-sense, it would be clearer to use the adjective form *divine* rather than the noun form *God,* since the former term does not limit the Unlimited to the limited, which the latter term does.

Edward Schillebeeckx makes a like point when he writes that

> Since 1953 I have firmly opposed the formulation "Christ is God and man" and also the confusing expression "the man Jesus is God." The proper formula would be: "Jesus Christ is the Son of God *in humanity*." The deepest sense of revelation is that God reveals himself in humanity. We cannot seek farther, above or beneath the man Jesus his being-God. The divinity must be perceptible *in* his humanity itself.[14]

To repeat: To say that "Yeshua is God," if both the subject and the predicate, Yeshua and God, are understood as nouns, clearly means that Yeshua and God are coextensive, that there is no Yeshua that is not God and there is no God that is not Yeshua. Obviously that is *not* what Christians, whether early or current, mean to claim. Therefore, it would appear unavoidable to conclude that in this sentence although Yeshua is meant as a noun, *God is not meant as a noun* (for that would make God coterminous with Yeshua) but as an adjective. To make that clearly implied but confusedly disguised adjectival meaning explicitly clear, it would therefore be helpful to make the predicate specifically adjectival in form: "Yeshua is divine." Such a sentence is not non-sense and appears to capture precisely what Christians mean to say with the confusing sentence, "Yeshua is God."

What, however, of those passages in the New Testament itself that seem to state clearly that Yeshua is God and have been traditionally so understood? Such passages include Paul's Epistle to the Philippians 2:5–11, and the prologue to John's Gospel. Can they just be waived as the Hellenizing of the original Jewish understanding of Yeshua?

If it is *assumed* ahead of time that the concept of Yeshua as the incarnation of the second person of the Blessed Trinity existing from all eternity could have been in the mind of the Pharisaic Jew Paul in the middle of the first century, then certainly the words of the hymn that Paul recites in his letter to the followers of Yeshua at Philippi can be so understood.[15] However, Paul wrote three hundred years before the Council at Nicaea and four hundred years before the one at Chalcedon when this concept was hammered out—not by Jews, but by Hellenistic Christians who were triumphant over Jews and everyone else in the Roman empire. As E. P. Sanders has noted, "It is true that the early Church came to believe that Jesus was a transcendent being. . . . But it would be foolhardy—or worse—to rush to the conclusion that the historical Jesus must have corresponded to such beliefs."[16]

PRE-EXISTENT CHRIST?

Reasonable principles of interpretation would in fact indicate that the words of Paul should be understood in the way he and his readers would have understood them—and Paul was a Jew, indeed, "a Hebrew of the Hebrews, according to the Law a Pharisee" (Phil. 3:5).

Geza Vermes remarks that

To a Greek speaker in Alexandria, Antioch or Athens at the turn of the eras, the concept *huios theou*, son of God, would have brought to mind either one of the many offspring of the Olympian deities. . . . But to a Jew, the corresponding Hebrew or Aramaic phrase would have applied to none of these. For him, son of God could refer . . . to a good Jew; or to a charismatic holy Jew; or to the king of Israel. . . . In other words *"son of God" was always understood metaphorically in Jewish circles*.

He continues and makes the very interesting observation that, "If the medium in which Christian theology developed had been Hebrew and not Greek, it would not have produced an incarnation doctrine as this is traditionally understood."[17]

The Christian exegete James Barr supports this position when he argues that Paul and other Jews probably understood Paul's hyperbolic references to Yeshua in typically Jewish metaphorical fashion, but that as heard by Hellenistic ears these references probably were misconstrued in a non-metaphorical sense:

> It could be argued that this emphasis upon the Hebraic background of ideas may indeed have been present in the minds of instructed Jews like St Paul, but that the words which had this series of associations for him could for the most part be *understood* by Gentile Christian hearers, especially by the less instructed among them, in the normal Hellenistic sense of the words.[18]

In fact, the Jewish-Christians, the so-called Ebionites, "became convinced that they were witnessing in the Hellenistic communities a fatal misrepresentation of Jesus, a betrayal of his ideals, and their replacement by alien concepts and aspirations."[19]

Moreover, according to the Acts of the Apostles, Paul founded the Christian church at Philippi, having first gone on the Sabbath eve to the Jewish "place of prayer" (Acts 16:13), where those who first came to believe in Yeshua were assembled. Quite naturally the persons he met there were either Jews or Gentile "fellow-travelers," that is, Gentiles who were attracted to the Jewish tradition and way of life (known in the Acts as "God-fearers," *phoboumenoi,* or "God-worshipers," *sebomenoi,* or simply "Greeks," *hellēnai*). Hence, it was these two groups that comprised the great bulk of the first Christian churches outside Palestine, including the one that Paul founded and wrote to at Philippi and that met at the house of the *sebomenē* Lydia. Thus, Paul's words must be understood as coming from a strict Jew to prayerful Jews or pious Gentiles who were knowledgeable in and committed to the Bible and Judaism. Bearing that in mind, let us look again at the pertinent part of the hymn:

> Your attitude must be that of Christ Jesus.
> Though he was in the form of God, he did not deem
>   equality with God something to be grasped at.
> Rather, he emptied himself and took the form of a slave,
>   being born in the likeness of human beings. . . .
> Because of this,
> God exalted him . . . (Phil. 2:5–9).

Today many careful exegetes see an "Adam Christology," which was so prevalent at the time Paul wrote, operating here. Being "in the form of God" simply meant the same thing as Adam being "in the image of God," (Gen. 1:26). Rather than "grasp at" that level of being, that is, at "equality with God," before the Fall (which came about because Adam wanted to "grasp at" being "as God" Genesis 3:5), Yeshua chose to follow completely the path of Adam so as to redeem him, humbling himself and taking the "form of a slave" (Adam after the Fall). The poem reflects the symmetry that is always present in Hebrew poetry. Near the end of the poem God (not a person of the Trinity, but simply, "God," *ho theos*) "exalted," not "re-stored," him; Christ did not "re-take" his allegedly former divine place. Clearly here Jesus Christ is for the Jew Paul and his Jewish and semi-Jewish readers the "second Adam," not the pre-existent "second person" of the Trinity.[20]

LOGOS THEOLOGY

What, however, of the prologue to John's Gospel where it says, "In the beginning was the Word, and the Word was with God, and the Word was God. . . . and the Word became flesh" (Jn. 1:1,14)? Again, bearing in mind that this is a Jew writing largely for fellow Jews, it must be recalled that there were several figures and images used in biblical and early Jewish writings as *literary images* of the invisible God as made perceivable to humans. There is the Spirit (*ruach*) of God who already in Genesis 1:1 moves over the darkness in creation; and Wisdom (*hokmah*) who is present at creation (Prov. 8:22f.; Sirach 24:9); and God's Word who in numerous biblical (*dabar*, Hebrew) and post-biblical (*memra*, Aramaic) texts expresses God to humanity; as does God's *Torah* (teaching) in both biblical and post-biblical texts; and there is as well God's Presence (*shekhinah*) in post-biblical Jewish materials. It is within the context of this abundance of Jewish imagery of God's visible side turned toward humanity that John wrote and his Jewish readers understood him. However, these were all metaphors, not ontological substances, and that was likewise true of John's *logos*, the Word (*dabar*, *memra*).

To the Jews, the word of God was God speaking: God spoke and the world was created. Torah was God's word—indeed the ten commandments, the decalogue, means God's "ten words." For hundreds of years God spoke to Israel through the prophets. In brief, the whole Jewish experience of God was God speaking, expressing self, offering self for a relationship with human beings. "This self-expression of God had been going on for a long time before Jesus. It went back as far as humankind could remember. It seemed that God had always been speaking, from the beginning of the world."[21] Hence, as with Wisdom and the Spirit, it seemed to the Jews that the Word had been with God from the beginning. Indeed, again like Wisdom and Spirit, the Word was God as perceived by humanity; it "expressed God's own selfhood, and the one who encountered the word encountered God."[22]

Why, then, did those ancient Jews see Yeshua as God's Word become flesh? The answer is because their experience of Yeshua was that he was a diaphany of God:

Everything God has ever said is summed up in Jesus. It is all said there, every word. Not only are the teachings of Moses and the prophets summarized in the teaching of Jesus, everything God wants to reveal about who God is is shown in who Jesus is for us. Jesus is not just someone who has occasional words to say to us on God's behalf. He is in all the dimensions of his life God's self-revelation. Thus the word of God was enfleshed in a human life. . . . This is the Johannine vision as scholars reconstruct it today.[23]

DIALOGUE SUGGESTS A RESOLUTION

Here I would like to offer a possible resolution to the seemingly intractable problem between Christians and Jews over the Christian claim of the confluence of the human and the divine in *Yeshua ha Notzri*. My resolution of this problem has come out of interreligious dialogue; however, this dialogue was not between Christianity and Judaism, but between Christianity and Buddhism.

As a result of his long dialogue with Buddhism, the Japanese Protestant Christian Katsumi Takizawa (1909–1984) distinguished between what he termed the primary and the secondary contacts of God with the human self. The primary contact is the unconditional fact that God is with each one of us, is the very ground of our selves. Even though we may be unaware of it, this "contact" is real. The secondary contact occurs when we are awakened to that primary fact. At this stage we allow "the self to live in conscious accord with the will of God."[24]

According to Takizawa, Jesus was a man who was awakened to the primary fact—that is, he attained the secondary contact, and he did this so thoroughly and completely that he became a model for other selves. . . . Jesus was the person who in the Hebrew tradition played the same role as did Gautama Buddha in the Indian tradition. The ground of salvation is the primary contact of God with the self, and this is the common ground of both Buddhism and Christianity [and one might also add Judaism].[25]

By utilizing this distinction, another Japanese Christian, Seiichi Yagi, analyzes the "I" in the words of Yeshua, arguing as follows: Yeshua at times speaks in a way that clearly indicates the distinction between himself and God and at other times in a way that indicates a unity between him and God. This variance in language occurs in several places in the gospels, perhaps most clearly in John's Gospel. There Yeshua speaks of the unity between him and God, whom he calls the Father: "That all may be one as you Father in me and I in you . . . that they may be one as we are one, I in them and you in me" (Jn. 17:21, 23); "Anyone who has seen me has seen the Father" (Jn. 14:9); "Do you not believe that I am in the Father and the Father in me? The words I speak to you I do not speak of myself; but the Father who dwells in me does his works" (Jn. 14:10). Here, it is clear, when Yeshua speaks it is fundamentally the Father speaking through him. So complete has been the secondary contact that it is the language of the unity between God the Father and Yeshua that comes forth. Yet there is a distinction between them, for Yeshua obeys the Father when he says, "For I have not spoken of myself; but the Father who sent me gave me a commandment, what I should say, and what I should speak" (Jn. 12:49).

> In John 14: 10, Father and Son can be seen as two concentric circles in which the two centers coincide, whereas in John 12: 49, Father and Son appear as two centers in an ellipse, the latter obeying the former. . . . Christ is the Son of God insofar as the ultimate subject of the Son is the Father, but also insofar as the Father and the Son are distinguished from each other. They are paradoxically one.[26]

Yagi proceeds to note that these two types of relationship between Yeshua and God, the elliptic and the concentric, remind him of the two major kinds of Christologies in the ancient Church, the Antiochean and the Alexandrian. The Antiocheans (elliptic), he recalls, maintained that there were two centers in the person of Yeshua, the divine and the human; the latter obeyed the former, whereas the Alexandrians (concentric) insisted that both centers coincided. "The ancient church, therefore, maintained that both Christologies were true when, in the Council of Chalcedon, it declared that the divinity and the humanity of Christ were distinguishable but not separable."[27]

This kind of explanation, I believe, makes sense out of the apparently conflicting language of the gospels and helps to make that paradoxical language available to a contemporary person. If the Council of Chalcedon can be understood to be saying something of the same, it also helps to translate that Hellenistic ontological language into terms that likewise find resonance in a contemporary person's experience and thought patterns. However, it should be noticed that Yagi's explanation is largely in psychological rather than abstract metaphysical terms. Furthermore, what is said to be true in Yeshua's case, that the secondary contact with God was total (enlightment, *satori*), in principle can happen to every human being. In fact, Yeshua's language is full of exhortations to follow him, imitate him, be one with him and the Father.

In the final analysis, of course, this explanation is not entirely different from the one I offered above when I wrote: Yeshua was so completely open to all dimensions of reality — as all human beings are in principle — that he was totally suffused with an inpouring of being in a "radical" way that included the "Root" of all being, God. Thus he was thoroughly human because he was through and through divine — which is evidenced in what he thought, taught, and wrought.

"ONTOLOGIZATION" IN RELIGIONS

There is still something further that the dialogue between Christianity and Buddhism can teach us Christians in the understanding of our Christologies, and hence also about our relationship to Judaism.

The "ontologization" of Yeshua into the "divine" Christ, which occurred in Christianity as it moved from the Semitic cultural world into the Hellenistic, was matched by a similar development with the "ontologization" of Siddharta Gautama into the "divine" Buddha (*Buddha,* like *Christ,* is not a proper name but a title; it means "the enlightened one") as it moved from the Indian cultural world into the Chinese and Far Eastern. Connected with this was the development from the "internal" understanding of "salvation" to the "external," as discussed earlier. This in turn was like the movement from the "teaching Yeshua" to the "proclaimed Christ," from the religion *of* Yeshua to the religion *about* Yeshua the Christ, from the "Yeshua of history" to the "Christ of faith."

In many ways these shifts were also paralleled in Buddhism with the movement from the "internal" understanding of "salvation" (termed *jiriki,* "self-power," in Japanese) to the "external" understanding (termed *tariki,* "other power"); from the "teaching Gautama" to the "proclaimed Buddha;" from the religion *of* Gautama to the religion *about* Gautama the Buddha; from "the Gautama of history" (*Shakyamuni*) to the "Buddha of belief" (*Maitreya Buddha* and *Amida Buddha*).

Observing the same kind of developments occurring in such disparate religious cultures (one even being theistic and the other originally nontheistic) should make us Christians ask ourselves what deeper grasping toward an underlying insight is represented by these "ontologizing" movements. One way perhaps to express this deeper insight is as follows.

Yeshua is the key figure through whom Christians get in touch with those dimensions of reality that go beyond, that transcend the empirical, the everyday. Fundamentally, this is what Christologies are all about. They are all attempts through the figure Yeshua to come into contact with the transcendent, the "divine," each Christology being perceived, conceived and expressed in its own cultural categories and images. Some do it better, even much better, than others; some do it badly. Of course, all are culture-bound; otherwise, they would not reflect and speak effectively to the people in that culture. However, concomitantly each Christology is proportionately limited in effectiveness in regard to other cultures, whether the cultural differences result from variations in geography, time, class, or other factors.

All Christians, of course, can and should learn from the insights, and failures, of all other Christians' reaching out for the transcendent in their Christologies and other theological reflections. But what is "religiously specific" about Christians is that these Christologies, these theological reflections, are, or at least should be, intimately connected and compatible with the person Yeshua of Nazareth — though of course (!) they are not limited to imitating him in cultural detail.

Hence, it should become clear to us Christians, and others, that in moving from talk about the "internal" to the "external," from the human to the divine, from Yeshua to Christ, we, like the Buddhists and others, are attempting to express an experienced reality that transcends our everyday human experience, and hence also our everyday human language. We claim that there is a deeper reality that goes beyond the empirical surface experiences of our lives, and for us Yeshua is the bond-bursting means — the "way to the truth and life," to paraphrase John's Gospel slightly — to become aware of that deeper reality (as for Buddhists it is Gautama). It is preeminently in Yeshua for us Christians that we encounter the divine, and therefore our move to talk about the divine in Yeshua. Hence, our attempt to speak of the divine in Yeshua, of Christ, is not a mistake, but rather the result of the need to try to give expression to transempirical reality.

However, at the same time, we must be aware that when we attempt to speak of the transcendent we naturally will have to use transempirical language — that is, metaphor, symbol and the like. The error we must be cautious to avoid in this situation is erroneously to think that when we speak about the transcendent we are using empirical language. We are not. We cannot. We must at the same time also be cautious to avoid being reductionist and erroneously think all talk about the transcendent is merely fantasizing, that since Yeshua was merely a human being then all later talk about the divine in him is simply romantic emoting with no referent in reality. As I have argued, the "ontologization" shift in fact is a response to an experienced profound reality. Rather than be dismissed, it should be held onto for the vital insight into the meaning of human life and all reality it strives for. However, it must be correctly understood for what it is lest it become an idol, an image falsely adored, rather than the Reality toward which it points. When it is correctly understood and affirmed, we will then have reached what Paul Ricoeur calls the "second naïveté," that is, the state of awareness in which the affirmation of the symbol, understood correctly for what it is, further unlocks for us the deeper, transempirical reality.

CONCLUSIONS

Thus, in summary it must be asked, What does the Christian do about all the traditions and doctrines that speak of Jesus Christ as God, the second person of the Blessed Trinity? As I have argued, they are not to be dismissed, but they are also not to be merely repeated with no further reflection. Merely to parrot the past is to pervert it. These doctrines must be taken with utmost seriousness, analyzed for the kind of language they contain, and for what reality they seek to express; they must be wrestled with and translated into our own contemporary thought categories. This is a large task that has only been begun.

In working out this task, it should be remembered that if it has been held appropriate by the great bulk of Christian scholars and Church authorities to apply the historical-critical and other contemporary critical methods to the Scriptures, said to be the word of God—and it has—*a fortiori* it is appropriate to apply the same methods to authoritative Church statements and doctrines, that are *not* held to be the word of God. That same exegetical process must be engaged in to learn the "good news" handed on through the medium of the thought categories of an earlier age.

As such a reconceptualization of Christian doctrines, especially Christology, into contemporary thought categories occurs—and it is occurring, though of course often with great resistance, as always happens with any major thought-paradigm shift—the relationship between Judaism and Christianity will also be profoundly affected, and I believe very much for the better.

If the above suggestions and line of thought have any validity in explaining how at least some Christians are coming to understand their Christologies, then many of the disagreements between Christians and Jews in this area will begin to disappear. Jews will not thereby become Christians, of course, for Yeshua for them is not the door to the divine that he is for Christians, but perhaps their charges of blasphemy and idolatry against Christians will thereby be dissipated. No small gain.

A Response to Leonard Swidler from Lewis John Eron

I am in full agreement with you that it would be "no small gain" for Jewish-Christian relations if Jewish charges of blasphemy and idolatry against Christians were dissipated. I think that your understanding of theological language as metaphorical language is correct and I approach the Jewish tradition in much the same light. I also appreciate your statement that as a result of this new approach to Christology "Jews will not thereby become Christians, of course, for Yeshua for them is not the door to the divine that he is for Christians."

Despite my general sympathy toward your theological assumptions and aspirations, I have a number of questions and observations:

(1) Of all the titles given to Jesus, it is not at all surprising that the title "messiah" achieved prominence. "Messiah" was the most potent title available in Jewish circles.

"Prophet," although an ancient and respected title, does not involve the active involvement in the world in the way the title "messiah" does. This is not to say that the biblical prophets were passive, they were not. In the post-exilic period, however, the image of the prophet as a social critic gave way to the image of the prophet as a bearer of Divine Wisdom and as an apocalyptic seer.

The prophet, particularly the prophet in Jesus' time, was one who foretold and described the eschatological time. Such insights naturally had behavioral implications, but the eschatological prophet was a reporter and a commentator and not necessarily an active figure. Moreover, although the gospels identify Jesus as a prophet, the title and function were not restricted to him. The New Testament and the early Church recognized other people as prophets as well.

In the time of Jesus of Nazareth, the role and function of the rabbi was still in its infancy. The rabbi, as the role developed, became the leading figure in Judaism. As mediator of God's Law, the rabbi merged in his role the function of priest, prophet, wonder-worker and sage. Yet this role, even in its later fully developed form, does not carry the full spiritual power as does the term "messiah." Ultimately, there are *many* rabbis who stand in the tradition. But the messianic figure or the few messianic figures, as testified in certain early Jewish writings, are unique.

Is Jesus the Christ? I would have to answer that he is because that is the terminology that Christians use to describe his role. However, I would also insist that the use and meaning of the term *ho Christos*, "the Christ," for Christians was not and is not the same as the term *hameshiach*, "the messiah," is for Jews.

Although the word *Christos* is the Greek translation of the Hebrew word *meshiach*, "messiah," which has the literal meaning of "one anointed [with oil]," these terms are not used in the Hebrew Bible or in the Jewish and Christian tradition to refer to someone who has oil on his head and face. Anointing someone with oil was in ancient Israel part of the formal appointment and investiture ceremony to high office, for kings or high priests. The use and meaning of the concept expanded to refer to someone appointed to the sacred task of the redemption of Israel. In this light, Isaiah of the Exile described the Persian monarch, Cyrus, as messiah. At the end of the biblical period, the term was employed to refer to those persons central to the redemption of Israel and the world at the end of time.

The Christian use of the word *ho Christos* (the Greek equivalent of the Hebrew term *hameshiach*) for Jesus is a particular Christian midrash on the biblical tradition. As midrash, it is tied to, although not part of, the use of the term *hameshiach* in the biblical tradition. As true as this midrashic interpretation may have sounded to the followers of Jesus, it did not appear accurate or convincing to the vast majority of Jews over the centuries. The Jews developed their own concepts of *meshiach*/messiah.

To be honest to the midrashic process and to honor our predecessors' attempts to find God through the tradition they bequeathed to us, we cannot use biblical or first-century understandings of the term *meshiach* to give meaning to the terms *messiah* or *Christ* today. We stand in dramatic tension to all our past and not to any specific moment.

This, I think, is what the rabbinic legend means when it states that all Israel stood at Sinai. The revelation at Sinai is the crucial event in the history of the people Israel, for it is that moment that gives religious and spiritual importance to the experience of the Jewish people and individual Jews. The history of the people Israel through the present draws on and feeds the founding experience of the people.

That the term *Christos* developed its own Christian resonances is more important than is the phenomenon that the earliest Christian use of the term *meshiach/christos*/messiah to describe Jesus may have been conceivable in the Jewish world of the first century. The task of the Christian theologian today is not to return to the first century. It is, however, to mold a contemporary meaning of the term *Christ* that uses the first-century understanding of the term in conjunction with the midrashic unfolding of the concept through Christian history and in light of present-day realities. I hope that this new Christology will be distinctively Christian. As a Jew, I do not want to see a Jewish Christology, but rather, a Christian Christology that is good for the Jews.

(2) The Jesus of History. Although I am neither a Christian nor a theologian, I have a number of problems with your focus on the historical Jesus as the center of Christian faith. The relationship between historical research and tradition and faith is of great importance to modern Jews as we develop a Judaism for our time. My comments on your interest in the historical Jesus come from a particular Jewish perspective. The issues I raise with respect to your statement are similar to the issues I deal with in my attempt to apply the results of historical research to my own tradition.

Were I a Christian, I would argue that the historical Jesus is important as a limit and a corrective to Christian theology. The center of the Church, however, is its experience of Jesus and not Jesus himself.

Not everything Jesus taught, thought and wrought is of equal importance. A great deal of Jesus' life experiences have not been preserved. Not all that is missing is trivial and coincidental. On the one hand, we do not have the menu of the Last Supper. It would have been an interesting social-historical datum but its loss is of no great spiritual impact. On the other hand, other life experiences that would have surely given us great insights into the man Jesus are not reported. The gospels tell us nothing, for example, of Jesus' relationship with Joseph as youth and adult.

Many apparently good, pious, righteous people were not impressed by Jesus. The information we have concerning Jesus has been preserved for us by people who found in Jesus a special connection to the divine. Our information is edited information. Our only source is the *kērygma*, the teaching and preaching about Jesus by people who found a connection to the divine in and through Jesus.

It is the *kērygma*, I feel, that keeps Christians from idolatry because it focuses on the experience of revelation that comes from contact with Jesus and not on Jesus himself. Our historical knowledge of Jesus can shape the Church's proclamation of Jesus but it cannot produce the Jesus who is the fountain of Christian faith. As historians, we both share similar reconstructions of Jesus in history. Yet, we react to these reconstructions differently. I come in contact with an interesting but marginal Jewish teacher of the first century C.E., and you experience a reality that "transcends our everyday human experience."

It is the *kērygma* that prevents Christians from losing their roots. The *kērygma* transmits the experience of the divine in and through Jesus from one generation of believers to another. The *kērygma* ties the individual Christian's experience of Jesus to that of the Church over time. It is his or her contact with the kerygmatic tradition that enables the individual believer to encounter the depth of experience his and her fellow believers have found in Jesus. The *kērygma* connects the individual Christians into the Christian fellowship of faith that is the Church, the body of Christ.

Our historical study does not provide a full picture of Jesus. It gives us the broad outlines. It provides us with a general idea of who Jesus may have been and what he may have taught. It very rarely gives us the specifics of his teachings, although it can put into context what we know from the New Testament and related literature. The historian's Jesus is not always a useful guide to religious faith and practice. Jesus provides a poor model for family life. What should the Gentile Church do when the historian's Jesus is a man whose message is directed to the "lost sheep of Israel" and has little interest in or concern with Gentiles?

Yet, history and the historian do not destroy faith. Rather, the historical task changes the focus of faith. It destroys absolutes and makes relative all human experience. It is both humbling and liberating. It humbles us by claiming that what we hold as true and firm is in truth conditioned by our unique experience. On the other hand, it liberates us by allowing us to cherish our moment as important in the flow of human time.

For the Church's understanding of Jesus, history has shown that there is a treasury of images of Jesus. Christians have drawn on this treasury and have contributed to it as part of their experience over time and space. These images stem from and reflect on the historical Jesus, the point of contact between the human and the divine for Christianity. They are, however, not limited to whatever picture of that obscure Jewish preacher we can develop. Rather, they stand in dramatic and dynamic relationship with it and with each other.

I think that you have shown this very clearly in translating the ontological language of the creeds into the dynamic, dialogic language of our time. Our historical image of Jesus does not free Christians from the theology of Nicaea and Chalcedon; nor does it bind them to it. Christians today are neither first-century Jews nor fourth- and fifth-century Greeks. The historian can show how their understanding of Jesus was framed by the philosophical understanding and the sociological conditions of their times. The contemporary theologians' task, as I see it, is to use their attempts to relate and apply their religious experiences to their times as models for the very similar, contemporary struggle.

The teachings of the historically recoverable Jesus should provide the broad outlines of the Church's task. A Church that is false to these teachings is false to its roots. On the other hand, a Church that restricts itself to the insights of a first-century master is false to itself.

Jesus' basic teachings that the divine presence is near to all who turn in repentance, that God is concerned with the oppressed, that the divine dominion is soon to be fully present, that the heart of the Law is love of God and love of one's fellows, that ethical and spiritual concerns are part of the Law, come out of his Jewish background. As Jesus is central to the Church, so are his literary, spiritual and cultural roots also vital for Christian authenticity. That means that the Church needs to honor not only the Hebrew Scriptures but also certain Jewish pseudepigraphic writings and, possibly, some aspects of popular Hellenistic culture.

It is only natural that Jesus' basic commitments seem to parallel those of the rabbis, for they share the same roots. This does not make Jews a peculiar sort of Christians or Christians a peculiar sort of Jews. Rather, it indicates the richness of this heritage that has produced vital, yet different, fruit.

The historical critique of traditional religion shows that religious, spiritual and moral truth (like scientific and philosophic truth) is available to us in only a relativistic sense. There is no one person or one moment from which we can take truth in its absolute sense. We stand in tension with our past and our future. In our search for truth, we make judgments concerning our past, knowing that our judgments themselves will be judged in the future. Despite our best efforts, we will at times be in error. We should expect a similar mixture of truth and falsehood in the efforts of our predecessors.

The radical nature of this observation is seen more clearly in Christianity than it is in Judaism. The Jewish tradition of arguing with God, as well as such traditional understandings that the Torah is no longer in heaven but is meant to be interpreted and used by people, reduce the sharpness of this observation for Liberal Jews. To be honest, the historically aware Christian religious thinker cannot merely say that at times the Church was in error. He or she must be willing to say that at times even Jesus may have made a mistake.

(3) Although it is true that Jews tended to ask axiological rather than ontological questions—questions of doing and not of being—this does not necessarily indicate that Jews of the first century ignored issues of an ontological nature. Unlike the Greeks who were developing a number of differing philosophical approaches to the basic questions of human existence, the Jews seem to have shared a common belief in a creator God, who by establishing a covenant with this people demands proper ethical and ritual behavior from them. This is a God who rewards and punishes and who provides a means of repentance for those who have erred.

Controversy among the Jews stemmed not out of what to believe but rather on how to implement these beliefs into everyday life. The Greeks and the Christians, too, asked axiological questions. A large literature exists of maxims, instructions, illustrative stories, and other literary forms that addressed the question of how one lives a good life.

Jewish halakhic development rests on and expresses theological beliefs. The work of Jacob Neusner and his students has shown how the various documents of rabbinic Judaism reflect differing understandings of fundamental theological concepts. These documents, at times framed as discussions of Jewish Law, show in their choice of topics and structure clear theological concerns.

The issue facing us today is not the old and overstated dichotomy between the Hebraic/Jewish concern with actions and the Hellenic/Christian concern with belief. The answers given by either model—and one could very well argue that they are really the same—to the basic questions of the relationship of the human to the divine are not satisfactory.

We live in an era in which the prevailing worldview is dialogic. We have a picture of a world that is bound together by the dynamic interrelationship of its parts. In popular language, we picture our world as holistic and organic. We are evaluated not by series of causes and effects but rather by our location on the matrix of existence. This is not the worldview of Israel in the first century nor of the Christian Empire in the fourth and fifth centuries. We cannot simply appropriate our religious heritages; we need to mold them and adapt them to our new situations. We can recast the theologies of our pasts for our use. We need to do so, however, with care, trying to understand clearly and respond honestly to both their issues and our concerns.

NOTES

1. Cf. Eduard Schweizer, *Jesus Christus* (Hamburg, 1972), pp. 19f.; Ernst Käsemann, *Das Problem des historischen Jesus—exegetische Besinnungen*, vol. 1 (Göttingen, 1960), pp. 187, 205. Ulrich Luz, professor of New Testament at the Protestant faculty of the University of Bern, Switzerland, makes the point even more sharply: "Not only did Jesus not declare himself to his people as the Messiah; more than likely he did not even consider himself to be the Messiah," in Pinchas Lapide & Ulrich Luz, *Jesus in Two Perspectives* (Minneapolis: Augsburg, 1985), p. 129.

2. Hans Küng, *Christentum und Weltreligionen* (Munich: Piper, 1984), p. 451.

3. E. P. Sanders, *Jesus and Judaism* (Philadelphia: Fortress Press, 1985), p. 2.

4. Geza Vermes, *Jesus and the World of Judaism* (Philadelphia: Fortress Press, 1984), p. 81.

5. This stance is taken by Küng, Schillebeeckx and many other prominent Catholic and Protestant theologians; see Leonard Swidler, ed., *Consensus in Theology?* (Philadelphia: Westminster Press, 1980). E.g., Hans Küng: "And for the Catholic Christian too this criterion can be nothing but the Christian message, the *Gospel* in its ultimate concrete form, *Jesus Christ, himself*, who for the Church and—despite all assertions to the contrary—also for me is the Son and Word of God. He is and

remains the norm in the light of which every ecclesiastical authority—which is not disputed—must be judged: the norm by which the theologian must be tested and in the light of which s/he must continually justify her/himself in the spirit of self-criticism and true humility" (p. 163). The Protestant theologian Ulrich Luz made the same point abundantly clear when he wrote: *"Christianity must appeal to Jesus if it wants to endure* without allowing itself to be transformed willy-nilly by anyone and by every historical epoch. It *must* appeal to Jesus, as long as it continues to affirm that God acted historically in Jesus and not merely in our momentary faith experiences and ideas." He added that he was "convinced that appealing to Jesus cannot be painless and without consequences for us in the present; rather, it demands that our churches modify their theology and practice." Lapide and Luz, *Jesus in Two Perspectives*, p. 159.

6. Edward Schillebeeckx, *Jesus* (New York: Seabury Press, 1979), p. 61. Schillebeeckx takes note of the distinction between the historical Yeshua and our apprehension of him and states that the former is the ultimate Christian norm: "It is not the historical image of Jesus, but the living Jesus of history who stands at the beginning and is the source, norm and criterion." He then argues that historical critical research was the means by which the earliest "reactions to," Jesus Christ risen i.e., the original Christian beliefs, measure up to the final standard, "the living Jesus of history": "historical critical research can clarify for us the Jesus of history." Edward Schillebeeckx, *Die Auferstehung Jesu als Grund der Erlösung* (Freiburg: Herder, 1978), p. 44. Stated in other words, our apprehensions, by whatever methods, of the historical Yeshua will always fall short of apprehending him fully. (Other critical methods will also contribute to our fuller, deeper and never ending apprehension of the historical Yeshua, e.g., literary-critical and psychosocial-critical methods.) However, the very best "penultimate" image of the real historical Yeshua is the very best "temporary" final norm we can have for what is authentically Christian—until a fuller image of the historical Yeshua is developed, and so on *ad infinitum*.

7. Schillebeeckx, *Jesus*, p. 62.

8. Cited in Vermes, *Jesus and the World of Judaism*, p. 44.

9. Joseph G. Kelly, "Lucan Christology and the Jewish-Christian Dialogue," *Journal of Ecumenical Studies*, 21, 4 (Fall 1984), pp. 693, 704, 708.

10. W. M. Thompson, *The Jesus Debate* (Mahwah, NJ: Paulist Press, 1985), p. 104.

11. Paul Tillich made a similar point when he wrote that the statement "God has become man" is not paradoxical but "nonsensical" because "it is a combination of words which makes sense only if it is not meant to mean what the words say. The word 'God' points to ultimate reality, and even the most consistent Scotists had to admit that the only thing God cannot do is to cease to be God. But that is just what the assertion that 'God has become man' means." Paul Tillich, *Systematic Theology*, II (Chicago: University of Chicago Press, 1975), p. 94.

12. A related notion about the genre of language used in various religious texts was stressed by Monika Hellwig in discussing the language of the Tome of Pope Leo the Great, which became so influential in the Christological language of the Council of Chalcedon: "Throughout this document, Leo argues directly from the language of worship and piety to the abstract formulations that came to dominate the Council of Chalcedon. There is, of course, no reflection on the nature of religious language. . . . One is compelled to ask whether there may have been a mis-

perception of literary genre. The poetic language of piety seems to be used as though it were a simple historical record of the already self-critically nuanced language of a systematic exposition." Monika Hellwig, "From the Jesus of Story to the Christ of Dogma," in Alan T. Davies, ed., *Antisemitism and the Foundations of Christianity* (Mahwah, NJ: Paulist Press, 1979), p. 123.

13. Ansfried Hulsbosch, a Dutch Catholic theologian—who unfortunately died at a relatively young age—took the evolutionary thought of Teilhard de Chardin seriously and developed an insightful Christology. His argument was that the divinity of Yeshua consisted precisely in the perfection of his humanity. He stated that Yeshua "is the Son of God in that this man is in contact with God in a way that separates Him from ordinary men. But this can mean nothing other than a special way of being-man, since the whole actuality of the mystery lies precisely in the sector of the human." Then he added that, "The divine nature of Jesus is relevant to the saving mystery only insofar as it alters and elevates the human nature. And whatever that is, it must be called a new mode of being man." See: Ansfried Hulsbosch, "Jezus Christus, gekend als mens, beleden as Zoon Gods," *Tijdschrift voor Theologie*, 6 (1966), 255. This article is summarized along with two other key articles from the same special number of the *Tijdschrift* by Piet Schoonenberg and Edward Schillebeeckx in the article "Soul-Body Unity and God-Man Unity," by Robert North in *Theological Studies*, 30 (March 1969), pp. 27–60; 36f.

14. Edward Schillebeeckx, "Persoonlijke openbaringsgestalte van de Vader," *Tijdschrift voor Theologie*, 6 (1966), pp. 276f. (North, "Soul-Body," pp. 40f.). Ulrich Luz stresses a similar point about the shift from the Jewish way of thinking to the Greek way and its impact on Christology. He states that "the confession of Jesus' divinity may have been unavoidable and quite pertinent for the Greeks and for Europeans of the previous centuries, whose thought processes had been shaped by Platonic metaphysics, even though the possibility of a conversation with Israel thereby became inevitably strained. However, this confession has always been problematic insofar as it has threatened to swallow the humanity of Jesus as well as the historical reality of his mission; theologically this is the case in its Monophysite form, but for me this is also largely true of its Chalcedonian, non-Antiochene form. In my opinion it is impossible for us to go on thinking as the Greeks once did, even though we have learned, and still can learn, much from them." Lapide & Luz, *Jesus in Two Perspectives*, p. 165.

15. The Catholic exegete Jerome Murphy-O'Connor, O.P., argues in great detail that the common belief that Phil. 2:6–11 speaks of Christ's pre-existence as God and his subsequent incarnation, is "a presupposition rather than a conclusion" that is unwarranted. "Christological Anthropology in Phil. 2:6–11," *Revue Biblique*, 83 (1976), 30ff. See also James D. G. Dunn, *Christology in the Making* (Philadelphia: Westminster Press, 1980), pp. 114ff.

16. Sanders, *Jesus*, p. 21.

17. Vermes, *Jesus and the World of Judaism*, p. 72.

18. James Barr, *Semantics of Biblical Language* (London, Oxford University Press, 1961), p. 250.

19. Vermes, *Jesus and the World of Judaism*, p. 26.

20. See ibid. and Thomas N. Hart, *To Know and Follow Jesus* (Mahwah, NJ: Paulist Press, 1984), pp. 94ff.; Schillebeeckx, *Jesus*; Piet Schoonenberg, *The Christ* (New York: Seabury Press, 1971); Piet Schoonenberg, " 'He Emptied Himself':

Philippians 2:7," in *Who Is Jesus of Nazareth? Concilium*, 11 (New York: Paulist Press, 1965), pp. 47–66.

21. Hart, *To Know and Follow Jesus*, p. 98.

22. Ibid.

23. Ibid., p. 99.

24. Seiichi Yagi, " 'I' in the Words of Jesus," in Paul Knitter and John Hick, eds., *The Myth of Christian Uniqueness: Toward a Pluralistic Theology of Religions* (Maryknoll, NY: Orbis Books, 1987), p. 117. Here Yagi summarizes this aspect of Takizawa's work and goes on to apply it to Yeshua and Paul, with some additional help from the Zen Buddhist Shin-ichi Hisamatsu (1889–1980).

25. Ibid.

26. Ibid., pp. 121f.

27. Ibid., p. 122.

8

Jesus and Judaism

LEWIS JOHN ERON

The answer to the question of the position of the figure of Jesus within Judaism today rests in no small measure on the fact that Jesus' acts and teachings played no significant role within Judaism after his execution.

The extra-Christian sources concerning Jesus are meager. Josephus remembers Jesus as a historical curiosity. The briefer reference in *Ant.* 22.200 merely mentions the death of James, who is identified as "the brother of Jesus, the so-called Christ." The longer reference, the so-called *Testimonium Flavianum*, *Ant.* 18.63f, although claimed by some to be of dubious origin, seems to have been composed by Josephus and was later subject to Christian interpolation. It adds little to our knowledge of Jesus and his followers, except perhaps to emphasize that Greeks as well as Jews were members of this group called "Messianists" (*Christianoi*) after their understanding of their founder, Jesus.

The rabbinic material on Jesus confirms the basic facts of his life. The sources are on the whole from the late third through the fifth centuries (Amoraic). On the whole, the material is polemical and reflects the rabbinic response to the claims of Christians. At times Tannaitic (first through third centuries) scholars who may have had contact with early Christians are cited, most notably, Rabbi Eliezer ben Hyrcanus (end of first and beginning of second centuries C.E.).

The earliest references seem to indicate the early rejection of Jesus' teachings by rabbinic Judaism. For example, the Tosefta, a collection of Tannaitic material, compiled later than but related to the Mishnah, relates that Rabbi Eliezer was arrested for stating heretical opinions. Although he was released, he was distressed concerning the accusation. In discussion with Rabbi Akiba, he remembered that previously he found acceptable a teaching attributed to Yeshua ben Pantira (Jesus of Nazareth) taught to him in Sepphoris by a Jacob of Kefar Sekhania. Rabbi Eliezer claimed that

104

by finding this teaching acceptable he transgressed the Torah, citing Prov. 5:6 and 7:26 as his proof texts (the temptations of the wicked woman). Thus, he believed his punishment was justified (t. Hul. 2.24).

This passage tells us nothing about Jacob of Kefar Sekhania. We cannot assume that he belonged to a group of followers of Jesus. He may have merely repeated a ruling of Jesus remembered in the Galilee. It does indicate that the rabbis from an early period (second century according to the attribution) considered Jesus' teachings outside of their tradition.

One could suggest various reasons why Jesus and his teachings did not find their home in the rabbinic tradition. On one level it may have been coincidental. Jesus was an outsider, a Galilean, and the center of first-century Pharisaic thought was Jerusalem. Jesus and his disciples were not central to the mainstream of the tradition.

I place Jesus in the context of Galilean "charismatic" Judaism. He was probably closer to the miracle-working, popular teachers of the Galilean countryside than to the teachers of the urban centers, primarily Jerusalem. Jesus can be best compared to Honi the Circle-maker, Hanina ben Dosa, Abba Hilkiah, and Hana the Hidden. Although the tradition remembers and honors these popular teachers, they are examples of pious people and are described as *hasidim* rather than as teachers in the rabbinic schools of thought.[1]

The apocalyptic nature of Jesus' teachings and those of his followers also worked to exclude Jesus from the post-70 rabbinic tradition. The de-emphasis of eschatological speculation in early rabbinic Judaism after the disastrous revolts against Rome would have served to exclude those teachers whose teachings stressed the immediate inbreaking of the Dominion of Heaven. Yet, messianic hope continued as a major component of rabbinic thought.

More important may have been the rapid spread of Christianity among Gentiles. Non-Jews became the predominant group among the followers of Jesus in a very short time. Within a few decades after Jesus' execution, Christian teachers were founding communities of followers throughout the Eastern Mediterranean. The rejection of circumcision and other Jewish requirements for entrance into the Jewish people as entrance requirements into the fellowship of those who followed Jesus by Paul and, perhaps, by the Antiochene community with which he was associated, helped create a group of followers of Jesus who were without any expressed commitment to the Jewish people. Yet, there still remained Jewish followers of Jesus.[2]

The decisive factor may have been the fact that after the conclusion of the Great Revolt with the destruction of the Temple in 70 C.E., Jesus' teachings no longer answered the needs of a Jewish community on the way to self-reconstruction. Not only was the eschatological nature of his teaching no longer believable, but his criticism of the Temple priesthood was no longer applicable in a period in which there was no Temple.

The rabbis of the Mishnah expressed their messianic hope and criticism of the Temple in creating in the Mishnah their vision of proper Temple worship. The followers of Jesus recreated Jesus' critique in their association of priestly and sacrificial functions with the person of Jesus himself, as most clearly seen in the so-called Epistle to the Hebrews.

The need to re-establish the Jewish community as a community in which its members could experience holiness after the loss of the Temple and the destructions resulting from the revolts formed, as Jacob Neusner clearly indicates, the program of the Tannaitic rabbis. The Pharisaic fellowship in which its participants attempted to extend the sanctity of the Temple into their everyday lives supplied a useful foundation for the rabbis' reconstruction of Judaism and Jewish life.[3]

The highly individualistic ethic promoted by Jesus could not satisfy this need. The Jewish community that Jesus addressed, though under stress, was a vibrant and strong community. He preached to a living, organic community with its social structure basically intact. He could dream of reforming this community through reforming its members. He could send his disciples wandering through the Land of Israel, calling on individual Jews to repent in light of the soon-to-be-coming Dominion of God, because there was an organized community into which they could be sent. With the destruction of that community, the message no longer made sense.

To the Jews, particularly to the Jews of the Land of Israel, Jesus' message did not provide the basis on which to reconstruct their communal life. Similarly, Jesus' teachings provided little help in determining the structure of the earliest churches. The problems of organization the early Christian groups faced are well represented in the New Testament. The growth of the Jesus movement from a wandering band of charismatic healers and teachers to established, stable, local communities of believers took the early churches beyond the teachings of their master.

Jesus, the Pharisees, and the other Jewish groups at the beginning of the first century were attempting within the same ethnic, cultural, and geographic Jewish arena to find ways to renew Jewish life. By the end of that century only the Pharisees' successors, the rabbis, survived to rebuild the Jewish community. The Jewish part of the Jesus movement faded, as did the other Jewish groups of its time. Its Gentile successor, the Church, organized itself independent of the activities of the rabbis, and found a way to preserve the memory of Jesus of Nazareth.

For Judaism today, Jesus and his followers have the position of other forms of so-called sectarian Judaism of the first few centuries B.C.E. and C.E. The gospels are significant, as are apocryphal and pseudepigraphic works such as Jubilees, Enoch, the Testaments of the Twelve Patriarchs, and others. This is not a negative position. As we Jews search our history for deeper understanding of the growth of Jewish life and culture, many figures are emerging not as religious figures, but as persons of historical interest and importance. We are looking again not only at our heroes but at our rogues as well. Jesus may well emerge as neither a hero nor a rogue but as another representative of a form of Judaism whose mutated seed ultimately found root in fertile foreign soil.

If one places Jesus in a Galilean context, many of the conflicts between Jesus and Jewish leaders and authorities can be explained as the social and economic conflict between the urban center and the countryside. This makes Jesus and his followers important for the study of Jewish social history, but not necessarily part of the rabbinic tradition.

The vast majority of Jews never meet the divine in Jesus either as an inspired teacher or as the redeeming Christ. Jews met and continue to meet the divine in other situations and experiences. Christian and Jewish ways to experience the power of divinity are based on different experiences. Those experiences both in the history of the tradition and in the lives of their followers provide the foundations for each cultural and religious tradition's unique view of the world. Jesus, though he was born a Jew and died a Jew, is not part of Judaism. He is part of Christianity.

For Jews to use Jesus as an important Jewish religious teacher is to take away from Christianity's special vision as well as to denigrate their own. The challenge Judaism faces is not for Jews to reclaim Jesus but for Jews to reclaim their own traditions. The inner Jewish need is first to rediscover those heroes, both men and women, who are clearly our own.

The use of the image of the crucified Jesus by modern Jewish artists and writers, such as Marc Chagall, in his *White Crucifixion* and Elie Wiesel in his novel *Night*, should not be seen as a welcoming home of Jesus. Jewish artists, particularly those as well grounded in Jewish tradition and imagery as these two, have a large repertory of Jewish symbols and images for Jewish suffering under tyrannical forces. The use of the image of the crucified Jesus does not reflect the acceptance of the historical Jesus as a Jew. Rather it is an angry, ironic condemnation of Christians and Christianity. It turns Christian symbolism on its head to accuse and condemn.[4]

Although rhetorically powerful, such a Jewish use of Jesus as the image for the suffering Israel ultimately is an impediment to dialogue. Christian shame and Christian guilt may have led some Christians to hold dialogue with Jews, but dialogue cannot be based on such a relationship. We must talk as equals. I cannot see myself or be seen as an equal by my Christian dialogue partner if he or she sees me as either one guilty of deicide or as the one able to forgive his or her faith tradition its genocide. Jewish use of the crucified one brings us only to the start of dialogue.

Likewise, for Christians to use Jewish religious symbols and customs steals from Judaism and exhibits a lack of faith and courage in the Church's own wealth of experience. Jews and Judaism cannot tell Christians who Jesus was. Almost two thousand years of vibrant development separate modern Jews from Jesus' contemporaries. Together, we can study the world in which Jesus lived. If Jewish participation helps Christians study that world in a positive light, then we can make a contribution, but we have no special key to the past.

Our historical knowledge of Jesus helps limit and define Christ as the meeting point of the human and the divine. As Sinai is a mountain in the wilderness between the Land of Israel and Egypt, Jesus is a first-century Jewish man. Christians cannot escape that fact. Yet, the Christ of the Church is much more. Study of earliest Christianity is the study of the first few steps people who saw themselves as Christians took in defining and living what was to them a new reality through their experience of Jesus Christ.

It is true that Jesus of Nazareth has been ignored in Judaism. His significance to Christianity has worked to his detriment in Jewish circles. It is important for Jews if they wish to recover another witness to a period in their history to approach Jesus and his teachings with academic sympathy. Jews need to discover and understand the historical Jesus as part of a need to understand their history. Likewise, the image of Jesus that grew in Judaism as a response to Christian polemics is also of value, for that, too, provides an insight into the development of our history.

Jesus, the Jew, neither binds us nor separates us. He is historically interesting. Jesus, the Christ of the Church, is the one who brings us together and draws us apart. It is because of Christ that religious Jews can meet with religious Christians, realize the depth of our experiences, and learn that we are truly not the same but refreshingly different.

A Response to Lewis John Eron from Leonard Swidler

I agree that the challenge Jews face is "to reclaim their own traditions." Just before you say this you also say that "the challenge Judaism faces is not for Jews to reclaim Jesus." I would agree with you here too, in that it is not a *challenge* that Jews face in this regard. However, I would like also to suggest that if, while remaining authentically Jewish, some Jews would wish to reclaim Jesus, even as a "Jewish religious teacher," it would not "take away from Christianity's special vision," at least, not as far as most Christians are concerned.

To be sure, this is an extremely delicate matter. Christians for millennia have been trying to foist Jesus in one guise or another off onto Jews. Jews know from long experience that they need to be thoroughly skeptical about any such Christian moves. Nevertheless, new, and positive, things have been happening on the religious scene of Western civilization in the two centuries since the Enlightenment—slowly, unfortunately, and mixed with some horrendous "counterattacks," but still positive and new. These new, positive factors need also to be taken into consideration in reflecting today on the place of Jesus in Judaism and Christianity.

Without entering into a discussion about the use of the suffering Jesus by some modern Jewish artists and literary writers, what has been mentioned, and even somewhat annotated, by both of us earlier should be recalled here: A large number of modern Jewish scholars and writers have been treating Jesus in a very positive manner—indeed, even in Israeli school books.[5] My citation from Leo Baeck above is just one of many scores from Jewish scholars who speak of Jesus as quintessentially Jewish. They feel that the life and teaching should not be neglected by Jews, but, as Shalom Ben-Chorin put it, should be "brought home."[6]

In all this, Jews, of course, do not see Jesus as the messiah or as divine. Christians are not offended by the positive Jewish treatment of Jesus, which nevertheless does not enter into the Christian religious orbit. If anything, I would say that Christians are generally flattered. This is a natural enough response: If you admire something or someone I admire, I feel complimented, not lessened.

Let me offer the example of one Orthodox American rabbi's reflection on Jesus as a messiah, a failed one, to be sure, but nevertheless very much in the Jewish tradition:

> Rabbinic Judaism finally judged Jesus to be a false Messiah. . . . The Rabbis concluded that Christianity is an alien growth, developed by those who followed a false Messiah.
>
> The Rabbis perhaps erred here. Understandably, they did not do greater justice to Jesus because they were surrounded by an enemy (= Christians) one hundred times larger than Jewry, aggressively proselytizing and persecuting the Jews in the name of Jesus's claims. Out of defensiveness, the Rabbis confused a "failed" Messiah (which is what Jesus was) and a false Messiah. A false Messiah is one who has the wrong values: one who would teach that death will triumph, that people should oppress each other, that God hates us [Jacob Frank is given as an example]. . . . A failed Messiah is one who has the right values, upholds the covenant, only did not attain the final goal [Bar Kokhba is given as an example]. . . . [Moses and Jeremiah are then discussed as Jewish "failures."]
>
> All these "failures" are at the heart of divine and Jewish achievements. This concept of a "failed" but true Messiah is found in a rabbinic tradition of the Messiah ben Joseph. The Messiah ben David (son of David) is the one who brings the final restoration. In the Messiah ben Joseph's idea, you have a Messiah who comes and fails, indeed is put to death, but this Messiah paves the way for the final redemption.
>
> Christians also sensed that Jesus did not exhaust the achievements of the final Messiah. Despite Christian claims that Jesus was a total success . . . even Christians spoke of a second coming. The concept of a second coming, in a way, is a tacit admission—if at first you don't succeed, try, try again.[7]

Christians may not see Jesus in quite the way Rabbi Irving Greenberg here describes him, but what is of interest to us here is the way Greenberg unhesitatingly places Jesus as a religious figure solidly in the Jewish tradition. He is one of a growing number of Jewish scholars who are doing so.

Earlier in the development of this part of our dialogue we raised the following question: Where would Jesus fit in the contemporary world if one or another key divisive event had not occurred? As you pointed out, the question would not be susceptible to a definite answer, but it certainly would be stimulating in that it would force one to question various, perhaps unwarranted, assumptions that otherwise would have remained unconsciously determining—and perhaps distortingly so. I think such an exercise may still offer us some stimulation at this point in our dialogue.

As I indicated before, I am convinced that the Roman destruction of Israel in 70 C.E. was a watershed event in the history of both what became known as rabbinic Judaism and of Christianity—and consequently of the whole history of the rest of the world, for without that event there never would have been a subsequent Christendom as we have known it, with its eventual domination of the world, nor even an Islam as we have known it (which drew on both a separate Judaism and Christianity).

More choices of how to be authentically Jewish would have remained available. Inner Jewish tensions would have been much less intense and mutual tolerance could have afforded to be much more magnanimous. Viable creative compromises and syntheses would have eventuated, thereby avoiding the extremist polarizations and splintering divisions that in fact occurred.

In that case, Jesus certainly would have remained solidly within the Jewish tradition, though perhaps more highly revered in one or more segments than others. He would have been not unlike, for example, the Baal Shem Tov within Hasidic Judaism, without being thought of as being outside of the Jewish community or tradition by non-Hasidic Jews.

If this line of speculation has any plausibility—and I am persuaded it does—then it should cause both Christians and Jews to pause and reflect whether Jesus could not in fact more accurately be perceived as a bond than a barrier between the two communities. It would appear clear from this exercise that it was not Jesus but other historical realities that brought about the divisions between Jews and Christians.

As a final comment, I would like to suggest that you underestimate the insight some modern Jews can contribute—if they have a mind to—to the Christian search for their own roots in the Jewish Jesus. You say that "Jews and Judaism cannot tell Christians who Jesus was" because "almost two thousand years of vibrant development separate modern Jews from Jesus' contemporaries." True, but nevertheless I would suggest that Jesus in some ways stands closer to contemporary religious Jews than he does to contemporary religious Christians: his theocentrism rather than Christocentrism, his focusing on the Hebrew Bible rather than the New Testament, his affection for the Torah, his rabbinic style of thinking and teaching, and his very language, among others, are all factors that would make him more open to understanding by many sympathetic contemporary religious Jews than by their Christian counterparts.

Of course, such an involvement by Jews would be an act of altruism, for by it they would essentially be helping Christians in their Christian search, and not their own. It would be a *mitzvah* that Christians in no way can expect, and for which, when offered, they should be extremely grateful: We are. It is incumbent upon Christians, of course, likewise to offer Jews whatever assistance Christians might be able to in matters of Jewish religious concern.

Beyond both of these mutual helping moves, however, Christians and Jews together need to explore new dimensions of what it means to be religious, to be authentically human, today. This ultimately is what dialogue is all about.

NOTES

1. Judah Naditch collected the rabbinic traditions concerning these figures and other early sages as part of his *Jewish Legends of the Second Commonwealth* (Philadelphia: The Jewish Publication Society of America, 1983), pp. 185–230.

2. For a discussion of how different entrance requirements and rituals led to separate early Christianity from early Judaism see: Lawrence H. Schiffman, *Who Was a Jew, Rabbinic and Halakhic Perspectives on the Jewish-Christian Schism* (Hoboken, NJ: Ktav, 1985).

3. Jacob Neusner, *Judaism: The Evidence of the Mishnah* (Chicago: University of Chicago Press, 1981).

4. Nineteenth-century Jewish artists, like Moses Jacob Ezekiel and Mark Antokolski, used the image of Jesus as Christ allegorically to refer to the people Israel as the bearer of high ethical teachings and hope for redemption to an unfriendly world. Their optimistic and idealistic hope that Israel, the Jewish people, would soon be not only full partners but, also, the leaders in the world's progress towards ultimate salvation was broken by the events of our century.

Both the nineteenth-century Jewish image of Jesus as the symbol for the soon-to-triumph spirit of the Jewish people and the twentieth-century Jewish image of Jesus as the martyred people Israel are critiques of Christianity. The twentieth-century image's message is blunt. It accuses and condemns Christianity of brutality and inhumanity.

The seemingly more irenic nineteenth-century image may unwittingly presage the twentieth's. It suggests that Christianity was unable to recognize and to follow its founder's message; this message did not survive in the Christian church but in the life and spirit of the people Israel. In the optimistic spirit of their age, these nineteenth-century Jewish artists could not or would not have recognized how serious this inability would prove to be.

Joseph Gutmann, "Jewish Themes in the Art of Moses Jacob Ezekiel," *Ezekiel's Vision: Moses Jacob Ezekiel and the Classical Tradition* (Philadelphia: National

Museum of American Jewish History, 1985), pp. 27–35. See also Z. Amishai-Maisels, "The Jewish Jesus," *Journal of Jewish Art*, 9 (1982), pp. 92ff.

5. Pinchas Lapide, "Jesus in Israeli Schoolbooks," *Journal of Ecumenical Studies*, 10, 3 (Summer 1973), pp. 515–531.

6. Shalom Ben-Chorin, "The Image of Jesus in Modern Judaism," *Journal of Ecumenical Studies*, 11, 3 (Summer 1974), pp. 401–430.

7. Irving Greenberg, "The Relationship of Judaism and Christianity: Toward a New Organic Model," Eugene Fisher, James Rudin, Marc Tanenbaum, eds., *Twenty Years of Jewish-Catholic Relations* (Mahwah, NJ: Paulist Press, 1986), pp. 201f.

9

Summary of a Jewish-Christian Dialogue on Jesus/Yeshua

The basic issue in this dialogue appears in the use of both the name Yeshua and the name Jesus to refer to the root figure of Christian faith. Leonard Swidler (Roman Catholic) uses Yeshua, the Hebrew form of the name, to stress the Jewish roots of Christianity and to emphasize that Yeshua was well integrated into the Jewish community of his day. Lewis John Eron (Jewish) uses Jesus, the Latin form of the name, to emphasize that despite the fact that Jesus was born, lived, taught and died as a Jew, his teachings found root in the Gentile Church and not in the Jewish people.

Swidler argues that it is essential for Christian faith that Christians not forget their Jewish roots. Eron argues that Jews can help in the Christian search for the Jesus of history, but Jesus, who is of primary concern for Christians, is of only tangential interest to Jews.

WHY CHRISTIANS NEED TO DIALOGUE WITH JEWS AND JUDAISM ABOUT JESUS

Leonard Swidler argues that for Christians to be true to their roots, they need to know that Jesus was a Jew. Whatever form of Christianity a Christian may follow, all are based on the life and teachings of Yeshua of Nazareth, a first-century C.E. Jew from the Galilee. Yeshua was born a Jew and stood in a close relationship with the early rabbinic Jewish tradition.

It is also important for Christians to be in dialogue with Jews. As a result of Christianity's Jewish roots and its long and not always friendly encounter with Jews and Judaism, it is vital for Christians to come to know Jews and appreciate them for what they truly are, rather than denigrate them for what Christians mistakenly think they are. Swidler argues that for Christians to hate Jews is for them to hate what Yeshua was, a Jew. Using Paul's image of the wild shoot grafted on the olive tree, Swidler claims that when

Christians hate Jews and Judaism, they hate themselves. They reject the live trunk on which they live.

Swidler concludes this section by discussing the significance of the name Yeshua. He argues that the name "Yeshua" captures the Jewish insight that *YHWH* (the Lord) is salvation. Swidler writes, "So, then, the very name Yeshua is an assertion that *YHWH* is the source of wholeness for all human beings, for all things."

THE PROBLEM OF A JEW TALKING TO A CHRISTIAN ABOUT JESUS

Lewis Eron suggests three reasons why Jews are interested in Jesus. The first is an apologetic attempt to facilitate Jewish entry into the modern Christian and post-Christian world. If Jews could show that Jesus was a good Jew, then Judaism should not be seen as threatening to the greater Christian society. The second reason comes out of a hope to eliminate the ideological basis of Christian anti-Judaism that has contributed to Christian persecution of Jews and to anti-Semitism. If Jews could show that Jesus was Jewish, then Christians should develop positive attitudes towards the people to whom their root figure belonged. Eron's third reason is for Jews and Christians to meet in dialogue as equals. He sees this reason as the most meaningful for Jewish-Christian understanding. The first two, by contrast, are not grounded in the experience of dialogue — that is, the attempt to learn who the other truly is. Rather, they serve apologetic and defensive purposes.

When Jews and Christians meet in dialogue, they should meet as members of vital faith traditions and for no reason other than to learn from each other. Dialogue is not negotiation. In dialogue, the Jewish partner should be interested in Jesus because of his or her respect for the Christian partner for whom Jesus is central.

Eron points out that a Jewish-Christian dialogue on Jesus is not a complete dialogue. Jesus, who is of central interest to Christians, holds only tangential interest for Jews. This is not to say that Jesus is not an important topic in Jewish-Christian dialogue; rather a Jewish-Christian dialogue that focuses on Jesus does not give full attention to the needs and interests of the Jewish partner. Eron concludes by noting that from a Jewish perspective Jesus holds historical, not theological, interest. In the context of the life experience of the Jewish people, however, Eron indicates, for someone to be of historical interest is a significant human accomplishment.

JESUS/YESHUA'S PLACE IN THE JEWISH LIFE OF HIS TIME

Eron and Swidler are in close agreement in their understanding of Jesus/Yeshua in the context of Jewish life of his time. Both see Jesus/Yeshua as a wonder-working preacher and teacher from the Galilee similar to other wonder-working Galilean *hasidim*, that is, "pietists," such as Honi the Circle-maker. Like them, Jesus/Yeshua was close to the Pharisees, the predecessors of the rabbis, but was not necessarily a member of the Pharisaic group.

On the one hand, Swidler stresses the similarities between Jesus/Yeshua and Pharisaic/early rabbinic Judaism to argue that Jesus/Yeshua is best understood within the early Jewish/rabbinic tradition. Eron, on the other hand, while agreeing with Swidler that the religious faith Jesus/Yeshua taught is strikingly close to that of the Pharisees/early rabbis, argues that it is not what Jesus/Yeshua shared with the Pharisees that made him significant but how he differed from them.

Both agree that Jesus/Yeshua was well integrated into the Jewish life of his time. As a Jewish teacher passionately concerned with the life of the Jewish people, Jesus/Yeshua addressed their concerns and hopes in terms that fit well within a first-century C.E. Jewish context.

YESHUA/JESUS: A TORAH-TRUE JEW?

Both Eron and Swidler argue that Jesus/Yeshua had a positive and accepting attitude to traditional Jewish law. Both of them point out that Jesus/Yeshua's twofold commandment of love—love of God and love of one's neighbor—is well attested in contemporaneous Jewish sources. The two of them understand that Jesus/Yeshua's teachings on the Law do not allow one to make a separation between Law and grace. Jesus/Yeshua, like the vast majority of Jews of his time, saw Torah, the practices and teachings of Judaism—poorly translated as "Law"—as an aspect of God's loving relationship with God's people Israel.

They differ on exactly what was Jesus/Yeshua's conception of "the Law." Swidler desires to place Jesus/Yeshua's conception of "the Law" within the early rabbinic tradition. He sees Jesus/Yeshua as a "proto-rabbi." Swidler describes Jesus/Yeshua as also being a *"hasid,"* a "pietist"—that is, someone dedicated to a supererogatory observance of ritual and moral law. As a hasid, Jesus/Yeshua advocated living in kenotic love.

Eron is reluctant to place Jesus/Yeshua within the early rabbinic tradition or to see him primarily as a teacher of the Law. He argues that although all Jewish groups of this period claimed loyalty to the Torah, there was no one understanding of what the details of Torah were. In addition, Eron is reluctant to use the later rabbinic term for Jewish law, *halakhah* for discussions of Jewish legal practice in the first century.

Eron holds that Jesus/Yeshua's approach to the Law was colored by the eschatological focus of his teachings. The sense that the Dominion of Heaven was soon to arrive led Jesus/Yeshua to support both hyperobservance of the Law and selective disobedience.

YESHUA: MESSIAH? CHRIST? HUMAN? DIVINE?

Leonard Swidler explores some of the implications for Christian theology of his interest in the historical Jesus. He differentiates between the "teaching Yeshua" or the "Yeshua of history" and the "taught Christ" or the "Christ of faith." Swidler believes that doctrines and beliefs concerning Jesus Christ must have their basis in the best image of the historical Yeshua that scholarship can produce. Swidler gives priority to what Yeshua thought, taught, and wrought over later reactions to him and doctrines about him.

Swidler's desire to base Christian doctrines about Jesus Christ in the historical Yeshua leads him to attempt to expand the dogmatic formulas created by the ancient ecumenical councils. In the work of the councils he sees the attempts of the elders of the Church to express in Greek philosophical, ontological terms the Christian experience of meeting the human and divine in Yeshua of Nazareth.

Swidler believes that a formula reflecting the dialogic, existential language of today is more useful to contemporaries than the essentialist language of the conciliar declarations. In this light, he restates the Chalcedonian formula that "Jesus is 'truly a human being and truly God,' *vere homo et vere Deus*," as "Jesus is 'truly human and truly divine,' *vere humanus et vere divinus*."

Swidler discovered through his encounter with Buddhism—in which he saw a move toward ontological formulations similar to what he saw in Christianity—that the move to ontological language is an attempt to grasp the human experience of that which goes beyond the everyday, the transcendent. For Christians, Christology is the attempt to express in the believers' philosophical language and cultural categories the experience of the transcendent, of the divine, which they encounter preeminently through the figure of Yeshua. All Christologies are, therefore, time and culture bound.

Swidler argues that Christians should not simply reject Christology, for it plays an important role in their religious experience. Christologies, however, should not be seen as definitively capturing religious reality in a, necessarily, culturally fixed formula. Rather, Christians would be better served by their various Christologies if they understood them as pointing to a deeper, ineffable religious truth (the encounter with the transcendent through Yeshua), and continually sought to re-express that encounter in culturally contemporaneous categories. This ever-living theologizing will make Christology not only more meaningfully relevant to Christians but also more understandable to Jews and other non-Christians.

JESUS AND JUDAISM

Lewis Eron stresses that Jesus is tangential to Judaism and the Jewish experience. If Jesus has importance, it is historical importance. For Jews today, Jesus and his followers are part of the tradition of so-called sectarian Judaism that existed in the last few centuries B.C.E. and the first few centuries C.E. The study of Jesus and the New Testament casts light on a dimly lit period of Jewish life.

The vast majority of Jews never encountered the divine in Jesus either as an inspired teacher or as the redeeming Christ. The challenge Jews face today is not to reclaim Jesus but to reclaim Jewish traditions and heroes more closely tied to the Jewish experience than he.

Eron suggests a number of factors to explain why Jesus and his teachings were not remembered in the rabbinic tradition. The decisive factor for him was that after the fall of the Jerusalem Temple in 70 C.E., Jesus' teachings no longer answered the needs of the Jewish community. Although Jesus' ethical teachings can fit nicely within the teachings of the rabbis, his apocalyptic vision and lack of a usable social program with which one could have reconstructed Jewish life after the defeat made his message irrelevant to the Jewish people.

Eron concludes by holding that it is Jesus, the Christ of the Church, rather than Jesus, the Jew, that binds and separates Jews and Christians. It is because Christians have found access to God through Jesus that Jews and Christians can meet each other as religious people who approach the divine in ways that seem at the same time to be comfortably similar and excitingly different.

Select Annotated Bibliography on Jesus and Judaism

For the last century or so, Jewish writers have increasingly been writing about Jesus in a positive vein (*"Die Heimholung Jesu"*). The best survey of this literature through the first three-quarters of the twentieth century is by the Swedish Protestant Goesta Lindeskog, entitled *Die Jesusfrage im neuzeitlichen Judentum, ein Beitrag zur Geschichte der Leben-Jesu-Forschung.* Uppsala: 1938; reprint, with added material, Darmstadt, 1973. More recent Jewish writings on Jesus are treated thoroughly by the Jewish scholar Shalom Ben-Chorin, who wrote "The Image of Jesus in Modern Judaism," *Journal of Ecumenical Studies*, 11, 23 (Summer 1974), pp. 401–430. The most recent coverage is found in the work of the Evangelical Protestant Donald A. Hagner, *The Jewish Reclamation of Jesus* (Grand Rapids, MI: Zondervan Publishing House, 1988). Hagner's expressed evangelical faith positions are largely separable from his broad, sympathetic/critical scholarship in this helpful book.

Flusser, David. *Jesus*. New York: Herder & Herder, 1969.
This small book by a Jewish New Testament Israeli scholar proved to be a breakthrough writing in Jewish-Christian relations. Flusser's learned and sympathetic presentation of Jesus as totally Jewish drew both Christians and Jews closer to him, and hence to each other. Still a good, brief introduction to the genre.

Havener, Ivan. *Q. The Sayings of Jesus*. Wilmington, DE: Michael Glazier, 1987.
This is a careful, scholarly, but very readable, analysis by a Catholic scholar of the sayings of Jesus known as "Q" that are embedded in the Gospels of Matthew and Luke. The Q community was the earliest Christian community (all Jews of course), of which we have any knowledge, who saw Jesus as a prophet, never as "the proclaimed" but rather always "the proclaimer." Q never referred to Jesus as the Christ; rather, salvation came through Jesus as revealing God and the kingdom. "The Q community was a group of Christian-Jews who knew of Jesus' death but attached no redemptive significance to it."

Kee, Howard Clark. *Jesus in History, An Approach to the Study of the Gospels*. New York: Harcourt, Brace, Jovanovich, 2nd ed., 1977.
This is a highly useful summary of the issues involved in the "search for the historical Jesus." Kee discusses and evaluates the evidence presented in the four gospels and the Q document and extra-biblical sources. He understands the various accounts of Jesus' life as witnesses to the faith of Christians at various stages of historical development rather than as kernels of objective historical information covered with various and conflicting religious claims. Nevertheless, Kee feels that

there is sufficient consistency within the various accounts of Jesus' life to enable him to draw a sketch of who Jesus may have been.

Lachs, Samuel Tobias. *A Rabbinic Commentary on the New Testament: The Gospels of Matthew, Mark and Luke*. Hoboken, NJ: Ktav Publishing House, and New York: Anti-Defamation League of B'nai B'rith, 1987.

Not only was Jesus a Jew, but the earliest groups of his followers came out of the Jewish community. Rabbinic materials, although composed and edited later than the compilation of the New Testament, contain earlier material and have been useful in illuminating the Jewish background to early Christian literature. Although not as detailed as Billerbeck's monumental work, *Kommentar zum Neuen Testament aus Talmud und Midrasch* (Munich, 1922–28; reprint, with Registerband, 1956), 4 vols., Lachs' work presents an English-speaking audience with an enlightening glimpse into the wealth of rabbinic sources without the strong anti-Jewish animus that marred Billerbeck's efforts.

Lapide, Pinchas. *Sermon on the Mount — Utopia or Program for Action?* Tr. by Arlene Anderson Swidler. Maryknoll, NY: Orbis Books, 1986.

Under the expert hands of Lapide, Jesus' "Sermon on the Mount" ceases to be eccentric, exotic and enigmatic; it becomes eminently sensible and practical. Lapide's knowledge of rabbinic writings and his ability to translate back into what must have been the original Semitic terms and phrases used by Jesus turns these mysteries to manifestos.

Lapide, Pinchas, and Ulrich Luz. *Jesus in Two Perspectives*. Tr. by Lawrence W. Denef. Minneapolis: Augsburg, 1985.

This is a more recent example of the dozens of creative books on the first century of our era written by Lapide in the last decade and a half. Steeped in both New Testament and rabbinic learning, the Orthodox Jew Lapide argues that Jesus did not declare himself to be the messiah, that the people of Israel did not reject him, and that Jesus never repudiated the Jewish people. The Protestant New Testament scholar Luz fundamentally agrees, and at times goes even further than Lapide: Christians can no longer think theologically in the ancient Greek fashion, but must return to the historical figure of Jesus — a Jew.

Lee, Bernard J. *The Galilean Jewishness of Jesus*. Mahwah, NJ: Paulist Press, 1988.

"There is little likelihood that Jesus had any conscious intention of founding a new religious institution either superseding Judaism or alongside it. . . . A Jewish sense of things early gave way to a rather more Greek sense of things as a framework for interpreting the meaning of Jesus." Since for this Catholic author the historical Jesus must be the basis of Christianity, it is vital to recover Jesus' *Galilean* Jewishness. He then proceeds to lay it out carefully. A sensitive, balanced work of honest scholarship.

O'Collins, Gerald, S.J. *What Are They Saying about Jesus?* New York: Paulist Press, 2nd ed., 1983.

Pawlikowski, John, O.S.M., *Christ in the Light of the Christian-Jewish Dialogue*. Mahwah, NJ: Paulist Press, 1982.

Borowitz, Eugene, *Contemporary Christologies, A Jewish Response*. New York: Paulist Press, 1980.

Jesus of Nazareth remains the focus of Christian theology. O'Collins presents a useful summary of current work by Christians on the meaning of Jesus as the Christ, i.e., Christology. Pawlikowski offers a more detailed study of contemporary Christian efforts in Christology, particularly in regard to the Jewish-Christian dialogue. Borowitz, a professor of theology at the Hebrew Union College/Jewish Institute of Religion in New York, provides a Jewish evaluation of contemporary Christian Christology, with a particular focus on ethical issues.

Rivkin, Ellis. *A Hidden Revolution*. Nashville: Abingdon, 1978.

The "hidden revolution" was accomplished by the Pharisees, according to the Jewish scholar Rivkin. Looking at the writings of Josephus, the New Testament, and the rabbinic writings, Rivkin finds a triad at the heart of Pharisaism: (1) the fatherly God so loved each individual soul that (2) he promised to save each soul and raise up each body of those (3) who followed his "instructions" (Torah). Rather than being opposed to Pharisaism, Jesus was very close to the best of it.

Sanders, E. P. *Jesus and Judaism*. Philadelphia: Fortress Press, 1985.

For the Protestant Sanders, we can know what Jesus "was out to accomplish . . . a lot about what he said, and that those two things make sense within the world of first-century Judaism." Sanders knows the New Testament and kindred materials, plus contemporary scholarship thereon, and the rabbinic and other Jewish materials. The result is a deep scholarly display of the utter Jewishness of Jesus: a charismatic, wonder-working teacher who preached the imminent coming of the Reign of God, without violence, especially for the oppressed, wherein even the wicked would have a place.

Sigal, Phillip. *The Halakhah of Jesus of Nazareth According to the Gospel of Matthew*. Lanham, MD: University Press of America, 1986.

This, unfortunately posthumous, monograph by a Jewish author is creative and controversial—probably the latter because of the former. Sigal sees as the forerunners of the post-70 C.E. rabbis not the Pharisees, as is customary, but a disparate group he calls the "proto-rabbis," of which both Jesus and his contemporary (and possibly, interlocutor!) Johanan ben Zakkai, the "founder" of rabbinic Judaism, were members. Jesus is learnedly presented as a charismatic, wonder-working, sagely reflective proto-rabbi. Sigal's challenges should be taken seriously.

Sloyan, Gerard S. *Jesus In Focus*. Mystic, CT: Twenty-Third Publications, 1983.

Written in an eminently readable style for a general public, though based on profound scholarship (deliberately printed without scholarly notes, however), this book presents Jesus at every turn as the committed Jew he was. *"Tolle, lege!"*

Sloyan, Gerard S. *The Jesus Tradition: Images of Jesus in the West*. Mystic, CT: Twenty-Third Publications, 1986.
Pelikan, Jaroslav, *Jesus Through the Centuries: His Place in the History of Culture*. New Haven: Yale University Press, 1985.

The image of Jesus has not remained static since the end of the apostolic period. As the earliest Christian communities produced images of Jesus in light of their own historical experiences and religious understandings, so have faithful Christians of all succeeding generations. The Protestant Pelikan's and the Catholic Sloyan's surveys of the evolving image of Jesus in the Christian experience are helpful, readable scholarly presentations.

Swidler, Leonard. *Yeshua: A Model for Moderns.* Kansas City, MO, 1988.
A presentation by a Catholic for the general reader, based on his scholarship, which claims that the historical Jesus (Yeshua) should be the measure of what it means to be Christian. Because that historical Yeshua turns out to be thoroughly Jewish, Swidler presents a detailed summary of contemporary scholarship on the Jewishness of Jesus, and draws implications for Christians. Yeshua's "feminist" attitude is spelled out, and the question of whether one can attain "salvation," i.e., live a (w)holy life, only through belief in Yeshua is answered in the negative.

Vermes, Geza. *Jesus the Jew.* Philadelphia: Fortress Press, 1981
This is an excellent scholarly analysis of the gospels by a man who was born into a secular Jewish family, became a Christian, a Catholic priest, and then returned religiously to his Jewish origins. He carefully analyzes the titles given to Jesus and finds the best description of him to be a wandering Galilean Jewish charismatic wonder-working teacher, who was totally Jewish, though of a particular sort, and obviously an extraordinary religious individual.

Vermes, Geza. *Jesus and the World of Judaism.* Philadelphia: Fortress Press, 1984.
Written a decade after his first book on the Jewishness of Jesus, Vermes here continues his analysis of the same topic. Like his previous book, this is a careful, scholarly presentation, a mine of keen insight and knowledge by a scholar who knows the New Testament, rabbinic writings and the Dead Sea scrolls intimately.

PART II

A Jewish-Christian Dialogue on Paul

Gerard Sloyan   **Lester Dean**

10

Introduction: The Problem of a Jew Talking about Paul

LESTER DEAN

"Paul an apostle of Christ Jesus to the church at. . . ." It was with words similar to these that Paul usually introduced himself in the letters that have become a part of the Christian New Testament,[1] and it is with these words that I think we should introduce our Jewish-Christian dialogue about Paul. We begin with these words not merely because Paul opened his letters in this autobiographical manner. The reason we begin with Paul's introduction is that the usual interpretation of this autobiographical statement is a point of contention between Jews and Christians. "Paul an apostle of Christ Jesus to the church" is read with respect and approval by Christians but is read with disrespect and disapproval by Jews.

How are these words usually *interpreted* by Christians and Jews? In the following ways: "Paul"—the man adopted this Greek name when he converted to Christianity; he no longer used the Hebrew name Saul since he no longer wanted to be identified as a Jew.

"An apostle of Christ Jesus"—Paul had become a Christian missionary; he was no longer a Jewish Pharisee. He now preached the "good news" about the savior of the world, about the need to have faith in the second person of the Trinity who had been crucified and resurrected; he no longer tried to earn righteousness by trying to do the impossible, follow the Jewish Law. He was now part of God's spiritual "Kingdom"; he no longer waited and no longer hoped for a human descendant of David who would reign over Israel as king in a national Kingdom of God.[2]

"To the church"—Paul now associated with, wrote to, and was accepted by Gentiles; he was no longer accepted by Jews, but instead was persecuted by them. He founded and supported the Christian church; he was no longer a member of the Jewish synagogue and visited the synagogue only to preach the gospel.

According to the usual understanding of these autobiographical words, Paul was a Christian apostle, an ex-Jew. For most Christians today, the majority of whom are non-Jews, Paul is a hero because he showed the error of Jewish claims of superiority. Judaism with its observance of the Law was actually inferior to Gentile Christianity with its faith in Christ.

From a Jewish perspective, Paul was an apostate. He had willingly forsaken his Jewish tradition for Christianity, had counseled other Jews likewise to forsake Judaism and convert to Christianity, and had hoped that all Jews would ultimately lose their Jewish identity and become Gentile Christians. This is the Paul we Jews usually hear about from Christians. This is the Paul who alienates the Jewish reader. "Saul, rabbi from the school of Hillel to the synagogue" is a person about whom Jews wish to read, a person who might be the topic of a dialogue between Jews and Christians, but not "Paul the apostle of Christ Jesus to the church."

Such an understanding of Paul hurts us as Jews and puts us on the defensive. We ask, "Why did this person forsake the tradition of his birth, the tradition in which he was schooled, the tradition which we continue to find so precious?" We wonder, "What would Paul think of us? Would he condemn us for continuing in the tradition he renounced?"

We usually hear the following reply from Christians: "Judaism is a legalistic religion. A person can be saved only through faith in Christ. That is why Paul gave up Judaism. Paul knew that it is wrong to remain Jewish and believed that God would condemn those Jews who did not convert as he did."

Neither Paul nor our Christian "friends" seem to understand why we continue to reject the one *they* claim to be *our* savior. We are reminded that Paul was a good Jew and that he even persecuted the Church—but then he found a better way, the true way, the only way. There can be no real dialogue between Jews and Christians about Paul the apostle of Christ Jesus. There can only be debates about why Paul forsook Judaism, and why we Jews do not likewise forsake it.

The problems between Jews and Christians that arise from the above understanding of "Paul the apostle of Christ Jesus" contrast sharply with Jewish-Christian dialogues about Jesus, such as the one between Lewis Eron and Leonard Swidler. Their dialogue, like many other discussions between Jews and Christians about Jesus in the past few decades, began by recalling that Jesus (like Paul) was born a Jew. But Jesus remained a Jew, lived as a Jew among Jews, worshiped as a Jew in the Temple and synagogues, taught as a Jew, chose disciples who were Jews, and addressed an audience that was predominantly composed of Jews. We Jews can hold dialogue with Christians about Jesus' life, teachings, and audience—for all these were Jewish. But when we turn to Paul, how can we hold dialogue with Christians about his life after he forsook Judaism, or his Gentile audience, or his Christian teachings that are so far removed from Judaism? We are now confronted with the Jew Jesus and the Christian Paul, with the common view that Paul forsook the religion of Jesus to create a religion about Jesus.

It is this religion about Jesus that we Jews find so perplexing. It is a religion which seems to have such different views from Judaism about God, humanity, and the world. We hear that Paul spoke of a humanity that sins and that needs God—we Jews also know that humanity sins and is in need of God's forgiveness. But then we hear that according to Paul people are enslaved by the power of Sin because of the first sin of Adam; they can never obey God and must have faith in Christ as the only way to be freed from the power of Sin.[3] Jews affirm that people have the ability to obey God, the ability to choose to do either good or evil.

We hear that Paul urged people to act correctly, especially to love one another—we Jews also are commanded to act correctly and to love one another. But then we hear that according to Paul the Law cannot be obeyed, was only temporary, and is no longer in effect. Those who try to obey the Law are opposed to God's will because they rely upon human effort rather than divine grace. We believe that God intended Jews to obey the Law and that we have the ability to obey it. We obey the Law not to gain salvation but because it is God's will.

We hear that Paul said that God wants to help all humanity—we Jews also believe that God wants to help humanity. But then we hear that Paul said that this divine help is available only through the vicarious sacrifice of Jesus, the son of God, who died for the sins of the world. Only those who believe in Jesus will be saved. Jews respond that there are many ways to find God. Not just Jews, but the righteous of all the nations will be saved.

We hear that according to Paul, God loves all humanity, both Jews and Gentiles—we Jews also believe God is the God of all the world, of both Jews and Gentiles. But then we hear that according to Paul we Jews are now cursed rather than loved, cut off from God because we rejected Jesus Christ. This we can never accept. YHWH, the LORD, is our God, and we are God's people.

To this religion about Jesus, we Jews have said, and continue to say, "No, this is not what we as Jews believe." Furthermore, we declare that the religion which Christians say that Paul described as Judaism, a legalistic religion of self-works, of earning one's place in God's kingdom, is not Judaism. It is neither our religion nor that of our ancestors. We reject Paul the apostle, his religion about Jesus, and his false portrayal of Judaism.

If such is the case, then why am I, a Jew, engaged in a dialogue about Paul? The answer is that even this most basic starting point of "Paul the apostle of Christ Jesus to the church," may be improperly understood. Simply translating *christos* as Christ, *apostolos* as apostle, and *ekklēsia* as church does an injustice to Paul, for to Paul these words did not have the specialized Christian meanings that they have today. The work of Krister

Stendahl, E. P. Sanders, Lloyd Gaston, and Paul van Buren[4] are especially helpful in showing the errors in the traditional Christian understanding of Paul's identity. Paul never spoke of a conversion from Judaism to Christianity. Rather, he spoke of a calling, a calling like that of the prophets of the Hebrew Scriptures. Paul was called to be God's messenger to the Gentiles, proclaiming a Jewish message about the Jew Jesus. He did not reject Judaism. Paul, at least in his own mind, never ceased to be a Jew and wrote from a Jewish perspective to his predominantly Gentile believers. "Paul the apostle of Christ Jesus" was still "Paul the Jew."

This is not to say that Paul's beliefs did not change because of his faith in Jesus as Christ, but only that he and those around him, both Jews and Gentiles, whether believers in Jesus or unbelievers, perceived the Jesus movement to be within Judaism. Paul was first of all a Jew. He was a Jew who believed that Jesus of Nazareth was the Christ, but he was still a Jew. It is this starting point that permits a Jewish-Christian dialogue about Paul. Paul the Jew has been lost to the Church because of the transformation of Paul from a Jew into a Christian. This has caused the meaning of Paul's words to be distorted. It is only by starting with the identity of Paul the Jew, and only with the help of Jews in dialogue with Christians, that Paul's words can be understood correctly.

There are at least three reasons why Jews are needed if Christians are to understand Paul's letters correctly. First, the words of Paul have a long history of Christian interpretation. Christians know what salvation, justification, redemption, faith, works of the law, sin, and grace mean. The meanings for these and other terms are derived from the various Christian traditions and their theological vocabularies. Jewish readers have alternative meanings for the same words, meanings derived from Jewish tradition and a Jewish theological vocabulary. Jews have been reluctant to suggest Jewish meanings for Paul because Paul was seen as a Christian and not as a Jew. But if we begin our study with a Jewish identity for Paul, then Jewish meanings can and should be used as the primary meanings for Paul's theological vocabulary. This does not mean that Pauline thought must be confined rigidly to first-century Jewish norms, even if such norms could be established. Paul's letters were shaped not only by Judaism, but also by his vision of the risen Christ. But if Paul was a Jew, then we should begin our reading of his writings by assuming that his vocabulary and ideas were comprehensible to first-century Jews, not twentieth-century Christians. This would not necessarily invalidate later Christian interpretations of Paul, but it would make the proper distinction between Paul's thought and the later interpretations.

A second reason why Jews are necessary for a study of Paul is that we are not bound to any particular interpretation of the message of Paul. Jews have not been a part of the numerous intra-Christian debates about Pauline theology. We offer a new perspective for understanding Paul; this perspective is not threatened by denominational disputes that concern Christians.

A Jewish interpretation of Paul is still an interpretation, and will not be free from all error, but it will probably not make the same errors that Christian interpretations have made. Considering the horrible anti-Jewish sentiment that has been fostered by many of the Christian interpretations of Paul, Christians should feel compelled to seek alternative understandings of Paul. It is important that Jews help Christians try to find an interpretation that is free of anti-Judaism.

A third reason why Jews are needed in the study of Paul is our greater sensitivity to erroneous understandings of Paul, especially those that deal with Paul's portrayal of first-century Judaism. There was considerable variety within Judaism at the time of Paul, and modern Judaism — or even early rabbinic Judaism — is probably quite different from at least some of the forms of Judaism Paul knew and described in his writings. Yet when we Jews hear about Paul's description of Judaism as legalistic and based upon self-works, we are astounded. This is neither what we believe today, nor what is found in the Hebrew Scriptures, nor what is found from any of the sources at the time of Paul. Those Christians who base their views of Judaism primarily upon the gospels and Paul probably do not see any problem with these descriptions of Judaism. Just as Jews have helped Christians see the Pharisees and other Jewish groups of the gospels in a less negative, more realistic way, we can also point out discrepancies in Christian views of Judaism derived from reading Paul.

A Jewish-Christian dialogue about Paul offers exciting possibilities for Christians. Although debates about the degree of similarity or dissimilarity remain, the search for the "historical Jesus" has yielded a charismatic Jewish teacher and healer of the first century. Many Christians wish to make this Jewish Jesus the center of their faith. Yet such a Jesus seems to be opposed to the Christ of the Christian tradition, a tradition that looks to Paul, among others, for support. But the tension that many now see between Jesus and Paul may be due to incorrect interpretations of Paul. A Jewish Paul, interpreted according to Jewish ideas, may prove to be in harmony with a Jewish Jesus. Rather than moving away from the religion of Jesus (first-century Judaism) to a religion about Jesus (first-century Christianity), Paul could have remained dedicated to the Jewish message and hopes of Jesus. These hopes did not change, but were now centered about God's action in the life, death, and resurrection of Jesus.

Dialogue between Jews and Christians about Paul will bring a better understanding of Paul's message and will foster a less anti-Jewish understanding of Paul's description of Judaism. The first result is primarily of interest to Christians, while the second is important to both Jews and Christians. But there are at least two other results of a Jewish-Christian dialogue about Paul that are especially valuable for Jews. First, since we now see Paul as a Jew, his activities and message belong not just to Christian thought and history, but also to our own Jewish thought and history. There are few primary sources for Judaism of this time. Those Pauline epistles judged to be authentic by biblical scholarship are valuable sources for first-century Judaism.

There is a second benefit for Jews from a study of Paul. Jewish tradition, especially after the consolidating work of the rabbis begun at Yavneh, did not accept most of the beliefs of Paul. Yet there has always been diversity in Judaism: in the Hebrew Scriptures, in the rabbinic literature, and in the different movements today. Paul, properly understood as a Jew and not as a Christian, would be a minority opinion within Jewish tradition. Perhaps, since we Jews today are facing problems similar to those faced by Paul—such as how to relate to non-Jews who are genuinely interested in Judaism—Paul may be of help. This is not to say that Paul's answers will necessarily be ours today, but at least we can learn from our past.

The task before us is great and we begin our dialogue not knowing what we will find when we seek Paul the Jew. Perhaps neither Christians nor Jews will approve of our results. Yet it seems doubtful that the ideas of Paul the Jew can be any more harmful to Jews than the Christian interpretations of Paul the apostle. At the least the disputes we Jews now may have with Paul will be seen as disputes among Jews, not disputes between Christians and Jews. What would Paul the Jew think of us Jews? What was his opinion of Torah and of Jewish obedience to Torah? In the past we have heard Paul the apostle; now let us hear Paul the Jew.

NOTES

1. Rom. 1:1, 1 Cor. 1:1, 2 Cor. 1:1, Gal. 1:1, Phil. 1:1.

2. The term "Kingdom of God" or "Kingdom of Heaven" is a literal translation of the Greek *basileia tou theou* and the Hebrew *malchut ha shamayim*. The term is prominent in the gospels and in Christian and Jewish liturgies. In the previous dialogue between Eron and Swidler the term was translated as the "Dominion" or "Reign of God." Such a translation is grammatically possible, and perhaps preferable to "Kingdom of God" when used to refer to the message of Jesus, since many believe that Jesus was describing God's rule now, and not a re-established eschatological national kingdom of Israel ruled by a messianic king. However, when used in this dialogue about Paul, the "Kingdom of God" is meant to refer explicitly to that hope for a national kingdom. "Dominion of God" is too general a term and lacks the ties to Jewish and Christian eschatological traditions.

3. One of the first rules in dialogue is to allow one's partner to define his or her religious tradition. The following discussion is not meant to represent any given Christian tradition accurately, but to point to areas that Jews have found problematic. Some, perhaps all, may be Jewish misunderstandings that can be corrected through dialogue. At this point it is sufficient that these problem areas exist and are often based upon the teachings of Paul.

4. See the annotated bibliography for these and other relevant works on Paul.

11

Did Paul Represent or Misrepresent the Judaism of His Time?

GERARD SLOYAN

If we knew the total structure of Judaism of the first century of the Common Era, we could discuss this topic better. We do not know it well at all—we only know what it came to be two centuries later. We know that it developed into nothing like the content of Paul's letters, or the way he argued the meaning of the Jewish experience. It is easy to charge him with being thoroughly untypical of his time. But he had known Jesus Christ risen and lived him daily for at least fifteen years before we learn of the first piece of Pauline correspondence. The Jewish community, first apprehensive over the gathering Roman storm and then reeling from the blows of two imperial attacks (70 and 135 C.E.), had an entirely different experience from Paul's. Remember, he drops out of the scene in Rome around the year 60, while those bitter, destructive experiences that Jews mourn on the ninth day of Ab would not occur for another ten and another seventy-five years. The outcome in the writings Paul and the rabbis produced—his sparse, theirs voluminous—was totally different.

How would Paul have carried on his correspondence if he had remained a Jewish proselytizer, let us say in the mold of Shammai in a variety of diaspora settings? We do not know. Would his epistolary style have resembled that of the opinions attributed to Shammai? Would he have responded in a fiery way to all attempts to bring his new pagan adherents to Judaism to Hillelite positions? We can at best speculate on how he would have acted on the basis of the letters we have. It is, however, basically idle to speculate about the content of his correspondence in other circumstances, for in such a hypothesis he would not have "seen Jesus our Lord"

(1 Cor. 9:1). That vision of the Risen One made everything different for him.

Two bodies of evidence would be needed to answer the question of how Paul might have fit into the Judaism of his time, assuming his remaining within its ambit, imperfectly as we know it. He was a very young man when he was the zealous, observant Pharisee he claimed to be (Phil. 3:5–6). We would need to know something of how rabbinical argument was carried on by his peers who were engaged in the same venture as he. Any Jewish prose calculated to convince non-Jews of the worth of Judaism *from that period* would do. We do not have it.

Something even more helpful would be a contemporary account of what Jews did to keep the Law in its fullness, and whether there was a radical Judaism abroad that thought itself completely Jewish despite a quite different approach to observance. We assume that the Stephen party of Acts — Greek-speaking Jews, all — derives from an anti-Temple wing of Judaism that also had problems with modes of law observance among Aramaic-speaking Jews. But how different was it actually? Paul's belief in Christ Risen forced him from the one way of Judaism he clung to, Pharisaism (we have no hard evidence to say that it "became rabbinic Judaism"), to face the spectrum of legitimate ways to be Jewish. Was what we know from Acts of Hellenistic Jews in Jerusalem one such way?

St. Paul has been accused constantly by Jews over the ages of not adhering to the ancient faith. His response would surely be that after coming to believe in Jesus he did so more profoundly than ever before. Granted, his resurrection faith relativized everything for him. But it could not have relativized out of existence the allowable limits of being Jewish. In view of God's promises to his forebears he would have thought that impossible.

What were those limits? Did they change so notably for Paul after he became a "believer" (*pistos*) that no Jew could recognize them? If that were so it would hardly have advanced his cause. This was especially true since the Jewish church of Jerusalem, led by James, for all we know lived at perfect ease in the midst of fellow Jews. Believers in Jesus though they were, they knew that by that fact, coupled with their presumed adherence to *halakhah*, they were displaying one way to be Jewish. Paul to his last breath would have maintained that he was showing another.

A Response to Gerard Sloyan from Lester Dean

Throughout our discussion of Paul we must be aware of the limits of our knowledge. Sloyan correctly draws our attention to that limitation. When we consider the degree to which long-held views of Judaism and Christianity were altered and amended because of the relatively recent discovery of the Gnostic and Essene libraries at Nag Hammadai and Qumran, respectively,

I doubt that we can overemphasize our lack of knowledge. Perhaps in a few years the questions raised in our dialogue will be meaningless because of discoveries that will provide indisputable answers.

I agree with Sloyan that there is little to be gained by speculating on what Paul would have done or written had he not come to believe in Jesus as the Christ. There could be some benefit in attempting to determine his earlier Jewish background, for we would learn whether he might have been from the school of Shammai, the school of Hillel, or the school of some other as yet unknown rabbi. Since we know very little about the divisions within the early rabbinic movement, it is possible that we can learn more about these groups by studying Paul than we can learn about Paul by studying these rabbinic groups. Unfortunately, Christian interpretations of Paul have kept Jews from using his work as a legitimate source for Jewish history. I hope that this dialogue will help Jews have a new appreciation of Paul and his value for Jewish studies.

Clearly there were numerous Jewish groups in existence at the time of Paul, and these groups had different levels of Torah observance. At this time we do not know which of these Jewish groups Paul might have known, which groups he would have condoned, and which he would have condemned. Despite such lacks, I do think we can make some comparisons between Paul's writings and the Judaisms of his time, especially since Christians so often use Paul's writings as a source for their description of Judaism. What Christians and Jews both should remember is that Paul's letters are not an accurate description of Judaism, because of Paul's emphasis on Torah to the point of almost excluding all else. The gospels should not be used to create a biography of Jesus because they were not written with that intention. Likewise, Paul's letters should not be used to create a description of Judaism. That was not Paul's intention.

Sloyan suggests that Paul might be connected with the Stephen group. According to the author of Acts, Paul was present at the death of Stephen. However, I think that the suggested connection is founded not upon the possibility of Paul's participation in the martyrdom of Stephen, but upon certain alleged similarities between Paul's letters and the speech of Stephen found in Acts 7, especially an alleged common anti-Torah and anti-Temple sentiment. Although such a connection has been suggested by several scholars, I think that the so-called similarities are founded upon past Christian misunderstandings of both Paul and the book of Acts.

A lengthy discussion of the Stephen party of Acts is impossible within the limits of this dialogue. Such a discussion ought to include the difficult problems of determining the historical accuracy of the book of Acts. We should not accept uncritically the existence of an anti-Temple Stephen movement merely because such a group is described in Acts.[1]

According to Acts, written by a Gentile several decades after Paul, Stephen was a Hellenist and not a Hebrew, whatever those terms might have meant. The Stephen anti-Temple, anti-Torah party is a hypothesis based upon the charges of Stephen's opponents who claimed that he spoke "blasphemous words against God and Moses." According to the accusation, he spoke "words against this holy place and the law; for we have heard him say that this Jesus of Nazareth will destroy this place, and will change the customs which Moses delivered to us" (6:11–15). If these charges were true, and if the usual view of Paul is true—that he was also opposed to the Torah—then Paul and Stephen would be in agreement.

However, according to the author of Acts, the words quoted above are the words of men who were "secretly instigated" by Stephen's opponents. These are charges brought against Stephen, not the words of Stephen, and the readers were not intended to believe these charges. These charges, like all the charges brought against Jesus, Peter, Paul, and other Christians in the two volumes of Luke-Acts were introduced in order to be disproven. Even if they accurately recall the accusations made against Stephen, and there is considerable doubt about this, they should not be used as proof that there was an anti-Torah, anti-Temple movement within the early Christian movement. They show only that some outsiders erroneously described the movement in such a way. Unfortunately, the author of Acts did not know that these false charges against Stephen—and also Paul—would be accepted as fact when Christianity itself adopted an anti-Temple and anti-Torah stance.

When we look at the words of Stephen found in Acts, we find nothing to indicate that he spoke against either Moses or Jewish tradition. Rather, Moses is cited as the first of many whom the Jews rejected. He received "the oracles of life" to give to the Jews. Nor did Stephen speak against the temple sacrifices, the temple priesthood, or the temple building. He only quoted Isaiah 66:1–2, that God did not dwell in the temple; these verses would have been acceptable to all Jews. There is no evidence from this work that Stephen was opposed to Torah.

Stephen did claim that some Jews did not follow Torah and had killed Jesus. Paul made similar statements, but I think it probable that these were generally accepted views held by most within the Christian movement. They do not show a connection between Paul and a hypothetical Stephen group.

To return to Paul, he definitely believed that he was living a proper Jewish life. His experience of "the risen Christ" changed his life, and thus in some way changed his Judaism, although I would hesitate to agree with Sloyan that he was forced into a different form of Judaism from the Pharisaism of his youth. I am also not as sure as Sloyan that Judaism developed into "nothing like the content of Paul's letters." It is easy to see differences between Paul and later Judaism, especially if one wants to emphasize dissimilarity. But there are also similarities. What is important is that Paul felt he was within Jewish teaching. I do agree with Sloyan that it is not correct for Jews to criticize Paul for not being identical with later rabbinic thought.

Did Paul's belief in Christ force him outside of Judaism? Not in his opinion. Did it force Paul outside of what Jews at that period could accept? I agree with Sloyan that it did not. Did Paul's belief in Christ force him into a form of Judaism different from that of the Jerusalem church? Our sources of information for the Jerusalem church are so limited that we can only speculate. There were probably differences, but I tend to see more similarity among Paul and the other apostles than most Christian scholars see.[2] Finally, did Paul's vision of Christ force him outside of what we Jews today can accept? That we have yet to determine.

NOTES

1. See Johannes Munck, *Paul and the Salvation of Mankind* (Atlanta: John Knox Press, 1959), pp. 218–228. Although Munck focuses primarily on Stephen's speech in Acts 7, his conclusion is the same as is presented here, "nothing is related by Luke about Stephen (and the Hellenists) that has not already been related about Jesus; and we thus have to suppose that there was, according to Luke's sources and his own conception of the facts, no contrast between Jesus, Stephen, and the original Church as such," p. 225. I would only add Paul to the list (at least according to the view of the author of Luke-Acts).

2. For a recent example, "The theology of Paul and the theology of Jerusalem are completely different," Lloyd Gaston, *Paul and the Torah* (Vancouver: University of British Columbia Press, 1987), pp. 114–115. Munck is an exception: "No conflict existed between Jewish Christianity and Paul," *Paul and the Salvation of Mankind*, p. 279.

12

Paul's "Erroneous" Description of Judaism

LESTER DEAN

We know from Paul's autobiographical statements that he was born a Jew from the tribe of Benjamin (Phil. 3:5–6). Not only was he raised as a Pharisee, but he claimed to have been "advanced in Judaism" and "zealous for the tradition of his ancestors" (Gal. 1:14). Paul's Jewish roots are not disputed by either Jews or Christians.

Paul claimed to have been "called to be an apostle" in order to preach Christ "among the Gentiles"[1] (Gal. 1–2). He included this prophet-like commission in the letters he wrote to the assemblies of believers in Jesus outside Palestine. Except for Rome, these assemblies (which we might call churches, provided we do not equate the word *church* with our modern definition) had been established by Paul. Most of the members of these churches were Gentiles. Throughout our dialogue it is important to remember that Paul himself affirmed that his preaching of the gospel was intended for Gentiles, whereas Peter and others had been entrusted with the gospel to the Jews (Gal. 2:7–8). Thus, Paul's remarks were addressed first of all to Gentiles. The purpose of his letters was to solve problems that grew out of that mission to the Gentiles. He aimed to give ethical instruction to Gentiles, to justify his mission to the Gentiles, to discuss the relationship of Gentiles and Jews in the new Christian communities, and to explain the differences between the covenant requirements of Jews (following all the commandments of Torah) and the covenant requirements of Gentiles (following the commandment to love one another).

Although Paul's audience was composed primarily and perhaps almost exclusively of Gentiles, he made numerous references to Jews and to their religious beliefs and practices. We might call those beliefs and practices Judaism, provided we remember that Paul lived in the first century of the

136

Common Era. The Judaism—perhaps it would be better for us to say Judaisms—that Paul knew was related to the Judaism that the rabbis would create, but was far from identical to it.

Christians often base their knowledge of Judaism upon a study of the Christian Bible, centering upon their "Old Testament," the four gospels, and the letters of Paul. Unfortunately, the Hebrew Bible describes just the religion of ancient Israel, a religion far removed from either first-century or modern Judaism. The gospels are also a poor source for a description of Judaism. They are polemical responses, written to demonstrate the messianic identity of Jesus of Nazareth, an identity which most Jews did not accept then and do not accept now. In the gospels, the Jews and their religion are the counterparts to Jesus, often the direct opponents of Jesus. We can learn much about the early Christian communities' views of Judaism from the gospels, but we can learn little about Judaism itself.

Paul's letters are the third source of information about Judaism within the Christian canon. Many Christians use Paul's statements contrasting faith and the Law as a basis for understanding Judaism. When Paul wrote his letters to the Galatians and to the Romans, he argued that a person was "justified by faith," and "not by works of the Law." These verses are often quoted by Christians to show the superiority of Christianity over Judaism. Paul, the one-time Pharisee who persecuted the church, now proved that Judaism was wrong. Christians expected Paul the apostle to criticize the religion he had abandoned, and their reading of these verses fulfilled their expectations.

Based upon Paul's statements about faith and works of the Law, Christians have traditionally viewed Judaism as a legalistic religion of works in which one tries to earn God's favor. According to this description, Jews strive for righteousness by trying to follow the commandments of the "Old Testament." Christians knew that these commandments were impossible to obey perfectly because of "original sin"—a doctrine that Augustine derived from a poor Latin translation of Romans 5:12–14. The result of the Jews' attempt to obey the Law must be failure. Honest Jews should cry out in dismay as Paul did, "the very commandment which promised life proved to be death to me" (Rom. 7:10). This dismay should then have led Jews to an awareness of the inadequacy of Judaism and the need for faith in Christ.

Yet most Jews, from the time of Paul onward, did not seem to realize their impossible position, that of trying to obey the Law that they could never perfectly obey. Instead, Jews claimed to be righteous and to follow the Law. Since such claims were impossible according to Christian beliefs, Jews were either ignorant of their mistakes or else deliberately lying. At best, Jews must be blind self-righteous boasters. Christians reading Paul found what appeared to be a similar description of blind and boastful Jews: "You who boast in the law, do you dishonor God by breaking the law?" (Rom. 2:23). At the worst, since Jews were "a disobedient and contrary people" (Rom. 10:21), Christians claimed that Jews knew of their disobedience and deliberately rejected God and God's offer of forgiveness through faith in Christ.

Such a description of Judaism has always been challenged by Jews either as a misunderstanding of Judaism arising from Christian ignorance or, perhaps, as a deliberate misrepresentation of Judaism arising from the need to show the superiority of Christianity over Judaism. Judaism is not a legalistic religion, and Jews do not follow Torah, the Law, in order to boast about their ability to fulfill God's commands.

Although Jews do try to observe Torah, their observance of the Law does not mean that Jews are trying to "work their way into heaven." A Jew's relationship to God is based upon God's covenant established with the Israelites and their descendants. Jews believe this covenant is a covenant of grace, just as Christians believe the covenant of the "New Testament" is a covenant of grace. Both the Hebrew Scriptures and rabbinic literature affirm that the Jews did nothing to earn this relationship with God; it was God's choice. Thus a Jew's righteousness does not come from observance of Torah; it comes from being a part of God's covenant people.[2]

According to Jewish tradition, the commandments of Torah are considered to be divine rules of proper Jewish conduct binding upon all who are a part of God's covenant established at Sinai. Observance of Torah means that a Jew is obedient to God; nonobservance means that a Jew is disobedient to God. Observance is not something of which a Jew can boast; rather, it is the expected behavior. Observing Torah does not make the Jew righteous; but nonobservance shows that the Jew is disobedient and has violated the rules of the covenant with God. Disobedience can result in the loss of that covenant relationship with God unless the Jew seeks forgiveness, relying upon God's covenantal faithfulness and mercy.

Jews respond that Christian descriptions of Judaism derived from Paul are wrong. Judaism today is not legalistic, and no evidence for any form of legalistic Judaism has as yet been found in any other literature, including those few sources for the Judaism of the time of Paul. Thus, there is a discrepancy between the description of Judaism found by a Christian interpretation of Paul and the description of Judaism derived both from Jews themselves and from the literature of the period. This discrepancy can be explained in several ways. Perhaps Paul was describing a form of Judaism that is unknown to us today.[3] Perhaps Paul misunderstood the Judaism of his time. Or perhaps "Jewish legalism" was not what Paul was describing. I think that the latter is the most probable.

We should first remember that Paul did not intend to present an exhaustive description of Judaism. His statements about Judaism arose from the needs and situations of the congregations to which he wrote. In some passages he answered questions about Judaism posed to him by his Gentile audience (Rom. 10–11). At other times he countered the arguments of Jews opposed to the Christian movement (Rom. 2–3). In certain situations he quoted Jewish teaching in response to the "other gospel" which was preached by "false brethren" (Gal. 1–2). Finally, sometimes Paul introduced Jews and Judaism in order to explain his mission of preaching the gospel to the Gentiles (Rom. 4:9). We should not expect Paul's writings to present either a single or a comprehensive view of Judaism.

Nevertheless, certain terms are surprisingly absent from Paul's letters. *Covenant, repentance, sacrifice,* and *expiation* are seldom found in Paul's writing; yet these words were an integral part of Judaism at this time. On the other hand, the Greek word *nomos*, usually understood to be the equivalent of the Hebrew word *Torah*, and usually translated as Law, was mentioned frequently by Paul. Although Torah usually has a broad meaning for most Jews, a meaning that would include God's law, God's instruction, God's promises, and the history of God's actions with Israel, Paul seems to have overemphasized the legal meaning of Torah. This emphasis upon Torah as Law, accompanied by the neglect of covenant, repentance, sacrifice, and expiation, which should have been understood as part of Torah, necessarily means that a description of Judaism based solely upon Paul will be erroneous.[4] A reader of Paul would easily think that Torah was the only important element of Judaism.

Paul argued in both Romans and Galatians that a person was justified by God because of Christ's faithfulness and not by the works of the Law.[5] The usual interpretation of this is that a person could not rely upon human effort in order to be righteous before God. Rather, a person must be a part of God's gracious covenant made available through Christ. This relationship between righteousness and grace is almost identical to the relationship found in Judaism where righteousness is attained by one's participation in the covenant that God had graciously established at Sinai. The difference between Judaism and Paul is that Paul emphasized the covenant God established through Christ, rather than the covenant God established at Sinai; by contrast, there is agreement between Paul and Judaism about the relationship between Law and righteousness.

There is no evidence to support the view that Paul was attacking the accepted Jewish teaching of his time when he discussed the relationship between Law and righteousness. Since we have no indication that Jews thought that following the Law made them righteous, the most probable interpretation of Paul's discussion of Law and righteousness is that he was attacking a deviation from Jewish teaching. Perhaps some Jews had modified the relationship between Torah and righteousness in their missionary preaching to the Gentiles. Or perhaps some Gentiles had misunderstood the message of Paul or other Jews. Regardless of the source of the misunderstanding, we can conclude that Paul's Gentile converts were in error about Judaism, and Paul was refuting the resultant heresy by quoting Jewish teaching.

Although there is no disagreement between Paul and Judaism over the relationship among righteousness, grace, and the Law, there may be a difference in the meaning of righteousness (in Greek, *dikaiosunē*, in Hebrew, *tzadeka*). In Judaism, the word righteousness was primarily used to refer to the maintenance of the covenant status. A Jew was righteous as long as the covenant obligations were fulfilled—that is, as long as Torah was obeyed.[6]

Paul often used the word righteousness to refer to one's becoming part of the people of God; the person had been a sinner but was now righteous.[7] This use must have been derived from the original Jewish definition of righteousness as maintaining the covenant relationship. There was no term to describe a Jew's becoming part of the covenant people, for a Jew was born into the covenant. In contrast, Gentiles did not have a covenant relationship with God and were not part of God's people. According to Paul, God established a covenant with the Gentile believer in Christ. Such a person was now righteous and had a correct relationship with God. A Gentile who had faith in Christ did not have to convert to Judaism and become a Jew in order to become part of the people of God. Fidelity to Torah was the Jewish response to God's covenant, but it was neither a requirement for Gentiles to enter into the covenant with God nor a requirement for the Gentile after he or she had become a part of the Christian community.

Paul was also concerned with Christian believers' actions now that they were part of the people of God. In these cases he would have used the usual Jewish meaning of righteousness: the correct behavior which the covenant relationship demands. It is at this point that disagreement *may* exist between Paul and Judaism. For Judaism, maintaining the covenant is impossible apart from Torah. Yet Paul seemed, at certain times, to be opposed to Torah. Since opposition to Torah would be opposition to Judaism, we must next examine Paul's views of Torah.

A Response to Lester Dean from Gerard Sloyan

This treatment makes clear the variety of Judaisms abroad in Paul's day open to persons living under the covenant. It provides a reminder that the religion of Israel would receive a relative homogeneity only in the age of the *Tannaim* (composers of the Mishnah, edited c. 180 C.E.). Similarly, the understanding of the religion of Israel among the Gentile Christians who professed faith in its Scriptures would go in a direction that Jews would find unrecognizable. By the second century, the two communities were assigning meanings to the same, by then archaic, literature from two widely divergent points of view.

Although the Judaism of the youthful, self-described Pharisee Paul is irrecoverable, the possibility exists that it and not the observance of most of his contemporaries under the covenant was "legalist" and not merely legal. Paul's faith in Christ might then have returned him to the observance of Torah as Law in a way that was Israel's glory, as he repudiated the exaggerated observance of early manhood. In hypothesizing thus, one assumes that Pharisaism was not the forerunner of rabbinic Judaism, as the convention in modern scholarship has it.

If anything surprises me about Dean's corrective remarks in this section it is the seeming denial that Torah, understood as Law, was the most important element in the Judaism to which Paul adhered. Indeed, this halakhic understanding would shortly come to prevail, and not the aggadic-prophetic one that the Christians espoused. The charge of legalism is a heavy burden for any Jew to bear. One can only be sympathetic to efforts to be rid of it. It is, however, just as much an albatross around the Christian neck, although Christians are slow to realize this.

Jews generally, in this writer's experience, do not point to "covenant, repentance, sacrifices, and atonement" as if these were to be distinguished from Torah. This is not a usual way to respond to the false charge of legalism. Rather, faithful adherence to Torah follows covenanted status, as Dean stresses throughout, while repentance and its first-century expression in expiatory sacrifice fall within fidelity to Torah.

All Christians bear the weight of nineteen centuries of interpretation that pitted Paul's new condition of faith in Christ against his former one of "gain" that he came to count as "loss" (see Phil. 3:7–9). The contrast was never identified to the present writer in his formative years, however, as a direct antithesis between Law and grace. That is because he was reared in the Church to which the reformers were chiefly addressing themselves, and not to the Jews of sixteenth-century Europe, when the Pauline theology of polar opposites received its modern form. Catholic antagonism to Jews and Judaism before and since the Reformation has been quite shameful enough. I only make the point that the Paul of Christian tradition whom Dean describes so accurately (as contrasted with the historical Paul these essays are in search of) is not the Paul of every Christian tradition. I accept the burden of guilt of my Catholic forebears, while pointing out that it did not take the precise theological form here described nor indeed the "common Christian interpretation" at several points that Dean describes as a given.

As to the careful sorting out of the relation of faith, grace, and works in Judaism—so near-identical with that of the Western Catholic tradition with its edifice of law (as contrasted with legalism, a pejorative term to both Jews and Catholics)—I am grateful. I continue to speculate as to why Paul's use of *dikaiosunē/tzadeka* differed from that of the more familiar meaning of maintaining covenant status. Perhaps no one knows why, for lack of data contemporaneous with his career. But the term must have had some special force that recommended it to Paul for the extensive argument he mounted in Galatians and Romans. The simple extension of the normal use of the term to describe a Jew's becoming part of the covenanted people does not seem a sufficient explanation. One has to conclude its currency somewhere in the sense in which Paul employed it.

NOTES

1. See Krister Stendahl, *Paul Among Jews and Gentiles* (Philadelphia: Fortress Press, 1976), pp. 7–23, for a discussion of Paul's calling in contrast to the traditional interpretation of his conversion.

2. See E. P. Sanders, *Paul and Palestinian Judaism* (Philadelphia: Fortress Press, 1977) for the most thorough treatment of the error of claiming that Judaism was legalistic.

3. For example, Montefiore suggested that Paul was describing an inferior Hellenistic form of Judaism, while rabbinic Judaism descended from Palestinian Judaism; see: *Judaism and St. Paul* (London: Goschen, 1914), pp. 112–129; likewise, Parkes, *Jesus, Paul, and the Jews* (London, 1936), pp. 120–123, Sandmel, *The Genius of Paul* (New York: Farrar, Straus, & Cudahy, 1958), p. 59, and Schoeps, *Paul: The Theology of the Apostle in the Light of Jewish Religious History* (Philadelphia: Westminster Press, 1961). W. D. Davies' compelling criticism of this arbitrary division between Palestinian and Hellenistic Judaism shows the inadequacy of Hellenistic Judaism as the solution to understanding Paul; see: *Paul and Rabbinic Judaism* (Philadelphia: Fortress Press, 1980), pp. 1–16.

4. However, it is wrong to conclude that the lack of these words necessarily means a lack of continuity between Paul and Judaism as was argued by Montefiore in, *Judaism and St. Paul*, pp. 60–75, and more recently, J. Christiaan Beker, *Paul the Apostle* (Philadelphia: Fortress, 1980), pp. 182–183, and Gaston, *Paul and the Torah* (Vancouver: University of British Columbia Press, 1987), pp. 114–115. Paul was writing to Gentiles about Gentile problems. We would expect his statements about Judaism to be incomplete.

5. Some of the scholars who argue that *pistis Christou* should be translated as the faithfulness of Christ rather than faith in Christ are: M. Barth, "The Kerygma of Galatians," *Interpretation* 21 (1967), pp. 131–163; G. Howard, "On the Faith of Christ," *Harvard Theology Review* 60 (1967), pp. 459–484; J. J. O'Rourke, "*Pistis* in Romans," *Catholic Biblical Quarterly* 36 (1973), pp. 188–196; G. M. Taylor, "The Function of *Pistis Christou* in Galatians," *Journal of Biblical Literature* 85 (1966), pp. 58–76; R. B. Hays, *The Faith of Jesus Christ* (Chico, CA: Scholars Press, 1983).

6. Sanders, *Paul and Palestinian Judaism*, p. 205.

7. E. P. Sanders, *Paul, the Law, and the Jewish People* (Philadelphia: Fortress Press, 1983), pp. 6–9.

13

Did Paul Have Any Problems with the Law?

GERARD SLOYAN

Jews of all centuries since the first C.E., if they have heard of Paul of Tarsus at all, have heard of him as a false Jew, a betrayer of his people, the architect of a new religion. They have assigned all sorts of motives to his behavior. What is commonly agreed upon is that he attacked the Law of Moses directly, saying that it was no longer binding on Jews. Christians of all the ages, not knowing the full measure of Jewish antipathy to Paul, have nonetheless unconsciously agreed with Jews that Paul taught the abrogation of the Law with the coming of Christ. Some have said that his epistles, the text of which they at least knew, emphasized the replacement of the Law by grace. The works of the Law justified no one, they said, not only since the days of Jesus Christ; they had *never* done so. Jews had a legal religion that Paul correctly identified once Christ had been revealed to him. He saw its shortcomings precisely in that it was a set of precepts and demands. Believers in Jesus Christ had been liberated from all these. The cross had brought freedom where there had been slavery. The written letter that kills had yielded to a Spirit that gives life in a new covenant (2 Cor. 3:6). "The ministry of death carved in writing on stone [although] inaugurated in glory, [yields to] the greater glory of the ministry of the Spirit" (vv. 7–8). The former covenant condemned; the new ministry justifies (v. 9).

These statements of Paul, which I have quoted or paraphrased, seemed crystal clear to a Gentile church. He was their champion, after all, unlike Peter and James who had mysteriously devised an accommodation to the Law for Jewish believers in Jesus Christ. These apostles left almost no trace of "Jewish Christianity," so it is impossible to know exactly how they had come to terms with Law observance in the Palestinian churches. But the superseding of Jews by Gentiles in the Pauline churches, indeed everywhere, seemed to be the logical outcome of Paul's theory that a new covenant had replaced the old (2 Cor. 3:6) and that the alternative was a spirit of slavery leading back into fear (Rom. 8:15).

There is no evidence from Paul's letters that he found it hard to keep the Law and hence that he turned to a new covenant of grace as a means of being delivered from despair. This construction was put on his actions by an anxious late medieval Church that was going through crises of spirit not unlike those of Augustine's day, first as the Empire approached dissolution and later as Europe was rocked by the Black Death and the breakup of feudal society.

Paul had a large problem with Cephas' yielding to the circumcision party after having "lived like a Gentile" (Gal. 2:14) in Antioch regarding food laws. The immediate impression one can derive from this is that Cephas was expected to desert kosher laws, as a demand of his new faith in Jesus Christ. But a careful reading of Galatians shows that Paul and Cephas, "Jews by birth" (v. 15), are at fault in observing the dietary precepts only if they think that these works of the law justify and not faith in Christ alone. The only thing wrong with the Law, in Paul's mind, is that it is not Christ. He has been led by it to die to it (v. 19) in the sense that without being brought to Christ by it he could not know that its binding force on him is over. Paul's one fear is to nullify the grace of God, "for if justification were through the Law, then Christ died to no purpose"(v. 21).

Paul's declaration that his Galatian backsliders are under a curse if they rely on works of the law (3:10) is strong language. It is probably stronger than he would have used were he not enraged by the bad bargain that "some who trouble them and want to pervert them" (1:7) had tricked them into: works for faith, an unimproved state for justification. His starting point is that the grace of God in Jesus Christ is a free gift, not something that can be earned. It was held out to Abraham by God's promise. Hence, any hint that one is justified by the Law as one's inheritance, one's due, is false. That is why Paul makes its deliverance on Sinai a stop-gap caused by human transgressions. It had worth, to be sure, the worth of alerting Jews to their sinfulness while they awaited the fulfillment of God's promise through Abraham's seed (Gal. 3:19–29).

When one examines all the uncomplimentary things that Paul says about Law observance—his estimate of which continues to offend the Jewish soul—one sees that the flaws he finds in it are never absolute but always relative. He never defines the Law by what it is or by what it can accomplish, but by what it is not and what it cannot accomplish. It is not Christ. Only faith in him justifies.

Some thoughtful scholars have maintained that, since Paul's chief opponents are those who would lead his Gentiles astray, his strictures against the Law do not apply to Jews. Paul's strictures do not apply on the same terms. But they do apply. For him, Law observance does not put anyone in a right relation with God. Only faith in Jesus Christ does that.

A Response to Gerard Sloyan from Lester Dean

Sloyan begins his remarks by noting that most Jews who have heard about Paul believe he betrayed his people and his faith for Christianity. In my introduction to our dialogue I also criticize this common view of Paul and discuss some reasons why Jews should study Paul's writings. However, I think it is important to remember that Jews have heard about Paul primarily from Christians. Paul's letters indicate that even during his lifetime his message was misunderstood by both Jews, Gentile Christians, and Jewish Christians. However, after the first century the misunderstanding of Paul continued because of faulty Christian interpretations to which Jews listened and responded. From Sloyan's statements one might be led to the opposite conclusion, that Paul is misunderstood because of faulty Jewish interpretations to which Christians erroneously listen.

Law observance does not put anyone in a right relationship with God. Sloyan and I agree that this was both Paul's understanding and the view of Judaism in general. I hope that our readers will realize that both Judaism and Christianity affirm that a person gains a right relationship with God by being in God's covenant. Correct behavior is the appropriate response of a person who is in a covenant relationship with God. To use E. P. Sanders' term, Judaism and Christianity are both covenantal nomism; neither is legalistic.[1]

I do disagree with Sloyan's belief that most of Paul's statements about Torah apply to Jewish observance of the Law. I agree with the scholars he mentions who think that most of what Paul said was directed to Gentiles and not to Jews.[2] It was Gentiles, not Jews, who erroneously believed that following Torah would make them righteous. It was Gentiles, not Jews, who Paul believed were not to obey Torah. Paul's language to these Gentiles was strong, and the reasons for his prohibiting any Torah observance for Gentiles are difficult to understand. All we can know with certainty is that he felt Gentile observance of Torah would make God's act in Christ unnecessary.[3] Yet I am not comfortable with Sloyan's statement that following Torah would be a "bad bargain" for Gentiles. Rather, following Torah was not what God intended for Gentiles. For Gentiles — not Jews — it was a stopgap measure to show their sins and their need to rely upon the faithfulness of the God of Israel as demonstrated through the faithfulness of Christ.

I agree with Sloyan that Torah was not Christ, and for Paul it could not do what God had done through Christ.[4] But the purpose of Christ's death was not to provide a righteousness that was lacking in Judaism. Rather, God now provided a way for Gentiles, as Gentiles, to become children of God. In this context, following Torah was wrong, but wrong only for Gentiles.

In Paul's view, Torah did have a negative function for Gentiles because it could never allow them to be part of God's covenant unless they became Jewish proselytes.[5] But Torah also had positive functions, for both Jews and Gentiles. I think that Sloyan focuses too much upon the negative things Paul said—on what Torah is not and never could do—rather than considering all the positive things that Paul indeed said about Torah. The Law was good, it was one way that a person could learn what God required, it showed that God was just, and it pointed to Christ—as the way that Gentiles could now become children of God. Was Paul opposed to Jewish observance of Torah? To quote him, "By no means!"

NOTES

1. Sanders defines Judaism as covenantal nomism, while he defines Paul's pattern of religion as participationist eschatology. But he notes that "Paul's view could hardly be maintained, and it was not maintained. Christianity rapidly became a new covenantal nomism." *Paul and Palestinian Judaism* (Philadelphia: Fortress Press, 1977), p. 552.

2. For Christians who also direct Paul's statements about the Law to Gentiles and not Jews, see Krister Stendahl, *Paul Among Jews and Gentiles* (Philadelphia: Fortress Press, 1976), p. 2. "In none of his writings does he [Paul] give us information about what he thought to be proper in these matters for Jewish Christians." Also Lloyd Gaston, *Paul and the Torah* (Vancouver: University of British Columbia Press, 1987), p. 22: "Paul kept this agreement throughout his career, confining his preaching strictly to Gentile God-fearers and never encouraging Jews to abandon the Torah."

3. Often scholars base Paul's prohibition of Gentile Law observance on the belief that Gentiles did not have to become Jews in order to be part of the Jesus movement. For example, see Sanders, *Paul, the Law, and the Jewish People* (Philadelphia: Fortress Press, 1983), pp. 6–10. Paul surely believed this. However, such a belief does not explain why Gentiles did not have to follow Torah after they became Christians and were part of God's covenant. In Galatians Paul is addressing this question of the proper conduct of Gentile Christians and not discussing entrance requirements. His strong stance against Gentile Christian observance has not yet been explained satisfactorily.

4. Sanders' statement about Paul's view of Judaism is now often quoted, "this is what Paul finds wrong in Judaism: it is not Christianity," *Paul and Palestinian Judaism*, p. 552. I think that Gaston is more accurate when he suggests, "this is what Paul finds wrong with other Jews: that they did not share his revelation in Damascus," *Paul and the Torah*, p. 140. Paul was critical of other Jews; but he was not critical of Judaism. I am in complete agreement with Gaston when he states, "Paul's quarrel with his fellow Jews is never about Judaism as such but rather about a Jewish understanding of Gentiles," p. 14. The distinction is crucial if a positive, or at least a non-negative, view of Judaism is to be found in Paul.

5. Gaston suggests that Paul's negative statements about Torah were based upon a common Jewish view of that time that condemned Gentiles for not following Torah; see *Paul and the Torah*, pp. 9–11, 23–32. I think that Gaston has combined

two different views, those of Paul, and those of Paul's opponents. Although there is some truth to say, "For Gentiles, who do not have the Torah as covenant, Torah as law functions in an exclusively negative way, to condemn," p. 28, the use of the word "law" may be misleading. For Paul, Gentiles were cursed by Torah because they were not part of God's covenant. But now through God's faithfulness, Gentiles were part of the covenant and were no longer under the Law's curse.

14

Paul's Problems with the Law

LESTER DEAN

In our last section we noted Paul's emphasis upon *nomos*, law, usually understood to be the equivalent of Torah. We showed that the usual Christian view of a legalistic Judaism, a religion in which one earned righteousness, was neither an accurate description of Judaism nor a correct understanding of Paul's view of Judaism. Paul's statements that righteousness comes from God's faithfulness and not by works of law showed a relationship between righteousness, faith, and Torah that agreed with Judaism.

However, Paul's statements about Torah were not limited to correcting the Gentile misunderstanding that righteousness could be attained by following Torah apart from God's gracious covenant. Samuel Sandmel notes that the practical issue for Paul was "Should new converts be compelled to observe the Jewish practices?"[1] Paul's answer was to forbid Gentile Christian believers—at least in Galatia—from being circumcised and following Torah. "Now I, Paul, say to you that if you receive circumcision, Christ will be of no advantage to you" (Gal. 5:2). For Paul, following Torah was neither the requirement for Gentiles to participate in the new covenant available through Christ, nor the proper obedient way to remain in that covenant.

It was about this point, nonobservance of Torah by Gentiles after they had come to believe in Christ, that Paul met opposition in Galatia. Apparently both Gentiles and Jews were confused about Paul's position. Paul had preached the universality of God; God was the God of both the Jews and the Gentiles. If Torah represented God's perfect rules of conduct for the Jews, did it not also represent God's perfect rules of conduct for all people?

To support his argument that Gentiles did not have to follow Torah, Paul examined the reasons for the existence of Torah. He had to show that

148

Torah was not God's universal law for all humanity. In Galatians, Paul argued against the universality of Torah by showing that Torah was not eternal. The Law "came four hundred and thirty years" after God's covenant and promise to Abraham (3:17). Torah could not represent the unchanging absolute rules of conduct that God required of all those who were part of the covenant, since Abraham was part of the covenant but did not follow Torah.

Paul's argument that the covenant with Abraham came before the giving of Torah seems obvious if only the Hebrew Scriptures are studied. However, Paul was actually arguing against a view held by some Jews at this time. In the Book of Jubilees and the Testaments of the Twelve Patriarchs there were attempts to retroject specific Torah observances into an earlier period, such as having Abraham observe the Sabbath. According to these writings, Torah had existed before the creation of the world and had been followed by Adam and Eve, by Noah, by Abraham and Sarah, and by the other patriarchs and matriarchs. All those who had been righteous and who participated in the covenant followed Torah.[2] A similar view of Torah could have been derived from Sirach:

> In every people and nation I [Wisdom] have gotten a possession. Among all these I sought a resting place; I sought in whose territory I might lodge.
>
> Then the Creator of all things gave me a commandment . . . "Make your dwelling in Jacob and in Israel receive your inheritance."
>
> From eternity, in the beginning, God created me, and for eternity I shall not cease to exist (24:6–9).

Sirach then identified Wisdom with Torah. This Wisdom "is the book of the covenant of the Most High God, the law which Moses commanded us as an inheritance for the congregations of Jacob" (24:23–24). Torah, as God's Wisdom, had been offered to all peoples of the world, but only the Jews had accepted it. The Gentiles who had rejected Torah would be judged by it and condemned. The only hope of the Gentiles was obedience to all of Torah. These verses, perhaps combined with other Jewish *midrashim* about the offering of the Torah to the Gentiles, form the context for Paul's comments about the Law in Galatians.[3]

Paul was opposed to such a view and argued that Torah was not eternal. Torah came after the covenant with Abraham, and neither Abraham nor the other patriarchs and matriarchs obeyed the Law. Since they were a part of covenant but did not follow Torah, Torah obedience could not be a requirement for those who were part of the covenant with Abraham. Jews were part of the covenant with Abraham and also the covenant at Sinai. Torah observance was required of them because of the Sinai covenant. Torah observance was also limited to them since only Jews were part of the Sinai covenant. Gentiles who believed in Jesus were a part of the covenant with Abraham, but not the Sinai covenant. Thus Paul proved that Gentiles did not have to obey Torah.

In addition to arguing that Torah was not eternal, Paul also stated that "it was ordained by angels acting as an intermediary. Now an intermediary implies more than one; but God is one" (Gal. 3:19–20). Many interpreters believe that Paul was arguing against Torah because Torah was given by angels and not God. Since the Bible does not mention angelic intermediaries, scholars explain that Paul was quoting a Jewish midrash about the giving of the Law at Sinai.[4] Some even suggest that Paul viewed Torah as representing the will of angels, in contrast to the will of God.[5]

Such a negative view of Torah seems incredible. To make Torah the antithesis of God's will is contrary to the fundamental Jewish belief that Torah is God's will. It is also contrary to all the positive statements that Paul made about Torah. Paul did not believe that Torah was opposed to God's will: "Is the law against the promises of God? Certainly not" (3:21).

A Jewish midrash is the most logical explanation about Paul's claims that the Torah was given by angels. But such a midrash would be in direct opposition to the biblical texts. Furthermore, although there exist several midrashim about the giving of the Torah, in all cases God still gives the Torah directly to Moses. As Gaston notes, "That the law was given to Israel by angels must be called exclusively a Pauline concept, if indeed that is what Paul says."[6]

When Paul mentioned that Torah was given by angels, he was probably referring to a Jewish midrash about the giving of the Torah to the Gentiles. Such a midrash would have been quoted by his opponents to prove the necessity of Gentile obedience to Torah. Paul referred to the same midrash to argue against the belief that Gentile believers in Christ had to obey Torah.

The view that the Torah was offered to all the nations could be derived from the passage about Wisdom quoted from Sirach: "In every people and nation I [Wisdom] have gotten a possession. Among all these I sought a resting place; I sought in whose territory I might lodge" (24:6; NAB,7). In addition, in Sirach 17, God's giving of Wisdom and Torah at creation is linked with the appointing of "angelic rulers" for every nation.

From this and other biblical passages various midrashim were created in which God offered Torah to the other nations who refused it for various reasons.[7] There are passages that refer to the presence of the angels of the nations when the Law was given, but they do not state that the angels actually gave the Law to the nations. However, one midrash does end with words reminiscent of Paul:

In the hour that the Holy One, blessed be He, came down to Sinai, hosts and hosts of angels came down with him . . . from them the nations of the world chose for themselves gods. . . . But Israel said to the Holy One, blessed be He: out of all these gods we have chosen only you.[8]

This midrash is not, of course, identical to the one which Paul was quoting, but the similarity is sufficient to suggest that Paul was referring to the giving of the Law to the Gentiles, not to Israel.

Paul's opponents used this story to prove that all Gentiles had to follow Torah since they all had been commanded to obey it. Gentiles were disobedient to God if they did not follow Torah. They would be condemned by God and excluded from God's messianic kingdom for this disobedience. Thus the Gentile converts of Paul also had to be circumcised and follow Torah.

Paul did not deny that Torah had been offered to the Gentile nations through angels. However, instead of using the story to prove the necessity of Torah observance for Gentiles, Paul proved the opposite position. Because angels offered the Law to each of the different nations, there was an intermediary between the nations and God. The nations had been led into polytheism because of the angelic intermediaries, keeping them from worshiping the one true God. They had thus rejected God's covenant and were not responsible for keeping the Law. But Israel had had the special privilege of receiving Torah directly from God without an intermediary. Israel had accepted God's covenant and had agreed to follow Torah, while the Gentiles rejected both the covenant and Torah.

Paul's opponents had argued that God was one, and that meant that there was only one acceptable form of behavior before God, following Torah. Paul naturally agreed that God was one. But Paul argued that if God had intended one Torah for all the nations, then God, and not the angels, would have offered Torah to the other nations. The nations should not be condemned for not accepting Torah since they had not had Israel's special privilege of receiving it from God. Thus Paul proved that Torah observance was required of Jews, but it was not required for Gentiles.

If God did not intend Torah to be the rule for all humanity, then why was Torah given? Paul asked this rhetorical question, and answered, "It was added because of transgressions." "We were confined under the law, kept under restraint until faith should be revealed. So that the law was our custodian until Christ came, so that we might be justified by faith"(Gal. 3:19–24).

The traditional Christian interpretation of these verses is that Torah was given in order to prevent further sin. Since only Jews were given Torah, they alone must have needed this to keep them from sin. For many Christians this proved what they already knew about Jews by their rejection of Christ: Jews were the most wicked of all peoples. God, knowing their extreme wickedness, had used Torah to restrain the Jews. Christians, who were not as wicked as Jews, did not need the restraint of Torah.[9]

This interpretation is based upon the following assumptions: that the confinement, the restraint of Torah is to keep people from transgressions, and that the people who commit transgressions are Jews. However, Paul's argument in Galatians is that Gentiles must not obey Torah. If the reason for Torah was to keep people from sin, then it would seem appropriate, or at least allowable, for Gentiles to follow Torah. If Torah kept Jews from sin, then surely it would also keep Gentiles from sin. Gentiles might not need this restraint, but why would it be wrong for them to accept it? The traditional interpretation of the verses does not explain Paul's argument against Gentile observance of Torah. On the contrary, it would seem to be more supportive of Paul's opponents' views than of Paul's.

Paul talked of restraint under Torah, followed by a new freedom available through Christ. This new freedom was not freedom for Jews no longer to follow Torah, but freedom for Jews, including Paul, no longer to require Gentiles to follow Torah. Torah had demanded that Gentiles become Jews in order to be assured of being righteous. We do not know whether Paul engaged in missionary work among the Gentiles before his vision of the risen Christ, but if he had, he would have had to demand that those Gentiles who now believed in the God of Israel become Jewish proselytes and follow Torah. Torah had been given because of the transgressions of the Gentiles, not of the Jews; it had kept Gentiles, as Gentiles, from being a part of the people of God. Torah allowed only Jews to be part of God's people.

But now, Paul believed, righteousness had come to the Gentiles. Gentile believers in Christ were children of God and Abraham's descendants. Now there was a way for Gentiles, as Gentiles, to be part of the covenant with Abraham, through the faithfulness of Christ. Paul was convinced that Gentiles who believed in Jesus Christ were no longer required to become Jews and obey Torah in order to be part of the covenant and be righteous. Paul was now free from that past restriction of Torah.

Both Jews and Gentiles were now to be considered children of God; "there is neither Jew nor Greek" (3:28). The specific function of Torah as restraint, as guardian, keeping Jews and Gentiles apart, had now come to an end because of God's act in Christ. However, the end of this function of Torah should not be interpreted as meaning the end of all functions of Torah. Torah as a restraint, demanding Gentile circumcision and observance of Torah, was only one of several reasons Paul mentioned for the existence of Torah.

In Romans, Paul made more explicit the link between Torah and sin. In the early chapters Paul enunciated again the Jewish view that righteousness did not come from following Torah, but from God's grace:

> For no human being will be justified in God's sight by works of the law, since through the law comes knowledge of sin. But now the righteousness of God has been manifested apart from law, although the law and the prophets bear witness to it. . . . since all have sinned and

fall short of the glory of God, they are justified by God's grace as a gift through the redemption which is in Christ Jesus (3:20–25).

The works of the law do not provide righteousness; rather, Torah shows "God's righteousness." In this passage Torah is not a custodian or a restraint, but an instructor. It enables a person to see that God is righteous. One way that Torah shows God's righteousness is by allowing a person to recognize sin. Torah was one way for a person to know what God required of humans.

Torah names as sin those human actions that are contrary to God's will, but one does not need to know Torah in order to refrain from sin and follow God's will. "Gentiles who have not the law do by nature what the law requires" (Rom. 2:14). For Paul, Torah was one way of knowing about God, but it was not the only way. He accepted the view of Sirach, previously quoted, that knowledge of God was eternal and available to all. Paul simply equated that knowledge with the natural world instead of with Torah: "Ever since the creation of the world God's invisible nature, God's eternal power and deity, has been clearly perceived in the things that have been made" (Rom. 1:20). All people had a knowledge of God—Jews from Torah, and Gentiles from creation. This again supports Paul's view that Gentiles did not need to follow Torah.

Torah also shows God's righteousness by pointing to the way of gaining righteousness, through the faithfulness of Christ. Christ's death was foretold in Torah and in the prophets. Thus Torah has an important function of bearing witness, not just to God's righteousness, but to God's righteousness as expressed through the death and resurrection of Christ. Now God was shown to be righteous, for all humanity could be part of the people of God, Gentiles as well as Jews.

In the beginning of Romans 7, Paul returned to the restraining function of Torah that he had developed in Galatians. The laws of marriage establish the relationship between a wife and her husband, and she cannot change that relationship while the husband lives. Likewise, the laws of Torah establish the relationship between God, the Jews, and the Gentiles. Jews were part of God's people; Gentiles were not part of God's people. According to Torah, for Gentiles to have the proper relationship with God, they must become Jews.

But through the death of Christ, this restraining function of Torah came to an end, and the Gentiles could now become children of God. "You have died to the law through the body of Christ, so that you may belong to another" (7:4). Torah, and its requirement that all men be circumcised and follow Torah, is no longer binding upon Gentiles. Gentiles are free from the restrictions of Torah that separated them from God; they can now enter into a new relationship with God.

Paul then continued to discuss Torah and its relationship to sin. First he returned to the role of Torah as instructor: "If it had not been for the law, I should not have known sin" (7:7). But this was not the only relationship between Torah and sin. According to Paul, Torah could point out sin, but Torah could also be used by sin, "sin, finding opportunity in the commandment, wrought in me all kinds of covetousness . . . sin finding opportunity in the commandment, deceived me and by it killed me" (7:8, 11). Thus, in some way, Torah can be used by sin to cause a person's death. Paul even implied that this death was the result of Torah: "I was once alive apart from the law, but when the commandment came, sin revived and I died; the very commandment which promised life proved to be death to me" (7:9–10).

But is the Law sin? "By no means!" (7:7). Paul emphasized that "the law is holy, and the commandment is holy and just and good . . . the law is spiritual" (7:12, 14). Torah may be used by sin, but Torah is still holy and right; its contact with sin does not transform it into something evil that should be avoided.

Nor was Torah the original cause of sin; "sin indeed was in the world before the law was given" (5:13). Torah may somehow be used by sin to cause a person to sin, but sin would still exist without the existence of Torah. Furthermore, Torah itself does not cause a person's death: "Did that which is good, then bring death to me? By no means! It was sin working death in me through what is good" (7:13). Sin, not Torah, is responsible for causing a person's death.

This use of Torah by sin to cause a person's death is often cited by Christians to prove that Paul was opposed to anyone following Torah. Torah was itself good, but if anyone tried to follow Torah that very attempt would lead the person into sin. Although Torah promised life to a person, trying to follow Torah meant death.[10] The solution to such a problem was faith in Christ, which frees the person from being under the law, and thus frees the person from the power of sin.

Such an interpretation is problematic from a Jewish perspective, since it would automatically lead to a condemnation of anyone who tried to follow Torah. Such a view would almost certainly have made Paul an apostate in the view of most Jews, regardless of whether they were believers in Christ. Paul would necessarily have been opposed to Judaism, since it commands all Jews to follow Torah.

Yet if we look carefully at this interpretation, we note several problems. First, how can Paul argue that without Torah he would not have known sin? We noted earlier that Paul argued for a universal knowledge of God's law through creation. This was crucial for his argument that all humanity had sinned and could be rightly condemned by God, both Jews who knew Torah and Gentiles who did not know Torah. If a person knew sin only through Torah, this would imply that all Gentiles should follow Torah in order to avoid sin. But Paul was opposed to Gentiles following Torah!

Second, Paul spoke about "the commandment," *tēs entolēs* (7:8, 10, 12), not the commandments, and he quoted only one commandment, "You shall not covet" (7:7). Why was this particular commandment the only one which Paul mentioned? Why not mention the commandment to keep the Sabbath? It would seem to have been a better example since it could not have been deduced from nature.

Finally, Paul stated, "I was once alive apart from the law, but when the commandment came, sin revived and I died." How can Paul say that he was apart from Torah? He was not considering life after a person has faith in Christ, for he concluded the chapter with the solution to this problem, that deliverance comes by faith in Jesus Christ. Thus he must be speaking of his life before he was a believer in Christ, but he had been a Jew from birth and had never been apart from Torah. Even after he became a believer, Paul could say that he was not "without law toward God but under the law of Christ" (1 Cor. 9:21).

These questions suggest that the usual interpretation of Romans 7 is incorrect. Paul began the chapter talking of the role of Torah as a restraint that had proclaimed that Gentiles had to become Jews in order to be righteous. That restraint had been ended by the death of Jesus Christ. This restraint of Torah is still the subject of the rest of the chapter. Paul was not talking about Torah causing sin for Jews, and especially not about Torah causing sin for himself.[11] We should remember that Paul claimed that "as to righteousness under the law [he was] blameless" (Phil. 3:6). Paul was reminding the Gentiles in Rome, those who "knew the Law" but were not Jews who had to follow the Law, why they did not have to follow the Law.

Paul began writing to his readers, to the Gentiles who now had a relationship to God free from the restraint of Torah, using the second person plural "you," *humeis*: "my brethren, you have died to the law through the body of Christ" (Rom. 7:4). He then identified with his readers and switched to the first-person plural, "we," *hēmas*: "now we are discharged from the law" (7:6). Finally, he switched to the first-person singular, "I," *egē*: "I was once alive apart from the law" (7:9). This switch to first-person singular does not indicate that Paul was speaking autobiographically or from a Jewish viewpoint. Rather, he was continuing to identify with the majority of his Roman audience. Paul was now speaking from the viewpoint of a Gentile.

If, as I am convinced, Paul were speaking as a Gentile, then all of the previously noted problems are solved. Talking as a Gentile, he could speak about a time when he was apart from Torah, the time before he heard about Judaism. Prior to that time he had been a righteous person, following God's will as he had discerned it from his own nature. He had conquered sin; sin was dead and he was alive.

Then he, as a Gentile, met a Jew and heard about Torah. He heard of all that God had done for the Jews. He heard about all that God promised in Torah. He heard about all that God commanded in Torah. He also wanted to have a share in these promises. He desired to be part of God's people. He coveted the relationship that Jews had with God.

Suddenly he found himself in an impossible situation. He knew that he was a Gentile, not part of God's people, and he wanted desperately to become part of that people. Then he read the commandment, "You shall not covet." This was exactly what he was doing—he was covetous of the Jews. Sin revived and he died. "The very commandment which promised life proved to be death to me" (Rom. 7:10). The very desire to be part of God's people now was seen as sin, as condemning him, the Gentile, to death. He was in an impossible situation, which he then described in the following verses, ending with the cry, "Wretched man that I am! Who will deliver me from this body of death?" (Rom. 7:24). The answer, of course, was God acting through Christ.

Torah was good; it was one expression of God's will for humanity. But Torah also made it impossible for Gentiles, as Gentiles, to become children of God. But now "the law of the Spirit of life in Christ Jesus has set me free from the law of sin and death" (8:2). Torah kept Gentiles from God, but now "God has done what the law could not do" (8:3). Believers in Christ lived according to the Spirit. Now Gentiles could find that "the just requirements of the law might be fulfilled in us" (8:4). Now all, both Jews and Gentiles, "who are led by the Spirit of God are children of God" (8:14). Gentiles now could submit to God's Law, and fulfill its requirements. For Paul this would probably have meant obeying the "law of love," which Judaism had already proclaimed to be the heart of Torah; all the rest was commentary.

A Response to Lester Dean from Gerard Sloyan

I confess that I had to re-read Justin's explanation that the Jews uniquely required the restraints of Torah because of their wickedness (chiefly idolatry). The charge of Jewish anti-Christian activity in chapter 17 may explain, but it does not excuse, the bitterness of chapters 16 and 17. Each day's newspapers and television stories reveal that there is no limit to the folly of my co-religionists when it comes to complaints against Jewish behavior.

The hypothetical construct about the angels serving as intermediaries in offering Torah to the Gentile nations is attractive. I would only hope there is enough evidence for it in the passages cited from Deuteronomy and Sirach without recourse to Talmudic writings, the dating problems of which are well known. The supposition that a rabbinic commonplace is to the fore in Paul's mind as he writes to a Galatian church or churches largely Gentile in make-up raises an important question about all of Paul's correspondence. Is he so thoroughly Jewish in outlook that he cannot put himself in the shoes of his Gentile believers for a moment? Can he count on some Jews in every community to explain to a preponderantly Gentile congregation what lies behind his far from obvious statements like "[The law] was ordained by angels through an intermediary. Now an intermediary implies more than one; but God is one" (Gal. 3:19c–20)? Or are we wiser to assume that Paul's "Gentiles" were predominantly such by birth but in fact Jewish proselytes and God-fearers—if these were two distinct groups—who had heard much rabbinic argumentation long before they encountered Paul? No hard evidence exists to eliminate our ignorance in this matter. But if we accept the meaning here alleged for the cryptic passage about the angels, there must have been some readers among the Galatians for whom it was less cryptic than it is for us.

I find the discussion of Paul's problems with the Torah very satisfying because I, too, think they were minimal, if not exactly at the zero point. Uneasiness sets in, however, as I read the explanation that "you, my brethren" of Rom. 7:4 are his Gentile fellow-believers only. Their identification in context as "those who know the law" in verse 1, it seems, has simply not been noticed. It is so infrequent for Paul to identify his intended audience that this exception should be noted, whatever the context. It is highly unlikely that those who "know the law" are meant to be Gentiles only. Paul's switches in person and number, even his identifying sympathetically with the Gentile segment of the Roman church, would cause no difficulty if it were not for verse 1, which flies in the face of the hypothesis. The discussion of Torah throughout Rom. 7 seems to be saying that the "we" who are discharged from it (v. 6) are all, Jews and Gentiles alike, who have left the flesh behind (v. 5) and "serve . . . in the new life of the spirit" (v. 6). Confining the beneficiaries of Christ's death and resurrection to the Gentiles as if Paul cared only about them and the freedom from the Law it brought them disregards strangely the benefits it brought to Paul and Jews like him.

NOTES

1. Samuel Sandmel, *Anti-Semitism in the New Testament?* (Philadelphia: Fortress Press, 1978), p. 7. This distinction between following the Law as an "entrance requirement" (to borrow Sanders' term) and following the Law as the proper conduct demanded by God of all those who are within the covenant seems to be ignored by most Christian scholars. Yet I would suggest that the latter was the true problem that Paul faced. Note, for example, J. Christiaan Beker, *Paul the Apostle* (Philadelphia: Fortress Press, 1980), pp. 43–44. Beker notes that the Galatians are Gentile believers; thus the debate should not involve entrance requirements. But his reconstruction of the debate in Galatians centers on that issue, "They [Gentiles] can participate in the full blessings promised to Abraham if they join the people of the promise." Hans Hübner, in *Law in Paul's Thought* (Edinburgh: T & T Clark, 1984), p. 152, correctly argues that in Galatians Paul goes beyond the question of circumcision as an entrance requirement, but his suggestion that "Paul expends all his energy on decrying theologically the *condition* of those who exist under the Law" must also be rejected. Unfortunately, Hübner seems to need to justify past erroneous anti-Jewish Christian interpretations of Paul rather then to consider seriously the possibility that Paul was not anti-Jewish.

2. See: Lloyd Gaston, *Paul and the Torah* (Vancouver: University of British Columbia Press, 1987), pp. 25–28, 38–40, for a similar development. However, as I observed previously, Gaston makes no distinction between the view of Paul's opponents and the view of Paul. For Paul's opponents, Gentiles were condemned for not becoming a part of God's covenant as Israel had. The midrash in which God offers Torah to all the nations should not be seen as commandments without covenant, but rather, the offering of the same covenant to all the nations. Gentiles are condemned for rejecting this covenant, as shown by their rejection of Torah. The correct Gentile response was conversion and obedience to Torah. This was obviously not Paul's position. For Paul, Torah as the record of God's righteous acts on behalf of Israel demanded Gentile conversion. Furthermore, Torah as the Jewish message about the God of Israel demanded that Jews engaged in missions to Gentiles proclaim the need for Gentile conversion. But Torah also contained the promise to bless the Gentiles through Israel in the future. God's faithfulness to both Israel and the Gentiles was now available because of the faithfulness of Christ. This new act of God freed Paul from the old demands of Torah, through the Torah, which contained the promise that God would eventually bless the Gentiles; this is now fulfilled through both God and Christ's faithfulness: "I have died to the Torah" with its message that God's blessing is available only to Israel. It was in this sense that Paul was free and was an "apostate" building up the mission to the Gentiles which he had previously tried to tear down.

3. Gaston has noted the importance of Jewish midrashic traditions in understanding Paul:

> The Hebrew Bible is the starting point, and there then begins a tradition of midrashic interpretation of the Scriptural text. The task of the Pauline interpreter is not to contrast Paul and the Old Testament itself but to try to reconstruct something of the history of interpretation of the text and to locate Paul with respect to these midrashic traditions. Insofar as this can be done, Paul's own midrash, while creative, is not at all arbitrary and outlandish. In any case, unless there are compelling reasons to the contrary, it seems best to assume that Paul stands in continuity with the midrashic traditions of Judaism rather than in antithesis to them. *Paul and the Torah*, p. 5.

4. For example, W. Barclay, *The Letters to the Galatians and Ephesians* (Edinburgh: St. Andrews, 1962), pp. 31–32.

> In the days of Paul the Rabbis were so impressed by the utter holiness and the utter distance and remoteness of God that they believed that it was quite impossible for God to deal direct with men; therefore they introduced the idea that the law was given first to angels and then by angels to Moses. . . ."

See also H. D. Betz, *Galatians* (Philadelphia: Fortress Press, 1979), p. 169.

5. For one example of the grammatical and theological complexities which such a view requires see H. Hübner, *Law in Paul's Thought*, pp. 24–32. For Hübner, "the Law was promulgated by demonic angelic powers in order to drive man to perdition," p. 31. In order to understand Galatians 3 in such a manner he makes a distinction between "God's intention, the immanent or intrinsic intention of the Law, and the intention of the Law-givers," p. 30. Hübner notes that "Paul's whole

argument about the purpose of the Law sounds blasphemous to Jewish ears," p. 32. It would be more appropriate to say that Hübner's argument sounds blasphemous and completely contrived, the result of trying to interpret the passage based upon an erroneous presupposition.

6. *Paul and the Torah*, p. 37. See also L. Ginzburg, *An Unknown Jewish Sect* (New York: Jewish Theological Seminary of America, 1976), pp. 172–174; J. Jeremias, *TWNT* 4:870; Judah Goldin, "Not by Means of an Angel and not by Means of a Messenger," in *Religions in Antiquity*, ed. J. Neusner (Leiden: Brill, 1968), pp. 412–424.

7. For example, Mekilta Bahodesh 5, Lam. R. 3:1; Shab 88b; Exod. R. 5:9.

8. *Lam. 3:24*, Midrash Tannaim, ed. D. Hoffman, quoted by Gaston, *Paul and the Torah*, p. 200. Gaston finds the passage not directly helpful since it deals with the election of Israel and not with the relation of Gentiles to specific commandments; "it is covenant not commandments which are of concern," p. 40. As I mentioned earlier, one of the major flaws in Gaston's work is his need to separate commandments and covenant for Gentiles. This midrash is directly to the point, for by refusing the covenant the Gentiles are under no obligation to fulfill Torah. They will not be punished for disregarding Torah, although they will be punished for rejecting the covenant. But for Paul that is no longer a problem since through Christ God has extended the new covenant to the Gentiles.

9. This Christian interpretation of the Jewish need for the Law has a long history, found in Justin Martyr, *Dialogue* 20–23 and Chrysostom, *Or. c. Jud.* IV. For summaries of the position see: James Parkes, *The Conflict of the Church and the Synagogue* (New York: Atheneum, 1979), pp. 100–101 and Rosemary Ruether, *Faith and Fratricide* (New York: Seabury Press, 1979), pp. 150–153.

10. This is the view that the Law cannot be "qualitatively" fulfilled. See Bultmann, *Theology of the New Testament* (New York: Charles Scribner's Sons, 1951), vol. I, p. 264: "man's effort to achieve his salvation by keeping the Law only leads him into sin." The qualitative can also be combined with the quantitative problem, following all of the Law, as in Hübner, *Law in Paul's Thought*, "quantitative fulfillment is not possible because the Torah contains stipulations which must be 'qualitatively fulfilled,' " p. 41. Sanders, *Paul and Palestinian Judaism*, noted that such an interpretation of Judaism and of Paul is "the retrojection of the Protestant-Catholic debate into ancient history, with Judaism taking the role of Catholicism and Christianity the role of Lutheranism," p. 57. For a thorough discussion of the weaknesses of such views see Sanders, *Paul, the Law, and the Jewish People* (Philadelphia: Fortress Press, 1983).

11. See Sanders, *Paul, the Law, and the Jewish People*, for a lengthy discussion on the fallacy of reading Romans 7 in an autobiographical manner. For a summary of common interpretations of Romans 7 (1. universal human experience apart from Christ, 2. Paul's experience prior to believing in Christ, 3. Paul's continuing experience), see: James Dunn, "Rom. 7:14–25 in the Theology of Paul," *Theologische Zeitschrift* 31 (1975), pp. 257–273.

15

Did Paul Think That a Person Could Follow Torah?

GERARD SLOYAN

"I testify again to every man who receives circumcision," Paul wrote to
the Galatians, "that he is bound to keep the whole law" (5:3). He probably
had in mind his earlier quotation of Deut. 27:26 in the same letter, "Cursed
be everyone who does not abide by all things written in the book of the
Law, and do them" (Gal. 3:10). In the latter citation Paul is criticized by
Jewish scholars for having added the "all" (*holon*) to suit his argument,
since the Masoretic text does not have *qol*; or for being ignorant of how
the text read. But aside from the fact that the Bible's text was in a fluid
condition, any rabbinic polemicist of the time would cheerfully have modified a quotation, even to the point of reading it in an opposite sense, to
make his point. Crying, "altering the text," or "going against the clear
meaning" is an entirely modern response to rabbinic techniques of argument. In those days a text meant whatever the interpreter found most
suitable to his purpose.

The question at issue in the present essay is not whether Paul was being
faithful to widely accepted teaching about the necessity of keeping the
whole Law but whether he thought anyone was capable of doing so. Certainly he seems to have thought he had done so. Whether perfect Law
observance was possible does not seem to have been a theoretical problem
for Paul. He was, he says, "as to righteousness under the Law blameless"
(Phil. 3:6). If taken strictly, that is a claim of never having consciously
transgressed. The spirit of his claim about his former life is the same: "And
I advanced in Judaism beyond many of my own age among my people, so
extremely zealous was I for the traditions of my fathers" (Gal. 1:14).

Paul had great ego strength, as we say nowadays. In the words of Krister
Stendahl, he had a remarkably "robust conscience."[1] The only sin or short-

coming Paul ever seems to have been conscious of is persecuting the church of God violently and trying to destroy it (Gal. 1:13). The phrase in 1 Tim. 1:15, "And I am the foremost of sinners," may echo this tradition of his one grievous sin, but it is probably an exercise in literary revisionism — like the description of Moses by the Deuteronomist as "meek." As a genuine sentiment of Paul it is "not 'arf likely," as certain Londoners within the sound of Bow Bells might say.

There is, in brief, but a single piece of evidence that can be brought forward to support the notion of Paul's seeking deliverance from the burden of the Law in a state of discouragement. That passage is his soliloquy in Rom. 7 where he says: "I can will what is right, but I cannot do it" (v. 19b). Martin Luther's troubled conscience and the congeniality of the pericope to his scrupulous condition in youth are well known. Augustine's anguished pursuit of chastity is equally familiar. Luther had a great problem in avoiding sin and fulfilling all the requirements of his vows as a scrupulous young Augustinian canon. He assumed that his was the universal human condition; he was much relieved to see the apostle acknowledging it as *his* condition. But did Paul say what Augustine and Luther thought he said? Or was he only cataloguing a commonplace, namely the gap between human awareness of the right course of action and the hardship of following it, as part of his myth of Sin, the enemy of humanity that uses the Law as its death-dealing instrument?

Was Paul, perhaps, saying nothing in particular of his personal struggle and, indeed, not commenting at all on the discouraging challenge that the Torah posed for him? After all, we know of no time when Paul had lived without the Law, although he speaks of a time in Israel before Moses' day when he — meaning all pre-Sinai Hebrews — was "alive" in its absence (Rom. 7:9). Earlier in Romans, Paul had stated that all were under the power of Sin (3:9), but this is a cosmic statement about personified *hamartia* being pitted against Jew and Gentile alike. Paul never draws the conclusion that a pious Jew cannot keep the whole Law. Indeed, he seems to assume the opposite when he says that Gentiles — some Gentiles, presumably — do by nature what the Law requires (2:14). How can they fulfill what, in Luther's hypothesis, Jews cannot fulfill?

No, the inability of anyone, starting with Paul, to keep all the precepts of the Law does not appear anywhere in his letters. In light of its absence, Rom. 7:15–25 is seen to describe not a discouraged Paul whose career under the Law was one of failure, but an anguished "everyman" of any time in history or any religious persuasion. Consider the context: Paul is wrestling with whether that "good" Law had become death for him (7:13). Such a thing is impossible, he maintains. The Law might have served as the agent of human death but it was not the principal actor. Sin was that (vv. 11,13). The Law did not bring about "my death" (v. 13) in the sense that it was the consciousness of Paul's sins which brought him to spiritual ruin. In the mythical drama he poses he could not be less interested than he is in his sins. He cares about one actor, Sin, employing another, the Law (Good-in-Itself), to attack a third, the people Israel. The Law is spiritual, that is, something of God. It is put to use in attacking weak "flesh": "I am unspiritual, the purchased slave of Sin" (*Egō de sarkinos eimi pepramenos hypo ten hamartian*, v. 14).

The *I* and the *me* of this passage is not Paul in particular but the whole human race. He explains the universal human experience of the will but not the capacity to do good by describing the maiming effect of Sin on all humanity: weak nature made weaker. Why, then, is Paul wretched, crying out for deliverance from "this body doomed to death" (v. 24)? Not because he is living a life of personal discouragement or despair over Law observance, but because all humanity needs deliverance from the power of Sin. Only God through Jesus Christ can do this—has done it. (See v. 25a.) All praise to God, then, who in delivering humanity has nonetheless left it in its divided condition: the *nous* or rational part now committed to the law of God, the unspiritual part a slave to the law of Sin. (See v. 25b.)

We conclude: Paul thought it possible for a sincere Jew to observe all of Torah but had come to be convinced that since the death and resurrection of Christ it did not matter as it had before. Such perfection in observance can be the subject of a boast, indeed is made to be such by those whom Paul opposes, which is reprehensible. Only one thing now should be the subject of a boast: God's deed in Christ. As to the anxious Paul, fearful that neither he nor any Jew can keep the whole Law, such a one is a figment of the imagination of later centuries. He does not survive a sound exegesis of Rom. 7. A Jewish people weighted down, burdened by a Law they cannot keep is the creation of Christians in their various ages of anxiety. For Paul, Jew and non-Jew alike needed to be delivered from the weakening in their flesh that Sin has caused. But the Law for the Jews, as Paul conceived it, was only Sin's innocent tool. In itself there was nothing with which it could be charged before Christ came. Even then, its sole flaw was that it had been rendered redundant—not for every purpose but for the purpose of mending the human plight that Jew and non-Jew experience in common, the all but overwhelming power of Sin.

A Response to Gerard Sloyan from Lester Dean

Sloyan is correct to remind us that we should not criticize Paul for adding the word *all* when he quotes Deuteronomy 27:26. Paul's use of Scripture was acceptable according to his contemporary standards, even though we would be critical of such liberties today. The early believers in Jesus and the rabbinic polemicists whom Sloyan described used the same freedom in quoting and in interpreting Scripture. Jews and Christians today are both faced with the problem that their traditions are based upon methods of scriptural interpretation that are considered inappropriate by modern historical standards.

In contrast to some Christian scholars, I do not think that Paul included the word *all* in order to prove that it was impossible to follow Torah perfectly.[2] Any Jew could easily have written the same words. The purpose is not to show how difficult it is to follow Torah. Rather, the passage argues that a person does not have the freedom to select certain commandments to obey and others to ignore.

Sloyan and I both agree that Paul thought he had followed Torah and that he thought others could obey Torah. Romans 7 should not be read as an autobiographical statement of Paul. I also agree that for Paul the answer to the problem of sin was not Torah but was God's act through Christ. Righteousness came from faith in God's covenant established by Christ; it did not come from obedience to Torah. This is similar to the usual Jewish view that righteousness came from faith in God's covenant established through Moses at Sinai, and not by obedience to Torah. Torah was not the answer to sin, but I think it is inappropriate for Sloyan to say that Torah is redundant or to fault it because it does not solve what it never was meant to solve.

I must also disagree with Sloyan's conclusion that for Paul obedience to Torah did not matter. Torah was God's commandments to the Jews; Jews followed Torah even though they knew that their covenant with God, not their observance of Torah, made them righteous. Observance of Torah was the sign that a Jew obeyed God; observance of Torah meant that a Jew acted properly, according to God's will.

Paul's epistles are filled with exhortations directed at believers in Christ, calling for obedience to God and correct conduct. The believer's proper conduct was of great concern to him. Paul did not believe that Gentiles should be circumcised or follow Torah; Torah was God's commands to the Jews. Thus Paul, when he wrote to his Gentile audience, did not command them to observe Torah. If he had written to a Jewish audience which was not following Torah, presumably he would have commanded them to follow Torah, since there is no evidence in his letters to the contrary. Faithful Jewish observance of Torah would have been of great importance to all Jews, including Paul. The writings that we have from Paul are silent about Jewish obedience to Torah not because it was unimportant to Paul but because these writings were addressed to Gentiles and dealt with Gentile problems.

I also think that Sloyan's statements concerning boasting for following Torah need clarification.[3] Paul clearly thought that he had obeyed Torah blamelessly. By our standards, this statement would be a boast. But Paul was not concerned about Jews boasting that they had obeyed Torah. His criticism of boasting was directed against a different problem. Paul was arguing against Jewish boasts of superiority over the Gentiles, boasting about their relationship to God: "You call yourself a Jew and rely upon the law and boast of your relation to God" (Rom. 2:17). Jews claimed that this special relationship was shown by Jewish observance of Torah; thus, they could "boast in the law" (2:23).

Paul's answer was not that it was wrong to boast about following Torah, but that some Jews "dishonor God by breaking the law" (2:23). In contrast, some Gentiles were more obedient to Torah than some Jews: "Those who are physically uncircumcised but keep the law will condemn you who have the written code and circumcision but break the law" (2:27).

According to Paul, the Jews had some advantages, but they had no special relationship to God, for "both Jews and Greeks, are under the power of sin" (3:9). God was the God of the Jews and the Gentiles. Jews could not boast of a special relationship to God evidenced by their observance of Torah, "for we hold that a person is justified by faith apart from works of law" (3:27–30).

But Paul was quick to add that the end of this boast of superiority did not mean that the law could be neglected. "Do we then overthrow the law by this faith? By no means! On the contrary, we uphold the law" (3:31). Jews must not boast that they are superior to Gentiles just because they observe Torah, but this does not mean that they should not observe Torah. I think that Paul still believed that Jews, even Jewish believers in Jesus, were commanded to observe Torah. Observance is what was expected; there was no reason to boast.

NOTES

1. *Paul Among Jews and Gentiles* (Philadelphia: Fortress Press, 1976), p. 14.

2. This is the "quantitative" argument, that Paul believed following Torah was impossible because no one could follow all of it. See H. Hübner, *Law in Paul's Thought* (Edinburgh: T & T Clark, 1984), pp. 18–20, 151–153.

3. For this common view see Hübner, *Law in Paul's Thought:* "The Jews glory in salvation through their own activity, the Christians glory in the salvation wrought by God's activity," p. 110. Hübner does note that in Rom. 2–3 Paul seems to accuse Jews of boasting because they possess the Law and not because they fulfill it: "Paul is not denouncing a self-glorying by works of the Law, but precisely the opposite, viz., a self-glorying because of one's posssession of the Law but without works of the Law" (p. 114), yet this is still linked with the problem of Jewish "alleged" claims to have followed the Law, pp. 113–124. Hübner is close when he raises the question of "possession" of the Law, but his need to emphasize the traditional view of righteousness by faith and not by works, and that in reference to a legalistic Judaism, cause him to miss what should have been so obvious, the Jewish boasting about their covenant status and the Gentile noncovenant status.

16

Any Person Is Able To Follow Torah

LESTER DEAN

For Jews, following Torah is a privilege, a blessing from God. Before fulfilling any commandment Jews praise God for teaching us this commandment and for giving us this opportunity to do God's will. Following Torah is a joy. According to a passage in the Mishnah, God wanted to grant merit to Israel, so he "multiplied for them the Law and commandments" (m.Mak. 3.16). The large number of commandments shows God's love for Israel, and Jews willingly obey these commandments to show their love for God.[1]

Yet when we Jews talk with Christians, Christians are shocked at our attitude toward Torah. They believe that following Torah is a great difficulty, a burden that ought to be unbearable.[2] They claim that people cannot obey Torah, and Paul is often cited as the basis for this claim. They suggest that Christ is the way to be free of this great burden. When we once again state that Torah is a joy and not a burden, that we can and do obey Torah, we are often condemned as self-righteous boasters.[3]

The belief that it is impossible to follow Torah is based upon passages from Galatians and Romans. In Galatians, Paul reminded the Gentiles that a person must obey all of Torah: "every man who receives circumcision is bound to keep the whole law" (Gal. 5:3); "Cursed be every one who does not abide by all things written in the book of the law, and do them" (3:10). There is nothing unusual in Paul's remarks; any Jew of that time would have stated that a Jew must observe all of Torah. These verses do not state that it is impossible to follow Torah. On the contrary, they seem to imply that a person can and must do so.

Paul's statement about keeping all of Torah, and his addition of "all" in his quotation of Deuteronomy 27:26, do not show that he felt that it was impossible to follow Torah. Torah included commandments, but Torah was not just commandments. Torah also made provision for human imperfection. Keeping all of Torah included not only following its commandments, but also following its provisions when a person accidentally violated a commandment. Paul's use of the word *all* should not be used as proof that Paul thought God demanded an impossible perfect observance of Torah.[4]

However, in Romans Paul seemed to claim that it is not possible to follow Torah. He stated that it was impossible to do the good that a person wants to do: "For I do not do the good I want, but the evil I do not want is what I do" (Rom. 7:19). This is often interpreted to mean that even the person who tried to obey Torah failed, and this failure resulted in the person being condemned by God. Christ, as the end of the Law, was then the answer to this impossible, human situation.

Further proof of the inability to follow Torah is sometimes found in Paul's argument that faith, not works of the Law, is the source of righteousness. Why is it that works of the Law do not make a person righteous? Because human Sin keeps a person from perfectly observing Torah. God did what the Law could not do by sending Christ and freeing everyone from the impossible requirements of the Law.

If this was the view of Paul, it would be contrary to what we know of Jewish teaching of that time. The Hebrew Scriptures, post-biblical literature, and rabbinic literature all taught that a person can and should obey Torah. The Torah was given by God and obedience to it was, and is still, the sign of a Jew's acceptance of the covenant. God would not command the impossible; thus obedience was not impossible. Disobedience was a sign of the rejection of the covenant, while repentance and atonement were the means to obtain forgiveness for involuntary transgressions.

In Romans 7:12 Paul said that the Law is holy and just and then exclaimed (v.15) that the good that he habitually wanted to do (here he uses the verb *prassō*) he sometimes did not do (here he changes to the verb *poieō*). The verses may represent Paul's present feelings; or they could be a remembrance of his previous life before he became a believer in Christ; they could be a reflection on the general human condition, or they could be a comment upon the difficulties of Paul's Gentile audience.[5] In any case, the text seems to indicate that a person may want to follow Torah, but will not always do so.

However, the purpose of the passage is to condemn neither those who try to obey Torah, nor those who fail to obey Torah perfectly. Paul had been discussing two types of human life, one under the lordship of Sin, the other under the lordship of God. Although the believer in Christ was transferred from the realm of Sin into the realm of God, he or she still existed in a world that awaited redemption. Paul did not state that the person would be condemned for doing evil rather than good. The responsibility for unintentional sins was placed upon the power of Sin. Paul, in keeping with Jewish teaching, realized that humanity was not perfect and hoped for the time when there would be human perfection. He did not affirm that

God would punish humans who were not perfect, and he definitely did not say that those Jews who sometimes accidentally sinned were guilty of not following all of Torah.

Paul knew that human beings sin unintentionally, but this failure was not an excuse to give up the attempt to do good. "Are we to continue in Sin that grace may abound? By no means!" (Rom. 6:1); "Are we to sin because we are not under law but under grace? By no means!" (6:15). Immediately after expressing the problem of human Sin, Paul exhorted the believers in Christ to correct conduct, "to set the mind on the Spirit . . . for the mind that is set on the flesh is hostile to God; it does not submit to God's law" (8:6–7). God had provided the answer to the problem of Sin by sending Christ, and now "the just requirement of the law might be fulfilled in us who walk not according to the flesh but according to the Spirit" (8:4).

Paul knew that human beings can also act properly, and the "doers of the law will be justified" (2:13). This law may not be synonymous with Torah, for, according to Paul, "Gentiles who have not the law do by nature what the law requires" (2:14). Perhaps he was thinking of the essence of Torah, the command to love one another. However, the verse does show that Paul believed people could do good and fulfill the requirements of the Law without knowing Torah.

The view that Paul was a frustrated Pharisee, who thought that God demanded perfect observance but found it impossible to follow all of Torah, is contradicted by Paul himself. He claimed that "as to righteousness under the law" he was "blameless" (Phil. 3:6). Thus, Paul talked not only of Gentiles who fulfilled the requirements of Torah, but claimed also that he had been able to obey Torah. The passage shows no signs of frustration or despair about an inability to please God.[6] Furthermore, Paul blamelessly observed Torah before he became a believer in Christ! Paul may have observed that some people fail to obey Torah, but he could hardly deny the possibility.

However, Paul now found that such obedience to Torah was of lesser worth in comparison to what he now had as a believer in Christ: "But whatever gain I had, I counted as loss for the sake of Christ" (3:7). It was not his inability to follow Torah, but rather his new experiences after becoming a believer in Christ that led Paul to value belief in Christ more than obedience to Torah. The faithfulness of Christ had accomplished something that Torah could not accomplish, the justification of Gentiles. For this reason, Paul considered Torah of lesser value. But did this lesser evaluation of Torah mean that Jews ought not to follow Torah? This is the next question we must ask.

A Response to Lester Dean from Gerard Sloyan

Your treatment of the way in which Paul thought the non-Jewish world was brought into covenantal relation with God by what God did in Christ is so good that one hesitates to observe a consistent absentee from the conversation. It is this: nowhere is there mentioned the Jewish view over the centuries that Torah as a gift of God to Israel is a mixed blessing: a treasure and a joy but also a hardship, a yoke lovingly imposed but still a yoke. I do not find a single place in Paul's letters where he states that he feels free to set Torah aside for Jews. All the texts that Christians have pounced on as making this point prove to be ambiguous or say the opposite. But as Jews rejoice in the Law against the Christian claim that it is a burden they long to be quit of, Jews also question among themselves why their God should have bestowed this at times doubtful honor on them. Paul would be a strange Jew indeed if the thought never crossed his mind.

I was puzzled to see Paul portrayed as a thoroughgoing enthusiast for Torah observance when Christian, Jewish, and disinterested readers of nineteen centuries have not been able to find in his letters a person who rejoices in the Law unequivocally such as Dean makes him out to be. I say unequivocal, for mixed in with his praise and thanks for the Law there is always stress on its temporary character, its capacity for being manipulated by Sin, or its character as a written *gramma* fated to be succeeded by a living *pneuma*. It should have done Dean no harm to tackle head-on this relativization of Torah for Jews that I find in Paul. Mention of it is present but always in slightly elusive language.

I am in full accord with the view that Paul was not a frustrated Pharisee or a frustrated anything. The discussion of the hardships people experience in doing what they know is right, whether they be Jews or Gentiles, is entirely helpful. So, too, and especially, is the dismissal of the Christian canard that Paul's repudiation of "boasting" by Torah observants means that Torah itself invites boasting or, worse still, inevitably leads to it. In no other matter is the proverb *abusus non tollit usum* set aside by Christians with such fine careless rapture. Abuse is taken by them to be identical with use only in this case. To fail at keeping the Law is inevitable; to succeed is to make it the subject of a boast! Jews have been in a "no-win situation" at Christian hands for two millennia before this particularly apt phrase was coined.

NOTES

1. For a discussion about "The Joy of the Law" see: Schechter, *Aspects of Rabbinic Theology* (New York: Macmillan, 1961), pp. 148–169.
2. For example, R. Bultmann, *Primitive Christianity* (Cleveland: World Publishing Company, 1956), claimed that to take the commandments "seriously meant making life an intolerable burden. It was almost impossible to *know* the rules, let alone put them into practice," p. 66.
3. For Bultmann and others who hold this view the very attempt to obey the Law is sin, defined as "man's self-powered striving to undergird his own existence in forgetfulness of his creaturely existence, to procure his salvation by his own

strength ... he can find his salvation only when he understands himself in his dependence upon God the Creator." *Theology of the New Testament* (New York: Charles Scribner's Sons, 1951), vol. I, p. 264. This is another example of the qualitative argument: God demands that the Law be fulfilled in a manner available only to Christians, not to Jews; see note 10 of chapter 14. Jews do not object to the emphasis upon God as the author of salvation. Yet we are astonished how Christians can think that we have forgotten God and are trying to gain salvation by our own actions. The Jew who obeys the Law is constantly reminded of God by the various commandments. God's giving of the Law seems to be a horrible trick played upon humanity, making demands which cannot be kept and then, when the means to fulfill the demands are given—that is, through faith in Christ—suddenly the demands are removed and Christians are forbidden to observe the Law. It is not surprising that Hübner, following such a view of the Law, can claim that according to Paul the Law was given by *demonic* angels; see note 5 of chapter 14.

4. See note 3 of chapter 17.

5. See chapter 14 and also note 11 of that chapter.

6. See K. Stendahl, *Paul Among Jews and Gentiles* (Philadelphia: Fortress Press, 1976), pp. 12–15.

17

Did Paul Think That Jews and Jewish Christians Must Follow Torah?

GERARD SLOYAN

Paul consistently refers to the law of Moses as *nomos*. There is no good reason to think that he meant by it anything other than *torah*, however much that Hebrew term encompassed in his day. Sometimes it is said that he had a narrow view of *torah* (a word that means "instruction" or "teaching") in that he took it to mean only the observance of precepts. That the Greek word *nomos* is a legal term is a good part of the evidence cited for this view. But that, of course, is the way the Septuagint Bible, a translation done by Jews, rendered the word *torah*. There is nothing of a Christian plot about it. Further evidence alleged to support Paul's understanding of "the Law" as narrowly legal and not the totality of God's revelation is his coupling of the term "law" with commandment(s) (Rom. 7:8–10, 1 Cor. 7:19) and "works" or "works of the Law," whichever they are (Rom. 3:20, 27, 28; 9:11, 32), as if he thought the observance of precepts was paramount in the Mosaic books. He could be seen as prescient in this, for the Rabbis were not too much later to opt for the halakhic or legal parts of *torah* as having priority over the *aggadic* or narrative parts.

There is a problem in our not knowing how far advanced in the 50s the movement was that would emerge after the fall of Jerusalem as "Rabbinism" or "Judaism." That there was already stress on the observance of precepts in Paul's day we can be sure from the tenor of his writings. We can deduce this from his pointing out that being circumcised meant keeping "the whole Law" (Gal. 5:3). But the term "oral Torah" had not yet surfaced at this early date, nor had the rabbis isolated the 613 precepts of the written Law. That development would be reported on two centuries later. It is safe to say that certain commandments were fully binding in Paul's time; these included circumcision, the prohibition of swine's flesh and other animals proscribed by the Bible, the prohibition of incest, and above all the "ten words" delivered on Sinai; also included were certain positive precepts like the observance of the pilgrimage feasts (*Pesach* or Passover, *Shavuot* or Pentecost, and *Sukkoth* or Tabernacles), an annual charge to support the temple, and the relief of the poor.

Still, it is important to recall that in Paul's day the legal edifice of the third- and the fourth-century Rabbis had not yet been constructed, indeed that their founding father Johanan ben Zakkai had not yet arrived in Yavneh (he was to come just before the fall of Jerusalem in 70 of the Common Era). Much is attributed in the Mishnah (180–200 C.E.) to Hillel and Shammai who predated Jesus and Paul, but we do not know how much of the opinions their "schools" are said to hold were retrojections on the basis of their remembered general outlooks. All of this means that Paul's dictum, "the whole Law is fulfilled in one word, 'You shall love your neighbor as yourself'" may not have been as radical a summary of Torah in his day or as redolent of Christianity as subsequent developments in both traditions made it.

We cannot overstress our ignorance of the exact limits of the demands of the Law that were being put on Jews by fellow Jews in Paul's lifetime. The situation was certainly in flux and we do not know its outer limits. Paul is found guilty of serious departure from Jewish behavior by the standard of Mishnah and Talmud (roughly completed in Babylon by the year 500), which is often erroneously set for him. At the same time, he cannot be charged with a laxity in the observance of precepts that characterized diaspora Jews generally, as is sometimes done. There is no hard evidence to support a double standard in the mid-first century C.E., a strict one for Palestine and a loose one for the diaspora. The claims that the native of Tarsus Paul makes for his own zeal for the traditions of his forebears (Gal. 1:14; Phil. 3:5) should be taken at face value, whatever it meant to be a Pharisee in his day. That, we do not know.

As to whether Paul thought that the members of his churches who were ethnic Jews had to observe Torah, there is enough indication from his epistles to answer yes, if their consciences told them they had to; no, if they thought that all Jews had to; and by no means, if they supposed that Law-observance was a necessary complement to their faith in Christ.

Close examination of Paul's letters discloses that in ethical matters, at least, he assumes that Torah is still in full force for Jews and should be adopted by Gentiles. This extends from matters touching on sexuality, property, and truth or falsehood to what we might call folkways, e.g., proper behavior as to hair style and head covering (1 Cor. 11:2–16). The latter he calls "the traditions even as I have delivered them to you" (v. 2), the "you" being the presumably majority Gentile church of Corinth. Evidently, according to Paul even some nonbiblical traditions had to be kept.

Torah in ritual or dietary matters can be either traditional for Paul's churches — hence to be kept — or something forbidden to believers in Jesus. Jewish behavior was a matter that Paul practiced easily. "To the Jews I became as a Jew, in order to win Jews," he writes, "to those under the Law I became as one under the Law — though not being myself under the Law — that I might win those under the Law" (1 Cor. 9:20). This seems to hint at a distinction between ordinary Jews and a new class of Law observants ("those under the Law") who were perhaps the "separated" or *perushim* to which he gave his allegiance as a young man. In any case, Paul does not scruple at aligning himself with either group; hence, he cannot charge other Jews with doing what he himself did regularly.

The other thing Paul could not tolerate was Torah observance as something *required* of believers in Jesus, chiefly of Gentile believers as part of their joining the Jesus movement. Most of what we know about Paul's wrath in this matter emerges from his polemic against those who would make such demands upon his Gentiles. The imposition of bits of Jewish behavior is the "other gospel" or "perversion of the gospel of Christ" he speaks of (Gal. 1:7). Faith in Jesus Christ (2:16), and the Spirit which was given by hearing with faith (3:2), are the characteristics of the new situation. The works of the Law as justifying (2:16), i.e. putting you in a right relation with God, which was the legitimate mark of the old situation — can be a curse for those who rely on them (3:10). The Law is not of itself a curse for Paul. It becomes such only when that faith that should be reserved for God's deed in Christ has been reposed in it. As has been observed, Paul's sole quarrel with the Law is that it is not Christ.[1]

God has done something new in Christ, relativizing all that has gone before: "The Law is holy, and the commandment is holy and just and good" (Rom. 7:12). It "held us captive" (7:6) only because the new life of the Spirit succeeded it. The Law showed sin to be sin (v. 13); it thereby increased the trespass (5:20). It acted as a stop-gap until the promise made to Abraham could be fulfilled in his seed, Christ (Gal. 3:19). The Law was "our custodian until Christ came" (Gal. 3:24). Most important, perhaps, "the doers of the Law will be justified" (Rom. 2:13) and "all who have sinned under [it] will be judged by [it]" (v. 12). This has to mean that there is a Law-righteousness for Paul that was surpassed once faith in Christ became a possibility (Gal. 3:16).

Did Paul think that the Law is nonjustifying for the Jew, not just for the Gentile? It certainly seems so. Can the Jewish "believer" conform to the Law so long as this gives no scandal and is not thought by Jews to be justifying? This, too, appears to be true. Paul cited portions of the Law that he expected the people in his churches to abide by. It had continuing validity as a guide to action, this God-authored code of behavior sanctioned by centuries of helpfulness, provided it did not impugn the *novum* achieved by God in the realm of the Spirit outpoured.

What of the Jews in Persia of Paul's day, to take a hypothetical example, who had not heard the gospel? What of the Jews of the ages since Paul who had not or have not "heard" it in the sense in which Paul used that verb, that is, most of the Jews who would ever live? Paul would probably say that Law-righteousness continued and continues to be open to them — something on which he put a high value. He simply valued the gospel higher and could not imagine the Law to be binding on anyone, Jew or Gentile, who had genuinely "heard" the new thing God had done in Christ.

A Response to Gerard Sloyan from Lester Dean

Sloyan is correct in warning us not to judge Paul's observance of Torah by later rabbinic standards. There were various standards of acceptable Jewish behavior at this time, although, as Sloyan observed, we know very little about any of these standards. I also agree that the often mentioned view that Paul was a "Hellenistic Jew," meaning that he had a different and lax view of Torah observance, is based upon a dichotomy between Hellenistic and Palestinian Judaism that is not supported by historical evidence.[2] Yet we should keep in mind that our topic is not how any particular group understood and defined the requirements of following Torah, but whether Paul could accept any of these standards as a requirement for either Jewish believers in Jesus or for any Jews.

I disagree with Sloyan's opinion that Paul was flexible in his view of Jewish Torah observance. I think that Paul told Gentiles not to obey Torah, but that he expected Jews to obey. Paul could allow flexibility in regard to food offered to idols. He was dealing with a human concern. As long as eating food offered to idols was not interpreted to mean worship of that idol, Paul could be flexible and allow for the demands of conscience. He could not allow the demands of conscience in the case of those who believed they were worshiping idols when they ate the food, for then they would be guilty of idolatry and idolatry was prohibited by God.

The observance of Torah was not a matter that could be left to the demands of conscience. Torah was God's commandment to the Jews, binding in its totality only upon them, since everyone who was circumcised was "bound to keep the whole law" (Gal. 5:3).[3] It was not conscience that told a Jew to observe Torah, it was scripture itself, the very Torah that was read and studied and whose prophecies had been fulfilled with the coming of Jesus.

Torah observance was not to be considered justifying by Jews, but this would not have been the correct Jewish view in any case. Paul probably often had to explain to Gentiles the distinction between relying upon faith in Christ as the way of attaining righteousness and the observance of Torah as a sign of that righteousness. It is a distinction that the Church soon forgot. If a Jew had thought that righteousness came from following Torah,

Paul would surely have corrected the error. However, I do not think that Paul would have prohibited the person from following Torah.

Paul's remarks about becoming "all things to all men" have sometimes been used to argue that he lived as a Gentile in order to win Gentiles to the gospel. "To those outside the law I became as one outside the law — not being without law toward God but under the law of Christ — that I might win those outside the law" (1 Cor. 9:21).

The first difficulty in the text is to determine what group Paul was addressing as those "outside the law," were they Jews or Gentiles? If Paul has made a distinction between Jews and those under the law, "To the Jews I became as a Jew ... to those under the law I became as one under the law" (9:20), then he could have been speaking about this same distinction here. He might still have been living as a Jew, but now was referring to different standards of Torah observance. If this were the case, then Paul had not completely forsaken Torah.

If Paul were speaking about Gentiles, saying that at times he lived like a Jew, and that at times he lived like a Gentile, we are amazed. Did he really mean that he lived as a Jew when he was with Jews and that he lived as a Gentile when he was with Gentiles? Such a suggestion seems absurd, especially since he stated that he lived in this manner in order to win these different groups.[4] Jews would not have listened to a Jew who obeyed Torah when he was with Jews but who forsook Torah when he was with Gentiles. Gentiles would probably have questioned the integrity of such a person. Such actions would surely have confused Paul's Gentile converts.

Paul's language is difficult for us to understand: he is both not under the Law, yet under the law of Christ. We must avoid an overly literal reading of the passage. No one would suggest that Paul actually sold himself into slavery, even though he said, "I have made myself a slave to all" (9:19). Likewise, we should not expect Paul to have forsaken Torah even though he said, "I became as one outside the law." Paul was outside of the Law and dead to the Law only in relation to its requirement for Gentiles to become Jewish proselytes. He was not saying that he no longer followed Torah in order to win Gentiles to the gospel.

NOTES

1. E. P. Sanders, *Paul and Palestinian Judaism* (Philadelphia: Fortress Press, 1977), p. 482.

2. See note 1 to chapter 2 above.

3. Obviously Gal. 5:3 was addressed to Gentiles, but if Paul would demand Torah obedience from Gentiles, how much more from Jews?

4. See: Sanders, *Paul, the Law, and the Jewish People* (Philadelphia: Fortress Press, 1983), pp. 179–192. For the view that Paul continued to practice Pharisaic Judaism throughout his life see: W. L. Knox, *St. Paul and the Church of Jerusalem* (Cambridge: Cambridge University Press, 1925), pp. 122–123; W. D. Davies, *Paul*

and Rabbinic Judaism (London: SPCK, 1955), p. 70; and F. C. Grant, *Roman Hellenism and the New Testament* (Edinburgh: Oliver and Boyd, 1962), p. 136. L. Gaston, *Paul and the Torah* (Vancouver: University of British Columbia Press, 1987) likewise notes that Paul could have remained a member of the Sinai covenant, but ultimately is led to believe that Paul was an apostate who renounced the Sinai covenant and became like a Gentile so that his mission to the Gentiles would not be hindered, pp. 76–79. Gaston suggests that perhaps "Paul wanted to have it both ways, to understand himself as an apostate in relationship to his Gentile converts but as a loyal son of Israel in relationship to Jews," p. 79. However, Gaston does not believe Paul thought other Jewish Christians should follow his example and renounce the covenant. Gaston places too much emphasis on Gal. 2:18. Paul is not renouncing the covenant, but only the Torah requirement that Gentiles had to convert to Judaism.

18

Jews and Jewish Christians Must Follow Torah

LESTER DEAN

In the last section we found that Paul believed it possible for a person to obey Torah. In fact, he stated that he had followed Torah blamelessly. However, Paul then stated, "whatever gain I had, I counted as loss for the sake of Christ" (Phil. 3:7). He no longer had "a righteousness of my own, based on law, but that which is through faith in Christ, the righteousness from God that depends on faith" (3:9).

Likewise, according to Galatians, Paul and Peter, who were "Jews by birth and not Gentile sinners ... believed in Christ Jesus, in order to be justified by faith in Christ, and not by works of law, because by works of law shall no one be justified" (2:15–16). Paul had "died to the law" (2:19). "If justification were through the law, then Christ died to no purpose" (2:21).

This epistle to the Galatians contains Paul's most negative remarks about obedience to the law. He argued that "all who rely on works of the law are under a curse" (3:10). He said to the Galatians, "If you receive circumcision, Christ will be of no advantage to you ... You are severed from Christ, you who would be justified by the law; you have fallen away from grace" (5:2,4). "If you are led by the Spirit you are not under the law" (5:18).

The usual interpretation of verses such as these is that Paul no longer followed Torah after he came to believe in Jesus Christ. It is also usually believed that Paul counseled both Gentiles and Jews to abandon Torah. According to this interpretation, Paul saw that the following of Torah was in opposition to belief in Christ. The person who believed in Christ could not practice the Law. Obedience to Torah was an attempt to gain righteousness apart from Christ, an attempt that led both Jews and Gentiles away from Christ.

From a Jewish viewpoint such a criticism of obedience to Torah is heretical; it would be punished most severely. According to the book of Acts, the Jews thought that Paul taught "all the Jews who are among the Gentiles to forsake Moses, telling them not to circumcise their children or observe the customs" (21:21). It was for this reason that he was arrested in the temple (21:21–28). Thus Paul's personal example, his advice to believers in Christ, and his persecution by the Jews all seem to indicate that he was opposed to Jewish observance of Torah.

However, it is important to note the audience Paul was addressing when he opposed observance of Torah, especially in the epistle to the Galatians. Throughout the first part of the letter, Paul reminded his audience that he was called to preach among the Gentiles (1:16, 2:2, 7–9). He showed that all who believed in Christ were children of God and that "there is neither Jew nor Greek" (3:28). In chapter five Paul argued that his readers should not be circumcised; faith, not circumcision was what was important. These Galatians, who had heard Paul preach, these Galatians, who were children of God not because they were Jews but because they were believers in Christ, these Galatians, who were not circumcised, were Gentiles and not Jews, and Paul's purpose in writing to the Galatians was to discuss the observance of the Law by Gentiles.[1]

We have already discussed Paul's belief that Gentile believers in Christ were not to be circumcised nor to be under the law. They were only to fulfill the essence of Torah, the law of love: "For the whole law is fulfilled in one word, 'You shall love your neighbor as yourself' " (5:14). It appears that Paul was persecuted because he did not preach circumcision, that is, he did not require Gentiles to be circumcised, and his opponents preached circumcision only to avoid persecution (5:11, 12).

Jews today are sometimes critical of this reported persecution. Judaism of the later rabbinic period held that Gentiles were not required to be circumcised nor obey all of Torah. They only had to obey the seven laws of Noah. However, the opinions of later rabbis should not be used as a guide to Jewish beliefs at the time of Paul. The Hebrew scriptures spoke about righteous Gentiles, but the requirements for a Gentile to be righteous were not explicitly stated. As mentioned previously, for some Jews the justice of God demanded that the commandments of Torah be eternal and be offered to all of humanity. According to such a view, Gentiles must also obey Torah, and Jews who discouraged Gentile observance would have been persecuted, just as Paul claimed.[2]

Most Christian interpreters of Paul claim that his explicit prohibition of Torah observance for Gentiles also included Jewish believers in Christ and probably included all Jews. Such a prohibition of Torah observance, from a Jewish perspective, denies the possibility of Judaism. Judaism is based upon obedience to God's will as found in Torah; lack of observance is disobedience to God and God's covenant with Israel. If Paul told other

Jews not to observe Torah then he had definitely placed himself outside of Judaism.

However, Paul's position on Jewish observance of Torah should not be derived from his views about Gentile observance of Torah. Prohibiting Jewish observance of Torah because of Paul's argument that Gentiles must not follow Torah is often based on Paul's statements about the equality of believers in Christ. "There is neither Jew nor Greek, there is neither slave nor free, there is neither male nor female; for you are all one in Christ Jesus" (Gal. 3:28). It is argued that this "oneness" in Christ meant that all distinctions between Jews and Gentiles were abolished. Since Gentiles were not to follow Torah, Jews were also not to follow Torah.

Close examination of this verse does not support an argument that Paul made no distinctions between Jews and Gentiles. The verse also argues that both slaves and free persons and males and females are one in Christ. But Paul's equality of these groups did not mean that he abolished all distinctions between slaves and free persons or between males and females. In God's eyes, they "are all one in Christ Jesus," but Paul still returned Onesimus the slave to Philemon; he still commanded that women be veiled and keep silent in church. Since Paul allowed different conduct between slaves and free persons and between males and females, he could also have allowed different conduct for Jews and Gentiles.[3]

However, in some parts of Galatians Paul seems to speak about the relationship of Jews and of Paul, himself, to Torah. Paul and Peter, "Jews by birth and not Gentile sinners . . . believed in Christ Jesus, in order to be justified by faith in Christ, and not by works of the law, because by works of the law shall no one be justified" (2:14–16). These verses are sometimes quoted to prove that Paul and Peter now no longer followed Torah since they now knew that they were made righteous through faith in Christ and not through works of the Law. Thus Christian Jews, and, by extension, all Jews, should not follow Torah.

These texts are concerned with the relationship between law, faith, and righteousness, and not with the question of obedience to Torah. The question Paul was addressing was not whether a person should obey Torah, nor the correct attitude a person should have when obeying Torah, nor even whether a person could obey Torah, but whether righteousness comes from obedience to Torah. Paul was merely expounding Jewish teaching to his Gentile audience. Righteousness came from one's status within the covenant that God graciously established. Obedience to Torah was not the source of righteousness but was the sign of the acceptance of the covenant by Jews. Any knowledgeable Jew of Paul's age, or our own, would agree. The verses do not prove that a Jew should not follow Torah. They merely state that one does not gain righteousness by following Torah.

Paul also mentioned "our freedom which we have in Christ" and warned that false brethren wanted "to bring us into bondage" (2:4). He did not submit to these opponents and was vindicated when those "who were in repute added nothing to me" (2:6). The subject of this controversy, the freedom that Paul enjoyed, is not explicitly stated, but it is often taken to mean Paul's freedom from observing Torah. The verses are then taken to show that Paul did not follow Torah, that there were some believers in Jesus who felt that Jews should follow Torah, but that Paul was supported by the leaders of the early Church in his contention that he did not have to obey Torah. Thus, both Paul and the Jerusalem church agreed that Jewish believers in Christ should not obey Torah.

However, the primary issue of Galatians is the circumcision of Gentiles, not Jewish observance of Torah. Immediately preceding the verses about freedom, Paul mentioned Titus, a Greek who accompanied him but who was not forced to be circumcised. Since Titus was not circumcised, he was a Gentile and not a Jew. The freedom about which Paul spoke was not freedom from obedience to Torah but his freedom to accept Gentiles as part of the body of believers in Christ without circumcision. As we noted previously, Paul was now free from the restraint, based upon Torah, that Gentiles had to become Jews in order to be righteous. It was this that Paul had preached to the Gentiles, and it was this that the apostles in Jerusalem condoned. Paul was not free from following Torah, and the passage does not prove that the early Church sanctioned the principle that Jewish believers in Christ had complete freedom from following Torah.

Likewise, when Paul "through the law died to the law" (Gal. 2:18), he meant only that he no longer was bound to the past Jewish understanding that Gentiles must follow Torah if they are to be part of the Kingdom of God. Because of his release from this, Paul had a new life in which "Christ lives in me" (2:20). It was a new life, a new mission, a new calling to tell the Gentiles about Christ. It was not a new life in which Paul no longer followed Torah.

Paul stated that "if I build up again those things which I tore down, then I prove myself a transgressor" (Gal. 2:18). Paul was not saying that he had forsaken Torah and that he would be a transgressor if he now began again to follow Torah. He referred to his past persecution of the Church. He was now building up what he had tried to destroy.[4] He was now proclaiming that Gentiles need not become Jewish proselytes, whereas in the past he had argued that according to the Law Gentiles had to become Jews. It was this Law that he now transgressed, since God's faithfulness to the promise given to Abraham showed that the Law had come to an end as a barrier between Jews and Gentiles. Peter, when he first came to Antioch, had agreed with Paul's opinion that Gentile believers did not have to obey Torah. Peter had "lived as a Gentile," breaking Jewish Law by eating with the Gentile believers in Jesus in Antioch. He was confronted with his transgression when messengers arrived from James. Peter changed his mind and demanded that the Gentiles in Antioch be circumcised, and he refused to eat with them until they followed Torah. Paul did not condemn Peter for following Torah or for withdrawing from the Gentiles, but for trying to clear himself by denigrating the Gentiles. Peter claimed the Gentiles were at fault, rather than himself, arguing that the Gentile believers should follow Torah.

We have already discussed the restraining or confining role of Torah that came to an end with Christ (Gal. 3:19–25). This was not the end of Torah, but rather the freedom to preach to the Gentiles without the requirement of circumcision (3:19–25). Now God was also showing mercy to the Gentiles, for the role of Torah, as the restraining force keeping the Gentiles from God, had come to an end. Jews still followed Torah, but they no longer had an advantage over the Gentiles. Both came to God through faith in Christ.

Paul also argued that "everyone should remain in the state in which he or she was called," and this admonition included the question of circumcision (1 Cor. 7:17–24). Thus the Gentile should not become a Jew. "Let him not seek circumcision," is the main argument of Galatians. Neither should the Jew become as a Gentile: "Let him not seek to remove the marks of circumcision." If Gentiles must not be circumcised and must not obey Torah, and if Jews must not try to remove their circumcision, then Jews must obey Torah.

The charges brought against Paul in the book of Acts were mentioned earlier, that he was opposed to Jewish observance of Torah. The usual Christian understanding of Paul would agree with these charges. Paul had forsaken Torah, and he had taught other Jews likewise to forsake Torah.

However, according to Acts the Christian leaders in Jerusalem knew that the charges against Paul were false. Paul was a faithful Jew who lived "in observance of the law" (21:24). At his trial before the Sanhedrin, Paul pleaded his innocence, and the Pharisees found him innocent (23:1–9). At his trial before Festus he stated that he had offended against "neither the law of the Jews nor against the temple" (25:8).

Some scholars have noted an apparent discrepancy between this picture of Paul the faithful Jew in the book of Acts and the usual picture of Paul the opponent of Torah derived from the epistles. The result has been a discrediting of Acts.[5] Christian scholars have agreed with the interpretation that Paul was opposed to Torah. The Church knew the true Paul. The author of Luke-Acts, writing a half century after Paul, was in error.

But there is another possible solution to the discrepancy. The traditional interpretation that Paul was opposed to Torah could be wrong. We have argued that Paul followed Torah and that he supported Jewish observance of Torah. In Acts Paul is pictured as the observant Jew who was falsely accused of preaching that Jews should not follow Torah. This description, probably written within the lifetime of some of Paul's youngest followers, is correct. The anti-Jewish interpretation of Paul's epistles by the Church pictured Paul as the opponent of Torah, who taught that Jews should not follow Torah. This is the description that is in error.[6]

Finally, it is necessary to note our own preconceptions on this issue, and then compare them to the ideas of Paul and his audience. From a Christian viewpoint it is assumed that Paul was against following Torah, not just because of a Christian reading of Paul, but because Christianity became predominantly Gentile and followed Paul's rule that Gentiles should not observe Torah. Therefore, with few exceptions, Christians do not follow Torah. Paul, viewed as a Christian, would then have been opposed to observing Torah.

If we begin our study of Paul's writings thinking that Paul was a Christian, then we expect him not to obey Torah and we expect him to counsel Jews, as well as Gentiles, not to obey Torah. Since most Jews of the time, including Jews who believed in Jesus, would have followed Torah, we would expect him to argue forcefully that they should not follow Torah. We do not expect him to be silent on the issue since the usual Jewish behavior would contradict Paul's beliefs.

But if we begin our study assuming Paul was a Jew, then we expect him to obey Torah. We also expect Paul to favor obedience to Torah for other Jews unless he explicitly states the contrary. In general he should be silent about Jewish obedience to Torah, since Jewish behavior would agree with his beliefs. On the subject of Gentile obedience we expect him to express an opinion, since there is no single Jewish opinion on the subject at this time.

When we look at the writings themselves, we note that Paul never explicitly forbade Jewish obedience to Torah. Paul only prohibited Gentile obedience to Torah. This is what we would expect from Paul the Jew, and not what we would expect from Paul the second-century Christian. If Paul were against Jews following Torah, and especially if he were against Jewish Christians following Torah, we should have evidence of that belief from his letters. In the absence of explicit statements against Jewish observance of Torah we must conclude that Paul agreed with the accepted view, that Jews must follow Torah.

We began our dialogue noting that Paul should be viewed as a Jew and not as a Christian. Here at one of the most sensitive points in our dialogue we again see that Paul's writings make sense if we start with Paul the Jew. This does not mean that Paul was a Jew like Hillel or Shammai. He believed in Jesus as messiah and wanted his fellow Jews to believe as he did, but this does mean that Paul, the opponent of Judaism, is a contradiction, a fabrication arising from Christian anti-Judaism. Paul's letters have been used for too long to oppress the kinsfolk he loved. Paul the Jew faithful to Torah, Paul the Jew described in the book of Acts, is the true Paul.

A Response to Lester Dean from Gerard Sloyan

That Galatians has as its primary thrust the nonnecessity, even the nonacceptability, of Gentiles' conforming to Torah is, I think, clearly spelled out here. Less clear is the assertion that when Paul says he and Peter are not justified by works of the Law (Gal. 2:14–16) he means chiefly that Law observance does not of itself justify (as every Jew then or now knows). He appears much more to be rejoicing in his and Peter's new condition of being justified by faith in Christ. The impression unavoidably received from a careful reading of this Galatians passage and Philippians 3:9 is that Torah observance for Jews has, in Paul's mind, been reclassified. It does not accomplish what it once did. What God has done lately in Christ has not annulled Torah or rendered it a matter of little consequence but has put it in a less than essential role. I am convinced that Paul counseled no Jew to abandon the Law as part of telling Gentiles that they were under a curse if they kept it. He distinguished between Jews and Gentiles many times in his letters ("the Jew first, then the Greek"). But in the matter of the new life available to both he did not distinguish.

To conclude: nothing in any Pauline writing says to me that he thought a Jew should not follow Torah. I resist only the idea that Paul is more concerned to tell Gentiles what they must not do than he is to insist on the new equality Jews and Gentiles have available to them by responding in faith to the preaching of the gospel. Paul's meaning when he speaks of having died to the Law (Gal. 2:18) continues to be a puzzle to me (death to the old eon with Christ on the cross?), but I am sure it has to do with Paul himself, not with a conviction he had about Gentiles before and after he believed in Christ.

NOTES

1. See: E. P. Sanders, *Paul, the Law, and the Jewish People* (Philadelphia: Fortress Press, 1983), pp. 18–20; L. Gaston, *Paul and the Torah* (Vancouver: University of British Columbia Press, 1987), p. 136; J. C. Beker, *Paul the Apostle* (Philadelphia: Fortress Press, 1980), pp. 47–49.

2. See: Gaston, *Paul and the Torah*, pp. 22–30, for the Jewish view that Gentiles had to follow Torah. Gaston notes the problems Paul had in defending his gospel, but claims Paul was persecuted because his opponents falsely believed he taught Jews to abandon Torah, pp. 33, 77, 109. This is the view of Acts, but it is more probable that Paul was persecuted because of his teachings about Gentile freedom from Torah.

3. See Beker, *Paul the Apostle*, pp. 324–325.

4. See Gaston, *Paul and the Torah*, pp. 68–71.

5. For example, Philip Vielhauer, "On the 'Paulinism' of Acts" in *Studies in Luke-Acts*, ed. L. Keck and J. Martyn (Philadelphia: Fortress Press, 1980).

6. See: L. Gaston, *Paul and the Torah*, pp. 79, 136.

19

What Was Paul's Hope for the Jews?

GERARD SLOYAN

It would be a mistake to think, on the basis of Paul's seven extant letters (Rom., 1 and 2 Cor., Gal., Phil., 1 Thes., and Phm.) that we have evidence that in his experienced call to apostleship to the Gentiles (Gal. 1:16; 2:8; Rom. 15:18–19) he turned his back on his fellow Jews or the religion of Israel. He would have called himself a Jew to his dying day. He would have denied vehemently that he had been "converted" in the sense of having deserted the faith of the people Israel for a new religion. Above all, there is nothing in his letters to support the idea that he deserted Jews for non-Jews in a new ethnic allegiance, whether intellectual or emotional or both. His correspondence, rather, supports the idea that he was prepared to share the gospel with anyone who would hear it; that the Spirit of Christ had led him to spend his life with largely but by no means exclusively Gentile populations; and that he devoutly wished that the Jewish people, first called by God through Abraham to believe in the gospel which he preached, would do so in great numbers. He was mystified, uncomprehending, even angry that they did not do so. Nonetheless, his wrath did not take the form of giving up on the Jews or saying that God had done so. If anything, Jewish disinterest in the gospel whetted his desire that this people should come to "faith," his term for commitment to God through Jesus Christ.

Seeing that it was not happening, however, he concluded his one formal reflection on the problem by marveling at God's all-encompassing mercy, the divine response to the universal human disobedience in which the Jews, being part of humanity, had a share (Rom. 11:32). This mercy has been effectively shown to the Gentiles in the past and will be shown to the Jews in the future (vv. 30–31). God's wisdom, God's judgment, God's ways with the Jewish people elicited from Paul only open-mouthed awe, not judgment (which he thought was a divine prerogative) on what he considered Jewish "disobedience" (v. 31).

St. Paul's correspondence was occasional or contingent. He faced problems as they arose in the churches. He never set himself in his letters to summarize the gospel as he first presented it in a new location or as he thought it could best be proclaimed. We do not know how he made such a presentation. The author of Acts did not know either but, like a good historian of his time, composed what he thought Paul should have said on these occasions. We do not possess a systematic presentation by Paul on any question, be it the exact nature of life in Christ; the relation of faith to baptism; how the churches might have related to a larger entity, the Church; the way ethical decisions flow from one's having been crucified and hoping to rise with Christ; or the precise force of the legal metaphor "justification" or any other metaphor: reconciliation, salvation, sanctification, or cleansing. Above all, we do not know how a systematic treatise by Paul on the continuing covenanted life of Jews who did not believe in Jesus after the apostolic age would have read. He never faced the problem. It is entirely hypothetical for us to do so on his behalf; it is presumption to assume we know what he would have said.

We do know that Paul was apprehensive on two fronts as he prepared to go to Jerusalem before proceeding to Rome and Spain—perhaps in the year 57 or 58. He had collected "aid for the saints," meaning believers in Jesus Christ, in Macedonia and Achaia (Rom. 15:25–26) and solicited prayers that he would fare well among "nonbelievers in Judea" (Jewish nonbelievers in Jesus being most of the populace) and that his "service for Jerusalem" would be "acceptable to the saints," the Jews who did believe in Jesus (15:31). This epistle is clearly directed to Jerusalem by way of Rome. Traffic and correspondence from the capital of the empire to Judea's chief city was constant. The respected and relatively populous Roman church, which Paul had done nothing to found and had never visited, would be a good witness to the way he preached the gospel. Many Jewish believers in Rome, like Prisca and Aquila, would testify that his intemperate outburst recorded in the Galatian letter against foisting fragments of Law observance on his Gentiles was not to be taken for an attack on the Law itself. Paul was fully confident of the way he preached the gospel. He knew that an attack on the Jewish people or the Israelite revelation through Moses was no part of it. (1 Thes. 2:15–16 gives every evidence of being an interpolation by a later hand, although the two verses are textually unassailable.) He seems to have hoped that the Roman community would convey that to Jerusalem before he got there.

There are many scholars who think that the epistle to the Romans is effectively over at the end of chapter 8. They suppose the letter to be a doctrinal summary on how God's grace operates to achieve the justification of Jews and non-Jews alike by faith. I am among those convinced that the next three chapters are not an appendage to the previous eight, a mere bridge to the paranaetic chapters 12–15, but the heart of the letter and the reason he wrote it.

An attack by a Jew on the Jewish people, then as now, was thought to be a form of religious apostasy. An attack on the Law was an attack on God, hence nothing short of blasphemy, although an attack by some Jews on how other Jews were keeping the Law—or not keeping it—was a commonplace. After writing Galatians, Paul would have to be obtuse not to know that he was vulnerable in Judea on both charges. The outreach to the Gentiles may not in the first place have received very wide approval by ethnic Jewish believers in Jesus, who were at first the only ones. Paul's special techniques in this outreach were probably known to many in Jerusalem and repudiated heartily with each new report. He wrote to assure them that he knew as well as any Jew that the "sonship, the glory, the covenants, the giving of the Law, the worship, and the promises" are theirs, that "to them belong the patriarchs, and of their race according to the flesh, is the Christ" (Rom. 9:4–5).

He so loved his fellow Jews that he would wish himself accursed and cut off from Christ for their sakes (v. 3) if it would do any good. The wish is expressed *per impossibile*, but it is no less heartfelt for that.

Everyone knows how Paul's argument goes from there, developing the distinction he had made earlier between a Jew in appearance and a Jew who is one inwardly (Rom. 2:28)—circumcision being "a matter of the heart, spiritual and not literal" (v. 25). This, we know, became an argument the rabbis would make without any reference to Paul. The children of the promise, not ethnic stock, are reckoned as descendants of Abraham through Isaac (9:7–8). God it was who did the electing; therefore those who believe in Jesus depend "not on human will or exertion but on God's mercy" (v. 16) and they come "not from the Jews only, but also from the Gentiles" (v. 24). Paul's heart's desire and prayer was that his kinsfolk be saved (10:1). How is what he calls their "unenlightened zeal" (v. 2) to be overcome? By persistently proclaiming to them (vv. 14–21) the word (v. 8) of God's righteousness (v. 3), a righteousness based on faith.

Did Paul have anything against his fellow Jews for "not submitting to [what he conceived to be] God's righteousness" (10:3)? Indeed he did. He quotes Isaiah against them (65:1–2), who calls Israel "a disobedient and contrary people" (10:21). How, if ever, will God's foreknown Jewish people, who are not rejected (11:1,2), come to faith? Paul must have wrestled long and hard with this problem before he put forward his theory, on the basis of his thirty-plus years of experience. It is given in Romans 10:10. The Jewish people will enter into the fullness of their faith inheritance by means of a present remnant of Jews chosen by grace (v. 5)—Peter, James, Paul, Barnabas, and the thousands like them—through the divinely ironic device of Israel's jealousy at the salvation of the Gentiles (v. 11).

That, at least, is what Paul had in mind to do as he magnified his own ministry (vv. 13–14): make his fellow Jews jealous of his good fortune. The present "hardening" of Israel—a phrase from the Hebrew Bible—was ultimately a mystery of God to Paul. He speaks as if he knew something about it but ultimately he does not. The "gift and the call of God [to Israel] are irrevocable" (v. 20)—only that much is he sure of. God who gave the initial call to Israel will not finally be thwarted. Present disobedience can only mean future mercy (vv. 30–32) "until the full number of the Gentiles shall come in." What is that full number? It is a piece of apocalyptic rhetoric, of course, and means as many non-Jewish believers as suit the divine purpose when God calls a halt to the world as we know it.

Israel's hardening will continue, "and so all Israel will be saved" (vv. 19–20). When is that, and what does "all Israel" mean? This too is the language of apocalyptic speech, describing God's ultimate disposition of things in the final days. Apocalypticism has no interest in times or seasons or numbers as a demographer or a calendar expert would reckon them. It is only certain about what *will be* in God's mysterious future. "All Israel" could be as many Jewish believers in Christ as suit the divine purpose.

Israel, Paul's kinsfolk, are not rejected. They are sure to be brought to end-time glory, Paul knows, at God's good pleasure. How? It would be folly for anyone or for the whole Church to presume to say, least of all to say that it will be the way of public belief in Jesus Christ by great numbers of the world's now 18,000,000 Jews. Maybe no such thing will happen, yet the prophecy will be fulfilled in other ways, as by a remnant even smaller at the end than in Paul's day. The Church maintains only that it *will happen*; it knows it through the prophetic-apostolic voice of Paul.

A Response to Gerard Sloyan from Lester Dean

Paul quoted Isaiah 65:1–2, apparently seeing it as a prophecy about his present successful ministry among the Gentiles. Gentiles had found God through Paul's preaching of the gospel, whereas the Jews had said "No" to the gospel. Yet I think this is less a criticism of the Jews than a statement of fact for Paul. He and his readers at Rome knew that Paul's ministry to the Gentiles had been more successful than the ministry of Peter to the Jews.

We should note both what Paul quoted and what he did not quote from the Isaiah passage. He stopped the quotation after verse two, omitting the extremely harsh rebukes found in the following verses, which conclude with God's judgment and destruction of the sinful part of the nation:

I will destine you to the sword, and all of you shall bow down to the slaughter; because, when I called, you did not answer, when I spoke, you did not listen, but you did what was evil in my eyes, and chose what I did not delight in (65:12).

This, which so closely resembles the traditional Christian interpretation of Romans 10:20–21, was not quoted by Paul. Instead of the rejection and destruction of Isaiah 65, Paul immediately reminded his readers that God has not rejected the Jews. Romans 11:1 should not be separated from Paul's quotation of Isaiah 65, for Paul knew that his quotation could be misread as a negative statement about Israel. The Church did, in fact, choose to misread Paul, and the chapter division is one example of a subtle form of anti-Judaism also found in Christian translations of their scriptures. Paul's citation is not an accusation of those Jews who do not believe the message about Christ, but proof that Jewish disbelief was part of God's plan. Through this disbelief, salvation had come to the Gentiles; thus, Gentile believers should not be critical of Jews who do not believe the gospel.[1]

Whether Paul truly understood God's plan regarding the successful ministry to the Gentiles and the unsuccessful one to the Jews cannot be determined, but I do think that Paul thought he understood some of this mysterious plan. Not only was he sure that God's call was irrevocable, but he saw that his successful ministry to the Gentiles was founded upon an unsuccessful ministry to the Jews. The Kingdom of God would begin when the Jews believed the good news about Jesus Christ. If the ministry to the Jews had been successful, then the Kingdom of God would have already begun and the disobedient among the Gentiles would have perished. But divine mercy was extended to the Gentiles because of the Jewish "No" to the gospel.

Paul thought that his successful ministry would also cause some of the Jews to accept the gospel, but this Jewish remnant of believers was not the ultimate solution to the problem of the unsuccessful ministry to the Jews. Rather, the remnant was Paul's answer to the possible criticism that God's plan had been thwarted by the unsuccessful ministry to the Jews. Some Jews had believed, proving that the gospel had not failed.[2]

Paul did not explicitly mention Jesus or Jewish faith in Jesus when he reminded his readers that "all Israel will be saved" (11:26). From a modern Jewish viewpoint we could be tempted to suggest that Paul separated the future salvation of the Jews from faith in Jesus.[3] Although such an idea may seem attractive and helpful in granting a continuing validity to Judaism, I doubt if it represents the thought of Paul. Paul's acceptance of Jesus as the messiah meant that Jesus would be the messianic king, ruling over the people Israel and also over the Gentile believers. Salvation meant a participation in the Kingdom of God at the last days, rather than a being saved from hell and going to heaven at the time of one's death. For Paul, Jesus as messiah could not have been separated from the future salvation of the Jews. Jews would be saved when God established the Kingdom, when Jesus returned as the messiah and ruled on the throne of David in Zion. Thus all Jews would believe in Jesus, but this does not mean that any would need to forsake their Judaism. Even the idea of a Jew converting to Christianity would have been contradictory for Paul.

Paul did not include an apocalyptic timetable to indicate when this salvation would take place. I agree that he was convinced that it would happen sometime, not just because he said it would happen in this epistle, but because God, whose promises are irrevocable, had promised to save Israel. This promise of salvation, known through the words of the prophets of the Hebrew Scriptures, can be affirmed by both the Church and the Synagogue.

NOTES

1. See: L. Gaston, *Paul and the Torah* (Vancouver: University of British Columbia Press, 1987), pp. 132–133. I agree with his suggestion that Paul is criticizing Israel for not understanding that the mission to the Gentiles was foretold in scripture, but I doubt if we can limit Paul's criticism to that point. Israel also did not understand that Jesus was Christ and Paul knew that the future eschatological salvation of humanity would occur when Israel did believe.

2. Gaston, *Paul and the Torah*, p. 140, suggests that the " 'remnant' that is to be saved in 9:27 is the same as the 'all Israel' that is to be saved in 11:26," while the remnant of 11:5 are those Jews like Paul who are engaged in the mission to the Gentiles, pp. 142–143. Whether these suggestions are accepted, he is certainly correct that Paul did not use the remnant concept to disherit Israel. See also J. C. Beker, *Paul the Apostle* (Philadelphia: Fortress Press, 1980), pp. 334–335. Beker refers the remnant to Jewish Christianity but notes that "Jewish Christianity does not simply displace the Jewish people and does not represent their fullness; rather, Jewish Christians are the symbol of the continuing faithfulness of God to Israel."

3. See: K. Stendahl, *Paul Among Jews and Gentiles* (Philadelphia: Fortress Press, 1976), p. 4; Gaston, *Paul and the Torah*, pp. 143–150.

20

Paul's Hope for the Jews

LESTER DEAN

We have found that Paul described himself as a Jew and that he was not opposed to Jews following Torah. But Paul also believed in Jesus Christ, a belief not accepted by most Jews. Did Paul's belief in Christ change his view of other Jews who were not believers in Christ? What was Paul's hope for the Jews?

Paul's longest and most developed discussion about the Jews is found in Romans chapters 9–11. In this passage we find Paul's attempt to understand the "No" to the gospel voiced by most Jews and his hope for the Jewish people. Often only selected verses from these chapters have been read. Paul was distressed about the lack of belief of the Jews: "I have great sorrow and unceasing anguish in my heart. For I could wish that I myself were accursed and cut off from Christ for the sake of my brothers [and sisters], my kinfolk by race" (9:1–2). He wished that the Jews would believe in Christ and be saved, "my heart's desire and prayer to God for them is that they may be saved" (10:1), even though he realized that "only a remnant of them will be saved" (9:27).

Israel according to the flesh was a "disobedient and contrary people" (10:21). "They were broken off because of their unbelief" (11:20), and "as regards the gospel they are enemies of God" (11:28). The God of Israel was found by the Gentiles who did not seek God, and these Gentiles were now "Israel according to the promise" whom God loved.[1]

These verses were used as proof that the Jews rejected Christ, that they were then rejected by God, and that the Gentile believers in Christ — the Christian church — had replaced them and were heirs to all God's promises to the Jews. Such a reading helped form the displacement theology of the Church and helped create negative feelings and attitudes toward Jews and Judaism. Such feelings made it possible for Jews to be persecuted and murdered for simply being Jews.[2]

189

Any analysis of these chapters must first consider the situation and purpose of Romans. In the past Romans was often read as a universal epistle presenting Paul's systematic theology. However, such interpretations ignore the situational character of Romans.[3] Paul was concerned with specific problems of the Roman believers in Christ when he wrote the epistle; the writing must be read within this context.

In chapters 2 and 3 of Romans Paul showed that Jews and Gentiles were equal before God, since "God shows no partiality" (2:11). Jews had certain advantages, but they were not to feel superior to Gentiles. Romans 9–11 deals with the opposite problem, feelings of superiority of Gentile believers over Jews. Paul argued that such feelings were also wrong; Gentiles were not superior to the Jews, and had not taken the place of the Jews in God's divine plan. The displacement theology of the Church, which has persisted for almost two thousand years, is what Paul was, in fact, attacking.[4] The traditional interpretation of these chapters can be supported only if one reads selected verses and ignores the surrounding text.

Paul affirmed that being a Jew meant being a child of God: "the glory, the covenants, the giving of the law, the worship, and the promises" of God were given to the Jews and Christ was a Jew (Rom. 9:4–5). Paul later made a distinction between Jews who did not believe in Jesus and Jews who did believe in Jesus in order to answer the possible charge that Jewish unbelief meant God's word had failed. However, the list of benefits in Romans 9 was open to all Jews, whether or not they were believers in Christ. Paul would return to the problem of Jewish unbelief several times, but he continued to remind his Gentile readers that the Jewish "No" to the gospel was part of God's plan, that God had not rejected the Jews, and that in the future all Israel would be saved (11:1–2, 25).

Paul tried to understand and explain the negative response of most Jews to the gospel and to grasp this part of God's mysterious plan for humanity. He was afraid that Gentile believers in Jesus might reach false conclusions when they thought about Jewish unbelief in Jesus. One possible error was to conclude that the small number of Jews who believed in Jesus indicated that the ministry to the Jews had failed. If this were true it would be possible to question whether the gospel itself was true. Paul was preaching that Jesus was the Christ, the Jewish messiah promised in the Hebrew Scriptures. If this were true, then Paul's Gentile believers wondered why the Jews did not believe in Jesus.

Paul answered that "it is not as though the word of God failed" (9:6). The solution was to be found in the biblical idea of the remnant. It was true that most Jews did not yet believe in Jesus, but there were some Jews who believed. The prophets predicted that only a few Jews would believe in Jesus: "Though the number of the children of Israel be as the sand of the sea, only a remnant of them will be saved" (9:27); "At the present time there is a remnant, chosen by grace" (11:5). This showed that the gospel was true and that the ministry had not failed. Those Jews who had been elected and called by God did believe and were the remnant of Israel described by the prophets. They had been given the special task of proclaiming the gospel to the Gentiles.[5]

But Paul did not use this remnant motif to claim that the Jewish believers in Christ had replaced all the Jews, the collective nation, in God's divine plan. He definitely did not say that the church had taken the place of the Jews.[6] Paul talked of the *plērōma*, the fullness, of the Jews that would bring greater riches to the world: "If their failure means riches for the Gentiles, how much more will their full inclusion mean" (11:12); "A hardening has come upon part, *merous*, of Israel, until the full number, *plērōma*, of the Gentiles" enter the people of God (11:25). But in the future, "all, *pas*, Israel will be saved" (11:26). Just as nothing could separate the believer in Christ from the love of God (8:31–39), so nothing could separate the Jews from the love of God, for "the gifts and the call of God are irrevocable" (11:29).

The second error that Paul argued against was that this Jewish unbelief was due to wickedness, or some inherent shortcoming. God's mercy did not depend upon good or bad human actions, but upon God's will: " 'I will have mercy on whom I have mercy, and I will have compassion on whom I have compassion.' So it depends not upon a person's will or exertion, but upon God's mercy" (9:15–16). God will have mercy or will harden the heart of whomever God wills. Jews do not believe in Jesus not because they are evil, but because of God's hardening of their hearts.

The Jews "have a zeal for God, but it is not enlightened" (10:1–2). The "Gentiles who did not pursue righteousness have attained it, that is, righteousness through faith," but the Jews "pursued the righteousness which is based on the law and did not come to righteousness by faith" (9:30–32).[7] According to Paul, it was because the Jews wanted to remain righteous and faithful to God, not because they were evil, that they did not find it necessary to believe in Jesus.

It was fidelity to Torah that kept Jews from the gospel, a position Paul could easily have understood considering his past persecution of the Church out of fidelity to Torah. Paul had needed to see "the risen Christ" in order to realize that "Christ is the goal of Torah" (10:4).[8] It was only through God's mercy that he was now enlightened. The rest of the Jews were still faithfully following God's Torah, not seeing the connection between Christ and Torah that believers were now able to read in Torah. They had "eyes that should not see and ears that should not hear"; but did they stumble and fall? "By no means!" (11:7,11).

Paul did not portray the Jews as self-righteous legalists. Rather, they were obedient to God's commandments, faithful to the covenant God had established with them, waiting for God to fulfill the divine promises of that covenant. Since they did not see what had been revealed to him, that the death of Christ was itself part of that covenant, it would be an act of infidelity to God and the covenant for these Jews to have faith in Jesus.

The Jewish faithfulness to God, which Jews expressed by their rejection of the gospel, was also part of the divine plan. God had hardened the Jews, keeping from them the revelation about Jesus, so that God could have mercy upon the Gentiles.

It was this mercy and hardening of God that formed the basis for Paul's insight into God's mysterious plan for the Jews and the Gentiles. God had had mercy upon the Gentiles and had hardened the hearts of most of the Jews, thus postponing the establishment of the Kingdom of God so that "those who were not my people I will call my people" (9:26). But "God has not rejected his people," the Jews (11:1–2). The failure of the Jews to accept the gospel was part of God's plan; it was the way the Gentiles could participate in the kingdom promised to the Jews. If the Jews had accepted the gospel, if they had believed that Jesus was the Christ, then the messianic kingdom would have begun and the Gentiles would have had no chance to become a part of that kingdom.

For Paul, salvation for either Jew or Gentile took place in the future. He used *sōteria*, salvation, to refer to God's ultimate redemption of humanity and not—as is often the case today—to refer to an individual's conversion experience.[9] Paul hoped that *tinas*, "some," Jews would be saved because of his successful ministry among the Gentiles. "I magnify my ministry in order to make my fellow Jews jealous, and thus save some of them" (11:13).

However, the salvation of *pas*, "all," the Jews would be caused by the return of Christ as the Jews' deliverer, establishing the kingdom of God (11:26–27). It was then that all the Jews would recognize that Jesus of Nazareth was God's messiah, for at this point Jesus would fulfill the expected role of the messiah. Then the Jews would understand the mysterious divine plan that Paul now understood, that Jesus had been the messiah, that he had been crucified and that he rose again. They would see that because of their lack of belief in Jesus, the Gentiles were given the chance to enter the Kingdom of God. Jews would then be believers in Jesus Christ, God would have mercy upon them, and they would be grafted back into their natural place. This would then lead to the resurrection of the dead: "What will their acceptance mean but life from the dead?" (11:15).

Thus, Paul's hope for the Jews was the belief that God would have mercy upon all and that finally all Israel would be saved. For Paul, this did not mean that all Jews would convert to a new religion called Christianity. Rather, Jews would see what Paul also saw, that belief in Christ was a part of Judaism.

Christians, who form their view of the Jews based upon Paul's letters, have a choice. They can selectively read Paul out of context and view the Jews as "a disobedient people," "enemies of God," "cut off because of their unbelief"—the usual view of the past. Or they can quote Paul's true view of the Jews that "God has not rejected God's people," that "they have not fallen," that "God will have mercy upon all," and that "everyone who calls upon the name of YHWH will be saved."

Unfortunately, we cannot end our dialogue at this point. Paul did not know that two thousand years would elapse and Christ still would not have returned to establish the Kingdom of God. He did not know that Judaism and Christianity would become two different religions. Perhaps Paul's belief in Christ was compatible with Judaism. Christianity in most of its forms today does not seem so compatible.

What would Paul's view of the Jews have been had he known these things? Would he still have had the same hopes for the Jews? What has been the fate of those Jews whom God has hardened during these many years? Has God's plan failed? Were Paul's insights into that plan mistaken? The apostle did not write about such a situation, yet speculation might help Christians form a better view of Jews. In order to suggest a response we must examine what Paul believed happened when a person had faith in Christ.

A Response to Lester Dean from Gerard Sloyan

My only thought about this generally admirable treatment is that it could give the impression that Paul was concerned only for the Jews of the Roman church and elsewhere, not for the Gentiles also in his presumably mixed communities. If the Gentiles' sin has been lording it over the Jews over the centuries starting with the apostolic age, there is evidence in Paul's letter to Rome that he feared that the Jews of that community were lording it over the Gentiles (see Rom. 2, esp. v. 9). They not only had pride of place as receivers of the gospel but had recently added to their crown being the object of unjust persecution. Claudius' expulsion of them in his search for a scapegoat for his political troubles, and their return, was a very recent matter when Paul wrote. It lends greater plausibility to Paul's warning to them about the perils of relying firmly on the Law and priding themselves on God (2:17ff.), as if their sufferings set them above Gentile believers.

For the rest, I am sure that Paul's thought processes in chapter 11 are reflected accurately. The temporary "stumbling" that was, in effect, Jewish enmity to God was ultimately in the Gentiles' best interest. God, who had never deserted Israel, nor could, would know how to make it right on the last day. That the Jews should be in a state of envy over the faith of Gentiles who believe in Jesus may bring a smile to twentieth-century Jewish lips. But, then, neither modern Jews nor Gentiles are able to reconstruct the apocalyptic Jewish world that Paul inhabited. It knew many tensions between Jews and non-Jews but was quite innocent of the nineteen centuries of bitter struggle between Jews and Christians, of which, as Dean says, Paul could have known nothing.

NOTES

1. See: L. Gaston, *Paul and the Torah* (Vancouver: University of British Columbia Press, 1987), pp. 139–150.

2. For examples, see: R. Ruether, *Faith and Fratricide* (New York: Seabury Press, 1974); C. Williamson, *Has God Rejected His People?* (Nashville: Abingdon, 1982); A. R. Eckardt, *Elder and Younger Brothers* (New York: Schocken, 1973); J. Parkes, *The Conflict of the Church and the Synagogue* (New York: Atheneum, 1979); P. van Buren, *Discerning the Way* (New York: Seabury Press, 1980); and *A Christian Theology of the People of Israel* (New York: Seabury Press, 1983).

3. See K. Stendahl, *Paul Among Jews and Gentiles* (Philadelphia: Fortress Press, 1976), pp. 3–8 and J. C. Beker, *Paul the Apostle* (Philadelphia: Fortress Press, 1980), pp. 23–27, 159–163.

4. See Gaston, *Paul and the Torah*, pp. 144–147; Stendahl, *Paul Among Jews and Gentiles*, pp. 3–5; Beker, *Paul the Apostle*, pp. 74–76.

5. See L. Gaston, *Paul and the Torah*, pp. 142–143.

6. See note 2 of Chapter 19.

7. Righteousness by faith in verse 30 should be the object of the verb *ephthasen*, "come," in verse 32.

8. Reading *telos* as goal, not end, see G. Howard, "Christ the End of the Law: The Meaning of Romans 10:4ff.," *Journal of Biblical Literature* 88 (1969), pp. 331–337; see also Gerard S. Sloyan, *Is Christ the End of the Law?* (Philadelphia: Westminster, 1978).

9. See E. P. Sanders, *Paul and Palestinian Judaism* (Philadelphia: Fortress Press, 1977), pp. 447–480.

21

Was Paul's Chief Figure Justification by Faith or the Transfer of Lordship?

GERARD SLOYAN

The word *kyriotēs* ("dominion," "domination") does not appear in St. Paul. It does occur in Ephesians 1:21 and Colossians 1:16, but there it has to do with heavenly "powers" and not the dominion of Christ as Lord. This dominion of Christ, however, is very much a reality for Paul. The American scholar E. P. Sanders, at Oxford and now Duke after a career at McMaster University in Hamilton, Ontario, thinks that it is a central Pauline conviction but not the key to Paul's soteriology.[1] Another American, John G. Gibbs,[2] would not make it the main theme of Paul's theology. Sanders' difficulty is that "it does not explain how believers *participate* in Christ's death to sin and consequently will participate in his reign."[3]

If either thinker is correct, along with Wrede, Schweitzer, and others, then the view in possession in many circles that righteousness by grace through faith is Paul's central theme cannot be upheld. Ernst Käsemann[4] in Germany and John Reumann[5] in the United States are the most recent protagonists of the classical Lutheran position. Perhaps Paul's "central theme" cannot be determined. It was not a question that Christian history was interested in until the Reformation. Since then, the Reformers followed Luther in his identification of justification by grace through faith as the best candidate. Catholic polemicists did not nominate anything in its place so much as quarrel about fiduciary faith, or what they took to be the terms of the Reformers.

In our time, various Protestants like the four named above, two earlier in the century and two contemporaries, think that the Lutheran position is wrong. Sanders and Gibbs are in the Reformed tradition but a Swedish

Lutheran, Krister Stendahl, has been the most vigorous opponent of classical "justification-by-faith" thought. He thinks that Paul's paramount concern is the history of salvation described in Romans 9–11. Käsemann joins him—indeed, is even stronger than Stendahl—in holding that the history of salvation belongs with justification by faith as a partner, in the sense that Paul's prime concern is with the totality of those who will be saved.

The main theme of Paul's gospel seems to be the "saving action of God in Jesus and how his hearers could participate in that action."[6] Sanders calls the principal word for that participation *faith* or *believing*. But this is the human response. Paramount is the initiative of God. This, in Paul's view, was the solution to the *human plight* and was Paul's starting point.[7] He argued from the divine deed to human need, not vice versa. The outcome of faith in God's action in Christ is union with Christ, a participatory union that is real and not a mere figure of speech. Believers become members of Christ's body (1 Cor. 6:15, 10:16, 12:12f.) and have fellowship (*koinōnia*) with him. They are all one in Christ Jesus (Gal. 3:28), one body in Christ and individually members one of another (Rom. 12:5). Christians are "one spirit" with the Lord (1 Cor. 6:7, 10:16) and have participation in or fellowship with the Holy Spirit (2 Cor. 13:13). The frequently used Pauline phrase "in Christ" does not describe an individual mystical state but a "collective and objective event." Believers are "Christ's" (1 Cor. 3:23) or the Lord's (Rom. 14:8). They belong to Christ Jesus and follow the Spirit's lead (Gal. 5:24-8). The most general term for the transfer from a previous condition to being Christian is "to believe."

In Christ, one does not merely have past transgressions atoned for ("expiated") but dies to the power of Sin. The purpose of Christ's death is assurance of life with Christ, whether one is alive or dead at his coming. Redemption in Christ is primarily participation. (See Rom. 8:3f., 2 Cor. 5:21, Gal. 3:16.) Christ's death, as Paul treats it, achieves a change of dominion or lordship that guarantees future salvation rather than expiates past transgressions. (See Rom. 6:3–11, 7:4; Gal. 2:19f., 6:14.) Christians share Christ's sufferings so as to share his life. (See Rom. 8:17, 2 Cor. 4:10.) The transfer for believers is from the old eon to the new, dying with Christ and living to God, hence, no longer being under sin or "the powers."

A Response to Gerard Sloyan from Lester Dean

Any shift by Christians away from an emphasis upon justification by faith as the center of Paul's thought is welcome from a Jewish perspective, since "justification by faith" is usually followed with "not by works of the law." This then leads to the old charge of Jewish legalism, which we have already discussed in our dialogue. Because the charge of legalism has been so persistent and has led to such a false, negative view of Jews and Judaism, a change that will de-emphasize "justification by faith and not by works" should result in a more accurate view of Judaism, which should then improve Jewish-Christian relations.

I agree that Paul, like most Jewish thinkers, focused first of all upon God's deed. Judaism, like Christianity—at least in its earliest years—stresses the divine act in history rather than a philosophizing about human nature. In the past Jews—and some Christians—have criticized Paul for engaging in Greek ways of thinking.[8] The beginning of Paul's theology was found in his anguish over the human condition, usually understood in terms of his personal frustration with the "impossibility" of following the demands of the Law. Christ was then the answer to this problem. Sanders is correct when he argues that this was not how Paul thought. "There is no reason to think that Paul felt the need of a universal savior prior to his conviction that Jesus was such."[9] It was not anguish over the plight of humanity, but rather God's newest act within Israel's salvation history that was the turning point for Paul. Once again we find that Paul's thinking was Jewish.

At first Paul's participation language seems strange and foreign for a Jewish reader. But we must recall that Paul lived before the destruction of Jerusalem and the unification of Jewish thought around the teachings of the rabbis at Yavneh. If we start with the temple as the center of Jewish religiosity, Paul's participatory language sounds similar to a description of the sacrificial cult. But for Paul the person participated in the death of Jesus rather than in the death of the animal sacrificed at the temple. "In Christ" seems to be such a sacrificial use.

The major soteriological difference between this participation in the sacrificial death of Jesus and the participation in the death of a sacrificial animal is the believer's death to the power of sin. The temple cult was focused upon the past to atone or expiate past sins; it could not atone for future sins or change the human condition.[10]

Participation in the death of Jesus does provide atonement for the past, but it also changes the present, and this is what ultimately led Paul to challenge Judaism. Animal sacrifices could be repeated, but not the death of Christ. Thus the death of Christ must change humanity, else it is of no real worth. It is through participation in the death and resurrection of Christ—and only through that participation—that one is freed from the power of sin. This change of lordship in the present probably was a part of Paul's message about Gentiles now becoming part of the people of God. However, this freedom from the power of Sin could not be limited only to Gentiles. Paul's Jewish apocalyptic hope was for the transformation of all the world. Paul had intensified the Gentile presence in this transformation, but the transformation also had to include the Jews. It is here that Paul found Judaism lacking.

For Paul the power of sin had been broken, the new age was dawning. Unfortunately, that dawning has taken two millennia. The power of Sin is still with us. Paul knew that the kingdom had not yet arrived, and we Jews likewise know that it has not yet arrived. Until that kingdom is established, the power of Sin is still with us. Paul believed that the war against the powers of darkness had been won, but he also knew that the battle still raged.[11] Sometimes we Jews think that Christians forget that the kingdom is still in the future. We ask them to remember what Paul wrote, that "salvation is nearer to us now than when we first believed; the night is far gone, the day is at hand. Let us then cast off the works of darkness and put on the armor of light" (Rom. 13:11–12). Salvation is nearer, and it will surely come, but surely it has not yet come. As J. C. Beker noted:

> Paul refuses to go the route of realized eschatology, so that either Christ becomes the spiritual fulfillment of all God's promises (John) or the kingdom of God becomes identified with the institution of the church in its sacramentalism and clericalism. He also refuses to go the route of a purely futurist eschatology, where the Christian confession of the crucified and risen Christ and our participation in him degenerates into an affirmation about Jesus as a new prophet or a new lawgiver, who merely announces what eventually will come to pass and what must be done in the midst of a wholly unredeemed present. Paul's spirituality lives the tension of the seemingly contradictory claim that the Messiah has come but his kingdom in its fullness is still outstanding.[12]

NOTES

1. *Paul and Palestinian Judaism* (Philadelphia: Fortress Press, 1977), pp. 435, n. 25.

2. *Creation and Redemption* (Leiden: E. J. Brill, 1971).

3. *Paul and Palestinian Judaism*, p. 436 n.25.

4. "Justification and Salvation History," in *Perspectives on Paul* (Philadelphia: Fortress Press, 1971).

5. *Righteousness in the New Testament* (Philadelphia: Fortress Press, 1982).

6. *Paul and Palestinian Judaism*, p. 447.

7. Ibid., p. 458.

8. See note 3 of chapter 4.

9. *Paul and Palestinian Judaism* (Philadelphia: Fortress Press, 1977), p. 443. Sanders claims that instead of starting with the problem of human sin, Paul did the reverse, starting from the solution, Christ's death and resurrection, pp. 442–444, 474–476. The major problem with Sanders' statement is his emphasis upon Christ as "universal savior." I think that Paul may have already been troubled by the negative view of Gentiles held by many Jews, a view which we might paraphrase theologically as "the only good Gentile is a Gentile proselyte."

Gaston, *Paul and the Torah* (Vancouver: University of British Columbia Press, 1987) is correct in locating the suffering servant of Isaiah as Paul's starting point, p. 6. However, I would place greater emphasis upon Isaiah 52–53, and would not exclude the possibility of some form of revelatory experience similar to, but not identical to, that described in Acts, since Paul claimed to have "seen Jesus Christ" (1 Cor. 9:1).

Little can be said with assurance about Paul's life before his calling as apostle to the Gentiles. We know that he persecuted the Church, but he never discusses the reasons for that persecution. Most scholars uncritically accept the speculation that this persecution was because the Church was lax in following the Law. But we have no evidence of such nonobservance, and Paul never mentioned it. Perhaps the origin of this speculation was the combination of Paul's "conversion," his former "zealous" observance of the Law, and his later "freedom" from the Law. Yet the Church did follow Torah. Furthermore, there was as yet no one accepted definition of correct Torah observance, neither between the rabbinic schools, nor between the Pharisaic and Sadducean positions. If Paul did persecute the Church under the auspices of Jewish authority, it is doubtful if the reason for that persecution was the Church's nonobservance of the Law.

I would suggest a different reason for Paul's persecution of the Church, the problem of Gentile proselytes. Conversion to Judaism had both religious and political consequences because of the status of Jews within the Roman empire. Unauthorized conversion of Gentiles by believers in Jesus would have been considered a serious problem by both the Jewish and the Roman authorities and could have been the reason for Paul's persecution of the Church. After his vision of Christ, Paul realized that Jesus was the suffering servant whose death atoned for the sins of the nations and brought them into a new covenantal relationship with the God of Israel. Christ's death was then the solution to the problem of unauthorized Gentile proselytes, since Gentiles no longer had to convert to Judaism or to obey Torah.

10. For the importance of the cult in the early Jewish-Christian understanding of the death of Jesus see: Sanders, *Paul and Palestinian Judaism,* pp. 463–468 and Gaston, *Paul and the Torah,* pp. 111–115. Both Sanders and Gaston argue that Paul goes beyond the early atonement understanding of the death of Jesus. Gaston noted that for Paul Jesus died for persons, while for the Jerusalem church Jesus died for sins. Likewise, atonement and righteousness refer to forgiveness of sins for Jerusalem, but for Paul these terms refer to Gentile incorporation into the people of God. I would suggest that Paul's new insight was extending the sacrificial death of Jesus to the Gentiles. Paul's participation language and also his change of lordship language result from combining these themes.

11. See J. C. Beker, *Paul the Apostle* (Philadelphia: Fortress Press, 1980), pp. 346–347.

12. Ibid., p. 346.

22

Transfer of Lordship, Solution or Problem?

LESTER DEAN

When we engage in dialogue we often find that what we once thought were points of disagreement become points of agreement, and this has been true for our dialogue about Paul. Starting our dialogue viewing Paul as a Jew, we have found that much of the usual opposition between Jews and Christians about Paul is really opposition about Christian interpretation of Pauline thought.

We have found only minor disagreement between Paul's writings and Judaism. Paul believed that it was possible for people to obey Torah; he did not urge Jews to forsake obedience to Torah. The evidence available from his epistles suggests that he expected Jews, including Jewish believers in Jesus, to continue to obey Torah. His future hope for the Jews was the Jewish hope that the messiah would soon come, saving them from their enemies and establishing the Kingdom of God. Paul's basic variance from this Jewish belief was his conviction that he knew the identity of the messiah, Jesus of Nazareth, who had been crucified and raised from the dead.

The agreement we have found may surprise both Jewish and Christian readers, but agreement should be expected when we start reading Paul from a Jewish, rather than a Christian, perspective. Are there then no major areas of disagreement between Paul and Judaism? Are we fair to Paul if we make him merely another Jewish writer of the first century? We should not forget that this Paul, who was a Hebrew, an Israelite, a descendant of Abraham, "five times received at the hands of the Jews 39 lashes," and was "in danger from my own people" (2 Cor. 11:22–26).

Paul the Hebrew, the Israelite, the descendant of Abraham, was also Paul the servant of Christ. The gospel he preached proclaimed that Jesus of Nazareth would return as the messianic king of Israel, establishing the

Kingdom of God. Although this belief in the messianic identity of Jesus was not shared by most Jews at the time of Paul—and fewer Jews since that time—this belief was not in itself the major point of conflict between Paul and his Jewish contemporaries. Furthermore, it need not be the major point of conflict between Jews and Christians today.[1] Both Jews and Christians hope for the coming of the messiah. Christians believe they know the identity of the messiah who will come; we Jews are not sure of that identity. One day we will all know.

But the gospel Paul preached proclaimed more than the identity of the future messiah. Paul preached Christ crucified and raised from the dead, events that according to Paul fundamentally changed the relationship between God and humanity. Belief in Christ changed the person; he or she participated in the death and resurrection of Christ, gaining freedom from the enslaving power of sin.

A major focus of Pauline thought—according to E. P. Sanders, the center of his thought—is this transfer of lordship from the realm of sin to the realm of God.[2] For Paul, righteousness often meant this change in lordship; the righteous person was now part of the people of God, rather than part of the enemies of God. In the past they had been "slaves of sin," but they were now "slaves of righteousness," "slaves of God" (Rom. 6:17–22). This transfer terminology probably arose from Paul's message about Gentiles now becoming part of the people of God. But Paul also shared an apocalyptic worldview that led him to universalize the need for this transfer of lordship.[3]

Paul personified sin and its power, using images from Jewish apocalyptic thought. He saw a great struggle between "Good" and "Evil" in which human beings failed without divine aid:

> I do not do the good I want, but the evil I do not want is what I do. Now if I do what I do not want, it is no longer I that do it, but sin which dwells within me . . . I delight in the law of God, in my inmost self, but I see in my members another law at war with the law of my mind and making me captive to the law of sin which dwells in my members (Rom. 7:19–23).

As mentioned previously, such a view is merely a recognition of the universal human condition of imperfection. We try to please God but we all fail. As such, void of the many layers of Christian interpretation about "original sin," the verses present typical Jewish thought of the period. Paul, like other Jewish writers, knew of this universal problem. He also knew of its solution, faith in Christ, and it is here that his thought was shaped, not by Judaism, but by his belief in Jesus Christ.

For Paul the solution to the problem of the power of sin is participation in the death and resurrection of Christ: "For the law of the Spirit of Christ has set me free from the law of sin and death" (Rom. 8:2). The believer in Christ has already been changed: "If Christ is in you, although your bodies are dead because of sin, your spirits are alive because of righteousness" (8:10). The victory over sin, which would be fulfilled when Jesus returned as messiah, had already begun.[4]

The death and resurrection of Jesus was neither just a fulfillment of past prophecy, nor merely the prelude to the future return of Jesus as the messiah. The death and resurrection of Jesus had meaning in the present. Through faith, the believer in Jesus also died to the power of Sin and was raised as a servant of God and of Jesus Christ.[5] It was for his belief and proclamation of this role of Jesus in the present that Paul was persecuted by the Jews of his time. Those Jews then, and we Jews today, find that such a belief contradicts the heart of Judaism, that we Jews are part of the people of God, that we are made righteous because of God's covenant given to Moses at Mount Sinai, and that we need no other divine act to free us from the power of Sin.

According to Paul, being a Jew by birth did not necessarily make that person a "real Jew," part of the people of God.

> He is not a real Jew who is one outwardly, nor is true circumcision something external and physical. He is a Jew who is one inwardly, and real circumcision is a matter of the heart, spiritual and not literal (Rom. 2:28–29).

God was the God of the Jews and the Gentiles; both were able to be part of God's people. Paul claimed that the distinction between Jew and Gentile was meaningless to God, for all who believe are part of the people of God: "In Christ Jesus you are all children of God ... there is neither Jew nor Greek ... for you are all one in Christ Jesus" (Gal. 3:26–28).

Paul extended God's grace beyond the Jews to the Gentiles, and argued that not all Jews were necessarily part of God's people. Neither of these represented a departure from Jewish teaching. From at least the time of the prophets there had been the belief that more than mere physical descent was necessary for remaining in God's covenant. By the post-exilic period the distinction between the righteous and the wicked was no longer based solely upon national lines — all Jews are righteous and all Gentiles are wicked. Now correct conduct determined whether one was righteous or wicked. Most Jews were righteous, and most Gentiles were wicked, but there were also wicked Jews and righteous Gentiles. The prophets condemned the wicked in Israel and comforted the righteous Gentiles. "My house shall be called a house of prayer for all peoples" (Isa. 56:7).

Both Paul and the prophets agreed that obedience to God was the basic requirement for being part of God's people. But Paul's definition of faithful obedience differed from usual Jewish teaching. According to Judaism, for Jews to remain a part of God's people they had to participate in God's covenant established at Sinai. Following Torah was a sign of that faithful obedience. In contrast, according to Paul faithfulness to God was shown by belief in Jesus Christ. Non-believing Jews were disobedient and were excluded from the people of God: "They were broken off because of their unbelief" (Rom. 11:20).[6] According to Paul, belief in Jesus was not just a way for the Gentiles to become righteous and be included in God's people. Belief in Jesus was a necessary part of obedience to God for both Jews and Gentiles. Jewish obedience to Torah was not enough.

For Paul the covenant at Sinai was inferior and surpassed by God's new act in Christ: "God has made us competent to be ministers of a new covenant" (2 Cor. 3:6). "But whatever gain I had, I counted as loss for the sake of Christ. Indeed I count everything as loss because of the surpassing worth of knowing Christ Jesus my Lord" (Phil. 3:7–8). It was this new covenant, rather than the covenant at Sinai, that allowed "the just requirement of the law to be fulfilled."[7] "God has done what the law, weakened by the flesh, could not do" (Rom. 8:3–4). God, through Christ, had finally destroyed the power of Sin.

Although Paul stated that some Jews were cut off because of disbelief in Jesus, the metaphor of the olive tree also contained the hope for the restoration of those branches that were cut off: "And even the others, if they do not persist in their unbelief, will be grafted in" (Rom. 11:23). Furthermore, the metaphor is immediately followed by Paul's statement that "all Israel will be saved." Thus Paul did not envision a permanent exclusion of Jews due to unbelief in Jesus. The present state of the Jews was a temporary situation that would be resolved by the imminent *parousia*.[8] It was not the natural or expected situation and the Gentiles should not "become proud, but stand in awe" (11:20). Jewish acceptance of Jesus will mean "life from the dead," the establishment of the messianic kingdom of God (11:15).

Paul did not present a systematic view about the relationship between belief in Christ and the present status of Jews who did not accept this belief. There is no indication that he believed that his excluding nonbelievers in Christ from being part of the people of God was contrary to Judaism. Apparently he saw this exclusion of Jews as part of God's mysterious plan of salvation for the Gentiles. But we should note that whenever he mentioned the exclusion of the Jews he then added his certainty that the Jews would be saved. His belief in this future salvation was just as sure as his belief that Jesus Christ would be the instrument of that salvation. Jesus would return soon to save all Israel.[9]

The delay of the *parousia* and the death of some believers in Jesus caused concern for some believers. Paul answered their questions with the Pharisaic belief in the resurrection of the dead. Those believers in Jesus who died would be raised again so that they could participate in the Kingdom of God. Death could not thwart God's plan for the believer in Jesus, for death had been conquered by the resurrection of Jesus.

We have no similar record of Paul's thoughts about the fate of Jews who died but did not believe in Jesus. Perhaps Paul did not consider the problem of how or whether dead Jews could become believers in Jesus when he returned as the messiah. We who live nearly two thousand years after Paul see a problem that was nonexistent for Paul. Faithfulness to the apostle might keep us from speculating about his view, but the many years of Christian anti-Jewish preaching require us to consider the problem. A sentencing of all Jews who do not believe in Jesus to an eternity in hell does not seem consistent with Paul's view that Jewish unbelief was temporary, part of God's plan, and that all Israel would be saved.

If we again start from the presupposition that Paul was a Jew, that he had not rejected his people nor thought that God had rejected the Jews, then we can offer the following as Paul's most probable view. Christ overcame death through the resurrection, and the believers in Christ overcame death through the resurrection. Since death could not thwart God's plan for Jesus or for the believer in Jesus, in the same way death should not thwart God's plan for the Jews. Those Jews who died before the time of Jesus would be resurrected and participate in God's kingdom. Those Jews who were alive would, of course, believe in Jesus as the messiah and participate in God's kingdom. Those Jews who died after the time of Jesus, but who did not believe in Jesus, would be resurrected and also believe in Jesus and participate in God's kingdom. "And so all Israel will be saved . . . that God may have mercy upon all" (Rom. 11:20, 26).

A Response to Lester Dean from Gerard Sloyan

This final treatment sets at rest any disquiet I may have had earlier that Paul was not being conveyed at full strength. He certainly is here—in the watchword of a modern newspaper, "without fear or favor." I find in this segment an excellent restatement of Paul's view of God's design for the Jewish people. Paul's concluding doxology of Romans 11:33–36 seems to me to give up on exact knowledge of what is in store in God's undisclosed future—a little less certitude than I find reflected in the treatment in chapter 18. Still, I have only praise for this final treatment: Paul's "solution," which he is convinced will be God's solution.

A final word. I was raised in a Christian setting that did not have the cheerful convention of consigning Jews to hell, not even the limbo or painless borderland (*limbus*) of Augustine's devising. Matters had sufficiently progressed in Catholic theology to the point where membership in the Church was not thought to be a condition of eternal life with God. In 1948, in fact, a proposition that said so, put forward by an overzealous Catholic named Leonard Feeney, was officially condemned by the Holy Office of the Roman *Curia*. As is well known, however, the popular teaching of medieval Christendom, which was defined as a proposition of Catholic faith at the Fourth Council of the Lateran (1215), is alive and well in certain circles. For this and other reasons I am pleased not to travel in them.

NOTES

1. See: P. Lapide and J. Moltmann, *Jewish Monotheism and Christian Trinitarian Doctrine* (Philadelphia: Fortress Press, 1981), pp. 59, 67–68; H. Matt, "How Shall a Believing Jew View Christianity?" *Judaism*, vol. 24 (1975), pp. 402–403; and L. Dean, "Rejection versus Revelation: Toward a Jewish Theology of Christianity," in *Breaking Down The Wall*, ed. L. Swidler (Lanham, MD: University Press of America, 1987), pp. 90–105.

2. Sanders, *Paul and Palestinian Judaism* (Philadelphia: Fortress Press, 1978), pp. 463–474.

3. Sanders, *Paul and Palestinian Judaism*, pp. 511–515.

4. J. C. Beker, *Paul the Apostle* (Philadelphia: Fortress Press, 1980), pp. 215–221.

5. Sanders, *Paul and Palestinian Judaism*, pp. 514–515, 522–523, 547–548.

6. L. Gaston, *Paul and the Torah* (Vancouver: University of British Columbia Press, 1987), p. 148, argues that Paul only criticized Jews for not believing in his mission to the Gentiles. But Paul not only states that branches are broken off because of unbelief, but also that others (the Gentiles) are grafted on because of belief. In such a context belief in Christ must be understood.

7. See: Sanders, *Paul and Palestinian Judaism*, pp. 551–552.

8. See: Beker, *Paul the Apostle*, p. 346.

9. See Beker, *Paul the Apostle*, p. 334–337, 343–344; Gaston, *Paul and the Torah*, pp. 145–150.

23

Summary of a Jewish-Christian Dialogue on Paul

Our dialogue about Paul began with a presupposition that might have surprised many readers: Paul viewed himself, and thus should be viewed by us, as a Jew and not as a "Christian." He considered himself to be a Jewish believer in Jesus Christ, rather than part of a new, rival religious tradition. With this as our starting point we found far greater agreement about Paul and his writings than most Jews and Christians. The Paul we have discovered is quite different from the great champion of the Gentiles who proved the superiority of Hellenistic Christianity over both Judaism and Jewish Christianity. We have found that many of the disputes between Jews and Christians about Paul were really disputes about erroneous interpretations of Paul.

Throughout our dialogue we have emphasized how little we know about Judaism at the time of Paul, especially in comparison to what it would become two centuries later. It is an error to compare Paul with a "normative" Judaism derived from Mishnah and Talmud, since these documents had not yet been written in the first century C.E. The various forms of Jewish conduct and belief that Paul knew—we know there were numerous Jewish groups in existence—must relate in some way to the Judaism the rabbis would create, but none of them was identical to it. We know neither their messianic hopes, their beliefs, their observance of the Law, nor their feelings about non-Jews. A knowledge of all these would be necessary to comprehend with any assurance the world within which Paul wrote.

A further problem we faced was the contingent nature of the correspondence we possess from Paul. Paul wrote his letters to deal with specific problems facing different local communities of believers in Jesus. Those who try to interpret Paul must consider the situation and purpose of each of his epistles. Often Paul seems to be directly responding to questions he has received from a local church. Unfortunately, half of the conversation is unavailable to us. In no case do we have a universal epistle presenting

Paul's systematic theology. We must be very careful in using one letter of Paul to interpret obscure passages in another epistle.

These fairly large factual gaps create imposing problems for us as biblical scholars and historians. Paul's writings must have been intelligible to his audiences. But for us there are several passages that seem quite obscure. Many of the disagreements in our dialogue can be traced to different interpretations in important but obscure areas. In such cases, the scholar must rely not only upon the few facts available but also upon her or his assumptions and the past history of interpreting the text. As Jew and Christian, we have different presuppositions and histories that produce different results.

The starting point of our dialogue was Paul's Jewish identity. Not only was Paul born a Jew, but he remained a Jew even after he claimed to have seen the risen Christ. We two are in agreement up to this point. There is some disagreement, however, about Paul's Judaism. Our lack of information about Judaism of this period has already been mentioned, and our ignorance includes that of the Judaism of Paul before he became a believer in Jesus. We can only extrapolate from the statements we have from Paul after he became a believer, remembering that the statements he made are now colored by his new faith in Jesus Christ.

Lester Dean notes that there was no evidence for a legalist Judaism before, during, or after the time of Paul. According to Judaism, a person was righteous, or had a right relationship with God, because of being a participant in God's covenant made with Israel at Sinai. Observance of the Law was obedience to God, the expected behavior of a person in a covenant relationship with God. Paul's arguments about being justified by faith and not by the works of the Law are in agreement with Judaism. There is no evidence from these statements that Paul had departed from Jewish beliefs or practices. Dean argues that Paul was simply attacking a distortion of Judaism held by his Gentile audience. He agreed with both Judaism and the predominantly Jewish Jerusalem church. However, in certain letters Paul emphasized the Law at the expense of other components of Judaism such as covenant, repentance, sacrifice, and expiation. This emphasis on the Law led Christian readers to an erroneous description of Judaism as legalist.

Gerard Sloyan is surprised at Dean's denial that the Law was the most important element in Paul's Judaism, especially since the halakhic understanding of the Law was the major focus of the later rabbis. It is possible that Paul's Judaism was legalist, in contrast to that of his contemporaries. Paul's vision of Christ forced him to change from the Pharisaism of his youth, whatever that might have entailed. His faith in Christ, he would say, returned him to the proper understanding of the Law. Sloyan also thinks that Paul's form of Judaism was different from that of the Jerusalem church that apparently combined faith in Christ with adherence to the Law, perhaps being similar to the Judaism of Stephen described in the Acts of the Apostles.

Much of our discussion centered around Torah, the Law. We both observed that Paul thought he had kept the Law and claimed never consciously to have transgressed it (Phil. 3:6; Gal. 1:14). There is no evidence that Paul found obedience to the Law difficult, or that he turned to God's new covenant available through faith in Christ out of despair or frustration with his life as a Pharisee. It was Augustine, Luther, and other Christians troubled by *their* faults who projected onto Paul guilt for not following the Law. The only sin of which Paul was conscious was his past persecution of believers in Jesus Christ.

Not only did Paul believe that he had followed the Law, but he also thought it possible for other Jews to observe all of Torah. Sloyan and Dean agree that a Jewish people burdened by God's Law that cannot be kept is the creation of later Christians, not Paul. Paul's statements that *all* the Law must be observed (Gal. 3:10, 5:3) prove neither that he felt it impossible to follow Torah nor that he was at variance with Jewish thinking. Most Jews of that time would have stated the same thing—that a Jew must observe all of Torah.

When Paul exclaimed, "The evil I do not want is what I do" (Rom. 7:19), his purpose was not to prove that those who try to obey Torah fail. The purpose of the passage is not to condemn either those who fail to obey the Law or those who try to obey it. Paul wanted to condemn the power of Sin itself as the cause of human disobedience of the Law. Paul was reflecting on the general human condition of living in a world in need of redemption. Sin, not the Law, is the cause of death; the Law is good, holy, and from God. All humanity needs deliverance from the power of Sin. Only by faith in Jesus Christ is there deliverance.

Paul criticized the Law, not because it could not be fulfilled, but because it could not do what faith in Christ did. However, we disagree about the specific fault Paul found with the Law. Paul's criticism, according to Sloyan, comes from his belief that only faith in Christ—not Law observance—justifies. The Law was now redundant for the purpose of delivering both Jew and non-Jew from the power of Sin. God had done something new in Christ, relativizing all that was before, including Torah. Law-righteousness was surpassed once faith in Christ was possible. Since Paul defined the Law by what it did not accomplish, there always was a negative aspect to the Law. It was manipulated by Sin and it had been succeeded by the life-giving Spirit.

Dean agrees that for Paul faith, not Law observance, justifies and frees one from the power of Sin. But he does not think that Jews, including Paul, ever thought that Law observance would do these things. Paul was expounding Jewish teaching about the relationship among Law, faith, and righteousness to a Gentile audience that had erroneously been led to think that righteousness could be earned by following the Law. Paul was not discussing whether it was proper for Jews to follow the Law, nor was he suggesting that Jews thought they gained righteousness when they did obey the Law.

When Paul criticized the Law, he was finding fault with its requirement that Gentiles had to become Jews in order to be acceptable to God. God's act in Christ provided a way for Gentiles, as Gentiles, to become children of God. It created a new covenant with a different entry requirement, faith rather than circumcision. Law observance was wrong, but only for Gentiles since they were not part of the covenant at Sinai. Dean notes that we should not focus only on the negative things Paul said about the Law. The Law was good, it was one way a person could learn what God required, it showed God was just, and it pointed to Christ as the way Gentiles could now become children of God. What Paul saw as relativized was not the Law, but the covenant God had made with the Jews at Sinai.

The various seemingly negative statements Paul made about Torah in Romans and Galatians were to support his argument that Gentile believers did not have to follow Torah. Dean suggests that Paul often made reference to a midrash of his opponents in which the Law was eternal and had been given to all humanity, making Law observance binding upon all. Paul argued that the Law was not eternal and that it was not God's universal Law for all humanity. Angels were the intermediaries through whom Gentiles received the Law—in contrast to Israel who received the Law directly from God—so Gentiles could not be condemned for not obeying the Law. Torah was given because of Gentile transgressions, to keep them from being a part of God's people. The past restraining function of the Law was the demand that Gentiles be circumcised and follow Torah.

In contrast to Sloyan, Dean is convinced that the "freedom in Christ" that Paul speaks about was not the freedom no longer to follow Torah, but the freedom no longer to require Gentiles to follow Torah. Paul criticized Peter, not for following Torah, but for changing his mind and demanding that the Gentiles in Antioch be circumcised, refusing to eat with them until they followed Torah. Paul explained that when Gentiles wanted to follow the Law they were coveting the special relationship the Jews had with God. Their desire to be part of God's people and to obey the Law was used by sin to condemn them, resulting in an impossible situation that God solved through the death of Christ.

Paul did not intend this prohibition of Torah observance for Gentiles to include Jews or Jewish Christians. Jews and Gentiles were equally children of God, but this equality did not abolish all distinctions between Jews and Gentiles. Dean feels Paul would have been no more flexible about the necessity of Torah observance by Jews than he was about the prohibition of Torah observance for Gentiles. Torah was God's commandment to Jews, binding upon them, but only upon them. The Jew was not to consider Law observance as justifying, but then no Jew should have viewed Law observance in such a way.

Sloyan does not accept the suggestion of Dean that in discussing the

Law Paul was primarily telling Gentiles what they must not do, or only stating that Law observance does not justify a person. Paul's freedom and death to the Law, Sloyan thinks, has to do with Paul himself and could extend to Jews like him. It was not confined to a conviction he had about Gentiles before and after he believed in Christ. Paul was rejoicing in his new condition of being justified by faith in Christ. When Paul wrote to "those who know the Law" he meant Jews primarily and any Gentile proselytes who had been schooled in it. All, Jews and Gentiles alike, are discharged from the Law, although Jewish believers in Christ do no wrong to keep it. The benefits of Christ's death and resurrection should not be confined only to Gentiles, as if Paul cared only about Gentiles and the freedom from the Law it brought them. Sloyan thinks that Dean disregards the benefits and freedom from the Law Christ's death brought to Paul and Jews like him.

It is true that Paul's statements against Law observance in Galatians were prompted by the actions of his opponents who tried to lead Gentiles astray by claiming they had to be circumcised and follow the Law. There is no record of Paul's explicitly prohibiting Law observance by Jews. But Paul's strictures against the Law also apply to Jews, in Sloyan's view, although not on the same terms. Jews should continue to observe the Law if their consciences say they must. However, Paul could not tolerate Torah observance as something *required* of believers in Jesus, whether Jew or Gentile. If Jews relied on Law observance as justifying, as necessary in addition to faith in Christ to put one in a right relation with God, then Law observance would be a curse. Paul was convinced that since the death and resurrection of Christ Torah obedience for Jews had been reclassified. It did not matter as it had before, and it did not accomplish what it once did.

In Romans, Paul mentions God's mysterious plan concerning Israel and the Gentiles. According to Sloyan, Paul spoke as though he knew something about the plan, but in fact he knew only that God's call to Israel was "irrevocable." Paul knew that God would not be thwarted. Paul saw the remnant of Jewish believers as the answer to God's faithfulness to the promises made to Israel. When Paul stated that all Israel would be saved, he was using apocalyptic language and was concerned to emphasize the certainty that Israel would be saved and brought to glory in the future end-time, instead of Israel's being rejected. "All Israel" would be the number of Jewish believers in Christ that suited God's purpose.

Dean believes Paul was sure not only that God's call was irrevocable, but also that the successful ministry to the Gentiles was founded upon an unsuccessful ministry to Jews. The messianic Kingdom would have been established with Jesus as its King if most Jews had believed in Jesus. The Gentiles who were now believers in Jesus would then have perished. But divine mercy had been extended to the Gentiles because of the Jewish "No" to the gospel. According to Paul, Jewish rejection of the gospel, which Jews then and now affirm to be faithfulness to God, was part of God's plan to allow Gentiles the possibility to be part of Jesus Christ's Kingdom.

The Jewish remnant was not Paul's ultimate solution to Jewish unbelief in Jesus but the answer to the criticism that God's plan had been thwarted because of that unsuccessful ministry. Dean does not think that the remnant took the place of the collective nation in God's plan. For Paul, "all Israel" means more than the small remnant who believed in Jesus. Paul was convinced that ultimately all Jews will believe in Jesus when Jesus returns to earth as God's anointed King in Jerusalem.

There is no systematic presentation by Paul about Jews who did not believe in Jesus. We have no record about his opinion of the fate of the millions of Jews who have not believed in Jesus since his time. It is obviously speculation to say anything on the subject and highly presumptuous to claim that we know what Paul would have said. Sloyan suggests that Paul would have believed that Law righteousness continued to be available for Jews — something that had a high value but not as high as the gospel.

Dean notes the anti-Jewish preaching by some Christians that claims that the Bible, including Paul's letters, condemns Jews who do not believe in Jesus to hell. Maintaining that these Jews were cut off permanently from God would not be consistent with Paul's view that Jewish unbelief was temporary, a part of God's plan, and that ultimately all Israel would be saved. Dean suggests that Paul would believe that those Jews who died before Jesus' return as Messiah will be raised at his return, will believe in Jesus as God's Messiah, and will participate in the kingdom Jesus would then establish.

The importance of transfer into the lordship of God (or Christ) was noted by both members in the dialogue. Paul proclaimed that Christ's crucifixion and resurrection from the dead fundamentally changed the relationship between God and humanity. Transfer into the Kingdom of God was the result of belief and participation in the saving action of God in Jesus and was Paul's solution to the human plight of being under the power of Sin. Believers in Christ were now "righteous," having become part of the people of God. It is union with Christ that guarantees future salvation.

Dean suggests that it was at this point that Paul stepped beyond the bounds of Judaism. For Paul, obedience to God was now primarily shown not by following Torah but by belief in Jesus Christ. Nonbelieving Jews, by this definition, were disobedient and excluded from God's people, although Paul did not envision a permanent exclusion of Jews due to unbelief in Jesus. With the imminent return of Jesus all Jews would become believers in Jesus. Such beliefs contradict basic beliefs of Judaism, that Jews are part of the people of God and that they are made righteous through God's covenant at Sinai. Paul saw the covenant at Sinai as inferior and surpassed by God's new act in Christ.

We have mentioned both similarities and differences of opinion about certain important areas of Paul's thought. Many topics have not been covered, not because we feel they are unimportant, but because we felt the need to discuss issues that have been points of conflict between Jews and Christians for nearly two thousand years. Our statements are not only the result of some years of study of Paul, but also the result of a dialogue that has continued for more than two years. It has been a dialogue in the true sense of the word, with each partner trying to listen carefully to the other. The views of both of us about Paul have changed as a result of this discussion. We know that we have not arrived at a complete understanding of Paul's thought, but we will continue the attempt. We invite all those interested to come and reason together with us.

Select Annotated Bibliography on Paul

Beker, J. Christiaan. *Paul the Apostle: The Triumph of God in Life and Thought.* Philadelphia: Fortress Press, 1980.

The subtitle accurately describes Paul's focus on Christ as the fulfillment in anticipation of the ultimate liberation of the creation by God. The contingent or occasional character is shown in a 100-page exegesis of Galatians and Romans and the coherence of Paul's gospel in a section of twice that length. Beker stresses the theocentric character of Paul's teaching and its futurist, cosmic eschatology (chapter 8). He presents fairly, against much liberal anti-Jewish exegesis of the last century, Paul's view of "The Destiny of Israel" (chapter 15).

Büchler, A. *Studies in Sin and Atonement in the Rabbinic Literature of the First Century.* New York: Ktav, 1967 (reprint of 1939 ed.).

A careful delineation of Rabbinic Judaism, which, like those of S. Schechter and G. F. Moore, shows the reality of modes of obtaining forgiveness and performing good works (*mitzvot*) in a way vastly superior to the depiction that has reached modern Christians via the Bultmann school's uncritical acceptance of the work of F. Weber (1897), E. Schörer (1886–90), P. Billerbeck (beginning in 1922) and W. Bousset (1903, 1925).

Dahl, Nils Alstrup. "Paul: A Sketch" in *Studies in Paul: Theology for the Early Christian Mission.* Minneapolis: Augsburg Publishing House, pp. 1–21.

———. "The Future of Israel," ibid., pp. 137–58.

———. "The One God of Jews and Gentiles (Romans 3:29-30)," ibid., pp. 178–91.

Three essays that are brief and that might even be called "slight" except for their unerring insight into Paul's view of his Jewish tradition and the influence of Augustine and the reformers upon it. They "did recognize fundamental elements of Paul's thought, but they placed these elements in a non-Pauline context, a context shaped by the history of the church, by its practices of penance, and by a consciousness of sin far more introspective than that of Paul and his congregations" (p. 21).

Davies, W. D. *Paul and Rabbinic Judaism: Some Rabbinic Elements in Pauline Theology,* rev. ed., New York: Harper and Row, 1965.

A pioneering work in English in which the author, although necessarily dependent on German and English translations for his rabbinic materials, shows that Paul's acceptance of Christ did not involve the rejection by him of the usages of his people nor a denial of community with them. Paul remained closely related to rabbinic

Judaism and, in accepting the gospel, did not discover a new religion antithetical to it, "as his polemics might sometimes pardonably lead us to assume, but the recognition of the advent of the true and final form of Judaism ... the advent of the Messianic Age of Jewish expectation" (p. 324).

Fuchs Kreimer, Nancy. "The Essential Heresy: Paul's View of the Law according to Jewish Writers, 1886–1986." Unpublished Ph.D. dissertation, Temple University, 1990.
   A rabbi examines Jews on Paul over a century and finds their commonest accusation to be that he was an apostate from the Law, whereas she sees Paul putting the claims of God above Law and peoplehood in a way that Jews might profitably consider.

Gaston, Lloyd. *Paul and the Torah*. Vancouver: University of British Columbia Press, 1987.
   The studies of Paul, followed by the author's translation of Romans and Galatians, in which he takes Paul's description of himself as Apostle of the Gentiles to mean that "Paul's churches and their successors were exclusively Gentile (with the possible exception of some Jewish apostates)" (p. 8). This leaves no room for a Paul of the letters who has anything to say about what the gospel means for believers among Jews. Gaston thinks them to be totally absent from Paul's horizon. He thus interprets "under the Law" as if Paul referred it to Gentiles; Paul's "we," as if it were written in solidarity with Gentiles; and so on. Aside from a few other such exegetical forays, the studies are highly illuminating.

Hübner, Hans. *Law in Paul's Thought*. Edinburgh: T & T Clark, 1984.
   Two chapters, "Nomos in Galatians" and "Nomos in Romans" (in which a development is discerned in Paul's thinking, the Corinthian correspondence having intervened), are followed by an "Elaboration" in which this study is proposed as preliminary to a draft theology of the use of the Old Testament by New Testament authors. Adopting the Reformation position as promoted by modern exegetes, Hübner thinks that in Galatians 3 Paul envisions the enslavement by the Law of Jew and Gentile alike, a carnal man who "in his illusion loses himself in the quantity he has to produce [whereas] true fulfillment of the Law is possible and real only as a fruit of the Spirit" (p. 41). Hübner finds Paul reducing Mosaic Torah in Romans 13 and abrogating its commandments which rest on a cultic approach in Romans 14 (pp. 84–85). The only attention paid to the new view of Paul's long assumed opposition to Judaism and the Law is a challenge to Sanders' interpretation of Galatians 3:10. Many exclamation points occur in this careful apologia for the tradition in possession!

Marmorstein, A. *The Doctrine of Merits in Old Rabbinical Literature*. New York: Ktav, 1968 (reprint of 1920 ed.).
   An extended discussion of rabbinic views of the merits of the patriarchs, including Joseph, versus those of the desert wanderers in bringing on the election of Israel and the giving of Torah. In much later times, the deeds of righteous Jews could merit for others. None of the rabbis supposed that belief in the efficacy of merits eliminated human responsibility of God's freedom and initiative. Assuming the latter, they sought only reasons why the Lord had so acted on Israel's behalf. The

first mention of the teaching occurs in the time of the Bar Kokhba revolt but Paul (whom Marmorstein does not explore) was born into a milieu that featured the Merits of the Fathers and appears to have relied on it for Romans 5:17–19.

Munck, Johannes. *Paul and the Salvation of Mankind*. Richmond: John Knox Press, 1959.

————. *Christ and Israel. An Interpretation of Romans 9–11*. Philadelphia: Fortress Press, 1967.

The earlier book is a compilation of studies published in the 1940s and 1950s, displaying in somewhat labored exegesis (similarly the second book) a scholar's emergence from one era into another. In *Paul*, chapter 4, "The Judaizing Gentile Christians, chapter 7, "The Manifesto of Faith: Comments on Romans," the last two sections of chapter 9, "Israel and the Gentiles," and chapter 10, "Paul and Jerusalem" are the most rewarding. Munck thinks that the number of Jews in Paul's churches was negligible.

Neusner, J. *The Rabbinic Traditions about the Pharisees before 70*. Leiden: Brill, 1971. 3 vols.

Not an attempted reconstruction of the history of pre-70 Pharisaism but an analysis of the rabbinic traditions about the Pharisaic masters who flourished before Jerusalem's fall and with whom Paul claimed a global affinity in the 50s. Neusner is the first to do a systematic analysis of the Pharisaic-rabbinic traditions from "formal, redactional, synoptic or comparative, and literary critical perspectives" (I, 1). For the nonrabbinic specialist, most useful for mastering the names of the teachers of the second temple period, as well as their major concerns and form of argumentation.

Räisänen, Heikki. *Paul and the Law*. Philadelphia: Fortress Press, 1983.

The freshest of the recent studies on this question. The author suggests that the numerous inconsistencies and even contradictions in Paul's letters rule out any linear development. Faced with the challenge of the Christian "restorers" after some decades of not promulgating ritual laws among his Gentiles, Paul argues that "a *divine* institution has been *abolished* by what God has done in Christ" while maintaining that "it is *his* teaching that really fulfills or 'upholds' the law" (pp. 264–65). Paul is a missionary and primarily a practical man of religion who develops a line of thought to influence the conduct of his readers. He did not have Scripture on his side but did not know this, possessing, rather, basic intuitions like that of Christian freedom. It is a mistake to create a consistent Pauline synthesis based on the Bible when his thoughts are what are of value for the Church.

Richardson, Peter. *Israel in the Apostolic Church* (SNTSMS 10). Cambridge: Cambridge University Press, 1969.

"The heart of this book, as a glance at the Table of Contents will make clear, is the [89-page] chapter on Paul" (p. ix). This exegetical study on the first- and second-century Christian literature both canonical and noncanonical as far as Justin, explores the gradual separation of the Church from Israel and its appropriation of that title to itself (first in Justin's *Dialogue*, 11.5; see all of 10–29). In discussing Paul, Richardson features all those places where Paul can and cannot identify with "Israel" or Judaism: and terms like "under the law" (= total observance). He disregards such contentions as that Paul was a Torah-true Jew throughout his life or that he repudiated the Law completely in favor of the gospel, letting his textual analysis point to an often necessarily uncertain path between the extremes.

Sanders, E. P. *Paul and Palestinian Judaism. A Comparison of Patterns of Religion.* Philadelphia: Fortress Press, 1977.
    An attempt in 400 pages to establish the "pattern" of Palestinian Judaism in Paul's day as "covenantal nomism," viz., what it took to get in and to stay in. This is followed by the same attempt in 100 pages as regards Paul, who taught a new form of covenantal religion that was more creation than covenant (the traditional term), more a transfer to the new eon and participation in Christ than dying to past transgression by faith in his death.

————. *Paul, the Law, and the Jewish People.* Philadelphia: Fortress Press, 1983.
    Essays on Paul's general relation to contemporary Judaism, his use of Scripture, the degree to which he was a practicing Jew during his career as apostle to the Gentiles, and his thought about his "kin by race" who did not accept Jesus as Messiah. The endnotes contain extended responses to critical assessments of his earlier book on Paul.

Schweitzer, Albert. *The Mysticism of Paul the Apostle.* New York: H. Holt & Co., 1931.
    A book the first draft of which goes back to 1906, with medical service in Africa intervening, 1913–27. The author sees Paul's great achievement of grasping "as the thing essential to being a Christian, the experience of union with Christ" (p. 377). Christianity is basically a Christ-Mysticism, a "belonging together with Christ as 'our Lord' "(p. 378). Christianity, in letting itself be Hellenized, was dominated by the idea of redemption based on the atoning death of Jesus for the forgiveness of sins, whereas primitive Christian belief had related redemption through Christ to a living belief in the kingdom of God. Schweitzer resolves Paul's seemingly inconsistent statements about the Law by declaring the Law's incompatibility with the final age that has begun with Christ for the elect among the Jews and the Gentiles.

Stendahl, Krister. "The Apostle Paul and the Introspective Conscience of the West," *Harvard Theological Review,* vol. 56 (1973), pp. 199–215.
————. Above and other essays published in *Paul among Jews and Gentiles.* Philadelphia: Fortress Press, 1976.
    A collection of papers, all valuable in their way but none so much as "The Apostle Paul and the Introspective Conscience of the West." Stendahl's essay establishes the falsity of reading Paul as a hero of introspective conscience on the basis of an autobiographical interpretation of Romans 7:13–25. A retired Lutheran bishop, he shows how Martin Luther, a canon of the Order of St. Augustine, shared the theology and some of the anxieties of his greater teacher in arriving at a similar understanding of Paul.

Epilogue

Two Jewish and two Christian scholars have here engaged in an ongoing dialogue stretching over several years concerning the understanding of Jesus and Paul and how that understanding should affect the relationship between Jews and Christians. We have, in fact, operated partly as historians attempting to return to the fork in the road that led from a common source to the development of our two distinct religions. In doing so we believe that we have come to know more about both who we ourselves really are and who our partners—erstwhile opponents—really are. As a result of our experiences, we are convinced that "interreligious historical analysis" is an essential step for Christian and Jewish self-understanding and the consequent relationship of each to the other. Hence, our desire is to share as much of our experiences as we can with our fellow Jews and Christians.

When we embarked on this path of dialogue we were convinced from our experiences and those of millions of others that the ancient road of debate and hostility was one that led not to truth but to distortion and falsehood—and all the horrible consequences that ensued therefrom. We aimed at effecting a reconciliation wherever the facts as we uncovered them allowed. We strove to find agreement with our partners as much as possible without violating our perception of the facts and our own Jewish or Christian integrity. We did this in the conviction that where we found that we could agree no further with our partners, there would be the point of real difference between us, rather than some pseudo-difference generated by some conscious or unconscious *a priori* motivation.

We learned that there are indeed real differences, but that is no surprise. We also learned that there are very real similarities, much more so than probably most Jews and Christians had ever thought possible—including some similarities that may be a surprise for many.

We found that we are in agreement that Jesus was clearly thoroughly Jewish—we found this was true as long as we were careful not to retroject later "normative" rabbinic Judaism or later Christian dogma into the pre-70 C.E. period.

We also agree that not only did Jesus understand himself as a Jew, but so did Paul. Indeed, they each thought of themselves as being very much within mainstream Judaism; each, of course, having his own specific understanding of what would best constitute authentic Judaism.

One of the perennial points of contention between Judaism and Christianity has been the Jewish affirmation of Torah, the Law, and Christianity's rejection of it—with the claim that in this rejection it was thereby following both Jesus and Paul. However, all four of us agree that not only did both Jesus and Paul understand themselves as faithful adherents of written Torah, but also neither of them thought keeping all of Torah was an impossible burden—which has often been the Christian claim.

Jesus, it is agreed, clearly thought Jews ought to keep the Law—as did also his immediate followers, according to the Acts of the Apostles. Again, it is important not to retroject later rabbinic "normative" practices into this earlier period. So far as we can tell from the documentary evidence, Jesus focused his ministerial attention almost entirely on the Jewish people. There is no indication that he addressed Paul's question of what Gentiles ought to do in regard to Torah—which lacuna doubtless led to the great dispute about keeping the Law reflected in the Pauline and other New Testament literature.

Further, it is agreed that Paul clearly thought that Gentiles need not, indeed, ought not, attempt to keep Torah. Sloyan believes that Paul thought that Jews, including Jewish Christians, *may* keep the Law; Dean believes Paul thought they *ought* to keep it, even though Paul and most other Jews agreed that keeping Torah was not the way one earned righteousness from God.

There is likewise agreement between Swidler and Eron that Jesus should not be a source of acrimony between Jews and Christians. Even the Christ figure, the divine dimension of Jesus, need not be a source of hostility between Judaism and Christianity if he is seen as a "way" to the God of Abraham, Isaac, Jacob, Sarah, Rachel, Rebecca, and Leah for the Gentiles.

All of us are in agreement that an apocalyptic view formed the mental world within which both Jesus and Paul lived. Hence, to understand them correctly this worldview must be taken into account. The thought of both of them must be constantly translated out of those first-century apocalyptic thought categories into contemporary ones if their insights are to have any significant relevance in living persons' lives.

It is our belief that when this translation is carefully done by Christians or by Jews, the resultant teachings and practices about the meaning of life and how to live according to that meaning will most often, if not always, turn out not to be contradictory (thereby engendering hostility) but either contrary, that is, simply different, or sometimes even complementary vis-à-vis those of Judaism.

For example, perceiving God's biblical self-disclosure through the midrashic lens of either the New Testament or the Talmud will, of course, result in varying perceptions of God. But in today's mental world we are aware that all knowledge is interpreted knowledge, is a view of reality from a particular standpoint in the world, and is therefore always partial and limited. Hence Jewish and Christian views of God and how to live in relationship to God and one another will more and more be understood as not necessarily being contradictory—canceling each other out—but as most likely being simply different.

Of course we should not *a priori* assume that Jesus' and Paul's views of God and reality were either in agreement or in opposition to the various views of their contemporary Jews, some of whom were the predecessors of rabbinic Judaism. That we can hope to learn *a posteriori*—if adequate evidence and appropriate analytic techniques are available—only with long and careful study and thought. The four of us hope that we have contributed a little to that process.

But beyond that task is the perhaps even more formidable one of comparing the translations of the Christian and Jewish messages into contemporary categories to determine whether they are fundamentally the same, similar, analogous, complementary, or contradictory. From this comparison we can determine how we Jews and Christians ought to relate to one another. This can be accomplished only through continuous, never-ending dialogue. To this enterprise we hope even more that we have contributed, and look forward to its stretching into an open-ended future.

Authors

LEONARD SWIDLER (Christian) holds a Ph.D. in history and philosophy from the University of Wisconsin and a Licentiate in Catholic Theology from the University of Tübingen. His books include *Jewish-Christian Dialogues* (1966), *Jews and Christians in Dialogue* (1975), *Jewish-Christian-Muslim Dialogue* (1978), *From Holocaust to Dialogue* (1981), and *Toward a Universal Theology of Religion* (1987). He is editor of the *Journal of Ecumenical Studies* and Professor of Catholic Thought and Interreligious Dialogue at Temple University.

LEWIS JOHN ERON (Jewish) holds a Ph.D. in Religion from Temple University and received rabbinical ordination from the Reconstructionist Rabbinical College. His doctoral dissertation, *Ancient Jewish Attitudes Towards Sexuality*, explored the relationship between the moral teachings of Jews and Christians in the first few centuries C.E. He has written a number of articles in the areas of Jewish-Christian dialogue, Judaism in the Hellenistic period, and Jewish sexual ethics. He is currently serving as Associate Rabbi at Temple B'nai Abraham in Livingston, NJ.

GERARD SLOYAN (Christian) has a Licentiate in Sacred Theology and a Ph.D. from the Catholic University of America, where he taught for seventeen years. Professor Emeritus of Religion at Temple University, he lectured in the New Testament and the early patristic period. He has published *A Commentary on the New Lectionary* (1975), *John* "Interpretation Commentaries" (1988), and *Jesus: Redeemer and Divine Word* (1989).

LESTER DEAN (Jewish) is a doctoral candidate at Temple University, specializing in post-biblical Judaism and early Christian origins. He is an instructor of religion at Temple University and Cabrini College and part of the staff of the *Journal of Ecumenical Studies*. He was the first recipient of the Chapel of the Four Chaplains Scholarship for Interreligious Dialogue and is the author of "Rejection versus Revelation: Toward a Jewish Theology of Christianity" published in *Breaking Down The Wall* (1987).

Index